management
of the
modern home

management
of the
modern home

second edition

Irene Oppenheim, Ph.D.

Macmillan Publishing Co., Inc.
New York

Collier Macmillan Publishers
London

Copyright © 1976, Irene Oppenheim

Printed in the United States of America

Earlier edition copyright © 1972 by Irene Oppenheim.

Macmillan Publishing Co., Inc.
866 Third Avenue, New York, New York 10022

Collier Macmillan Canada, Ltd.

Library of Congress Cataloging in Publication Data

Oppenheim, Irene.
   Management of the modern home.

   Includes bibliographies and index.
   1. Home economics. I. Title.
TX167.066   1976   640   75–11822
ISBN 0–02–389440–7

Printing: 1 2 3 4 5 6 7 8   Year: 6 7 8 9 0 1 2

To My Family

preface

The purpose of this book is to serve as a text for a first course in home management. It is planned around the needs of individuals and families today. Discussed are most of the important topics usually taught in home management courses: values and goals in the management process, decision making, using time effectively, the management of household work, the use of money, and food in the home. In addition, some topics of current concern that are increasingly being covered in home management courses are included, such as the home and the environment, the working woman, the low-income family, and the homemaker with a handicap.

Management of the home is rooted in the culture. There are vast differences in the way home responsibilities are managed in different cultures. Even within a culture there is considerable variation.

Today in the Western world we are in the midst of a social upheaval with youth as the leaders. Although many young people, and even more older people, retain the social values of the past, an increasing segment of young people are developing new social patterns. Whether one favors this trend or not, it is obviously having an impact on American life. For example, there is a definite trend for both young and old single adults to maintain independent households.

Part of this change is evident in the pattern of a woman's life today. At one time homemaking was a woman's major job for most of her life. Now, however, there is a growing tendency in the United States and other parts of the Western world for homemaking to be only a segment of a woman's life, not her all-consuming occupation from the time that she leaves her parents' home. Many women are marrying later, having fewer children, or deciding not to marry at all.

These changes have implications for home management in the future. Consider the changing roles of family members. A couple of generations ago the roles of men and women were much more clearly defined than they are today. Now it is no longer so certain who will tend the hearth and who will earn a living. More women are working in paid employment, while more men are sharing some home responsibilities.

I. O.

acknowledgments

I have received a great deal of help from many people in writing this book. In many cases I have indicated this where I have used specific material. There are some people, however, to whom I am very grateful, but whose help I have not acknowledged. Although I cannot mention each one by name, many colleagues, students, and friends contributed ideas.

Last, but not least, I want to thank my family—my parents, Dr. and Mrs. Samuel Gartner, my husband, Dr. Don Oppenheim, our three daughters, Ellen, Wendy, and Barbara, and my son-in-law, Steven Davidson—whose help and encouragement were important at every stage, and who have done so much to influence my philosophy of home management.

contents

part two
the use of resources   81

chapter 4
human resources   83

chapter 5
economic resources   121

chapter 6
environmental resources   145

part three
household operation   171

chapter 7
food   173

part one

---

an overview of home management

chapter 1

---

introduction to home management

The home, formerly the center of a great deal of production, is now primarily a consuming unit. Industrialization, which has so dramatically changed the world of work, has also revolutionized the life of the American family.

The Contemporary Home in the Social Setting

Families have moved off the farms and into cities and suburbs because these are where the jobs are. Industrialization requires that people be near the centers of activity. The family farm has become uneconomical. All over the country, family-run farms are being absorbed by large companies with costly machinery that till large areas or breed cattle using the latest scientific techniques.

Small family-run stores are disappearing too. Taking their places are large commercial bakeries, supermarkets, chains of drugstores, restaurants, newsstands, central dry cleaners with branch outlets, franchised ice-cream vendors, and many others.

Few people are their own bosses. The national trend is away from self-employment or individual ownership of farms or small business enterprises. Today the three largest types of employers are industry, commerce, and government.

Even the service professions are changing. Doctors, lawyers, and dentists are forming partnerships and corporations to provide better service to their clientele and also to enable them to take advantage of tax laws that apply to other types of businesses.

A large proportion of our nation enjoys a better income than at any previous period in our history. Most families have middle-income status. Moreover, *middle income* has been defined at an increasingly high level. At one time individuals were considered as above the poverty level if they simply had food and shelter. More recently, *middle income* has come to mean the ability to achieve a comfortable standard of living.

There is, however, a large minority of our population who do not have either adequate or comfortable incomes. Many of these families live in a cycle of poverty. When children grow up in such conditions, they are often unprepared or unable to take the action that would break the cycle and help them achieve a better standard of living.

The educational level of family members is rising. A generation ago a high school diploma was considered the entry card for white-collar jobs. Today many white-collar jobs require some posthigh school education. Most young people and their families recognize that education or job training are the keys to a good income.

The family unit is smaller these days than it used to be. Although there have been some short-term reversals in trends, the long-term picture is that families are having fewer children. The average couple now has only two children.

It is also becoming less common for several generations to live together. Generally, parents live with their young offspring. As children reach maturity they tend to leave home in search of a job, or to marry, or because they prefer to live alone, or to share an apartment with someone of their own age group. Older people, who are an increasing segment of the population, also often prefer to live alone.

People are extremely mobile. They move as the job situation changes. Some large companies transfer their employees frequently, as part of the training program. Vast migrations have taken place since the end of World War II. Many families have left the farms and rural areas around the country to seek work in cities. Black families have come north. Large numbers of Puerto Ricans have come to the mainland, where economic opportunities have looked more attractive.

Families also move around within urban areas. In some school districts it seems as if the families are constantly moving. This type of moving is generally done in an effort to get better housing, lower rent, more adequate schooling for the children, or easier transportation to work.

The production of housing has become quite complex. Few people construct their own homes. Most housing is put up by builders, using skilled craftsmen. The logistics involved in assembling and constructing the dwelling units often entail a complicated work schedule. Component parts, such as plumbing, heating units, kitchen equipment, and doors, are usually manufactured on assembly lines and brought to the construction site. Government agencies may issue work permits and inspect various

Figure 1.1(A). The majority of Americans use mechanical equipment to ease the job of laundering. (American Gas Association)

Figure 1.1(B). It is very different from the way these Brazilian women still wash clothes, much as people did centuries ago. (F.A.O. Photo)

stages of the construction process. Outside interests usually assist in the financing of construction costs.

There are new kinds of heating and cooling units to keep our homes comfortable in all kinds of weather. These require relatively little work on the part of the household to keep them in operation.

Each year brings new developments, fresh improvements, in home comforts and leisure equipment. Color television sets, tape recorders, humidifiers, and stereo systems help us enjoy the time we spend at home.

Our modern homes utilize the products of many industries in their daily operation. Today's homemaker takes it for granted that items like food, soap, or clothing will be readily available in nearby stores. The family's job has become the selection and purchase of those items that it feels are important to the operation of the home and satisfying to the members of the family unit.

Activities that were once an integral and time-consuming part of household operations are now done with mechanical equipment, and many are no longer done at home. Few people wash clothes by hand. Washing

Figure 1.1(C). Fabrics that wipe clean make it easy to care for many household articles. (3M Company Photo)

machines have become a common household item. They are also available in the basements of many apartment houses and at laundromats. Commercial laundries are used by many people. Dry cleaning of clothing, curtains, and other household items is generally done outside the home, either by a professional dry cleaner or in one of the coin-operated cleaning machines that are increasingly being installed in laundromats.

Our kitchens have many appliances to simplify the job of storing, preparing, and serving food—freezers, blenders, toasters, mixers, electric broilers and food warmers, to name only a few. Many mechanical tools, particularly those that are only needed periodically, are available for rent in urban and suburban areas.

Repair of household equipment is often done outside the home. Many household maintenance jobs require the services of a specialist.

Outside organizations perform some of the functions formerly done by the family. House painting, both interior and exterior, may be hired out. Some families employ people to help them with cleaning or gardening, at least occasionally. Service businesses have developed that will do jobs such as window washing, floor waxing, or heavy cleaning in private homes.

When the family moved off the farm it gave up most of the job of growing and preserving its own food. Quite a few families still enjoy putting up the products of their own farm or garden. But most people do not grow or preserve the bulk of their food. They buy it.

Much of the work involved in preparing meals has been taken out of the home. The tremendous array of canned, frozen, freeze-dried, and fresh foods available at local markets makes it unnecessary for a home-

Figure 1.1(D). The newest trend is for disposable garments for some
activities. The girl with the blond hair is wearing a polyolefin disposable smock. (Edmont-Wilson)

maker to spend long hours preparing food unless he or she chooses to
do so.

Frequently, the price of easy-to-use foods is competitive with the price
of the same food in a form that takes much longer to prepare. Frozen peas
are generally cheaper than fresh ones. Chocolate cake mixes will produce
a cake at less cost than most cakes made from scratch with basic
ingredients.

Many of the newer forms of food meet special needs that would be hard to handle otherwise. The frozen TV dinner with a complete main course, or main course and soup, is easy to prepare, and can enable a sick person, someone who is older and has limited energy, or a youngster with little knowledge of food preparation, to get a meal that is nutritious with little effort. They also can be used by people with limited cooking facilities. Some families have only a hot plate, or a stove that is not fully usable. While most people would agree that these prepared meals do not rival a good home-cooked meal in taste, and some are more expensive, they do have the advantage of making it possible for many people to have a better meal than if they had to prepare the entire dinner themselves.

Most of our clothing is bought from store racks. Clothes are produced by factories in quantity, and are available in current styles at a wide range of prices. Home sewing is a very popular activity for people, but it is far from being the principal source of clothing for most people in the United States today.

We go outside the home for much of our recreation. For young people there are sports, after-school activities, and groups of all sorts. Increasingly, members of each age group tend to seek recreational activities with their peers.

There is a rapid rate of social and technological change, which means we must learn to deal with new things at work, at home, and in recreational or leisure activities. It is predicted that this rate of change will continue and possibly accelerate.

The Scope of Home Management

Home management is a job with many facets. Many different types of things need to be done.

The Buying of Goods and Services

Today we buy most of the things we use. Thus, one of the major tasks in managing a home is to decide where and when to buy all sorts of items from food and clothing to cars, housing, life insurance, and credit for consumer goods. How should available resources be allocated to provide family members with the goods, services, and emotional relationships that will enable them to function effectively in the larger society?

The family has many kinds of resources to draw upon. Time, money, and energy are important, as well as the abilities, interests, and knowledge of the family members. Community facilities are still another category of resources.

Resources must be apportioned among the various family needs and desires. Few people have enough money to buy everything they want. Most of us have more ideas on how to spend money than we have funds. Therefore, money must be divided in some fashion among the many possible uses for the family and its members.

Most of us do not have enough time to do everything that we would like. There aren't enough leisure hours for recreation. Work in the household often takes much longer than we anticipate. The extra demands of a job and commuting to the job can eat up considerable time.

Our energy is limited. Although some of us have much more energy than others, particularly at some stages in our lives, none of us has unlimited energy. We are not always in a position to do everything in the manner that is most attractive or that costs the least amount of money. Most of us need to apportion our energy as well as our time and money.

We have a wide range of choice among many alternatives. Some products can be substituted for others. A particular product like television, for instance, is available in a great variety of models and prices. There are advantages in buying from each of several types of sources for goods and services.

Each household functions as a consuming and producing group. Whereas the producing role of families in the United States has decreased tremendously during the last fifty to one hundred years, the consuming role has increased enormously. Today we buy most of the things we use, rather than making and/or growing them. As a result one of the major tasks in managing a home is to decide where and when to buy all sorts of needs from food and clothing to cars, housing, life insurance, and credit for consumer goods.

The Care of Children

The care and nurture of children is still primarily a family job, although some aspects of it have been taken out of the home. Formal schooling begins earlier and lasts longer; children may go out of the home as early as nursery school age for a good part of the day and they generally stay in school until at least age sixteen or the completion of high school. Assistance in health care is given through health checks at school, such as hearing tests, eye tests, chest X-rays, and various types of inoculations. Public and private health facilities supplement these activities. Meals are served to children as part of the educational program. Many school and recreational programs have supplanted some recreation carried on by the family as a group.

For young families, one of the most time-consuming jobs is taking care of children. Young children have to be fed, bathed, dressed, and

Figure 1.2. The care of young children is a big job. (USDA)

watched carefully to keep them out of dangerous situations. Children need to be helped to learn to care for themselves. It is sometimes estimated that a new baby takes an additional eight hours of work each day. This time is reduced as children get older and can become responsible for doing more things for themselves, and even begin to help in the family.

The Preparation of Meals

The preparation of food for the family for one or more meals a day is still generally done at home. In most families the members eat their main meal of the day at home and the noon meal on Sundays.

Meals must be provided. This means that someone has to shop for food, prepare, serve it, and clean up afterward. Even with convenience foods and equipment like dishwashers and garbage disposals considerable time needs to be devoted to providing the family with food.

School lunches, factory cafeterias, and restaurants provide the noontime meal on weekdays for many people. Although it may be undesirable from a nutritional point of view, many people eat skimpy breakfasts or none at all.

The family may not all eat together. A commuting father may eat later than his children. A man working on the night shift may eat before his family. Sometimes the eating facilities are too small to permit all the members of the family to eat together.

The Care of the Household

A household doesn't run itself. Someone has to plan for its care and maintenance.

The amount of work involved in the care of the household will depend on the size of the home or apartment, how many people live there, what their ages are, how the home is furnished, whether it is located in an area with lots of soot and dirt, what is the age and condition of the house and its furnishings, whether the family entertains much, what are family standards for home maintenance, and who is available to care for the household.

Some families feel that it is important to maintain a home in spotless, gleaming condition. Others are much less interested in household upkeep and do the bare minimum. If you are looking for a house to buy and go to see a number of homes in a community, you will probably be amazed at the remarkable diversity in the care and maintenance of the homes. Possibly you are already aware of the great difference in standards among your acquaintances.

Household equipment must be kept in operating condition and replaced. A certain amount of time and money has to be spent on the buying of equipment in order to keep the household operating efficiently. Where do you go to buy these aids? What is a reasonable price? How much should you spend on service before deciding to replace an item? These are basic problems faced by families when making decisions about the use and maintenance of mechanical equipment.

Other Tasks

Many other activities are required in the operation of a home. Someone has to pay the bills, arrange for health and medical care for family members, coordinate activities within the family, and get the car (or cars) repaired. Toys and equipment may need minor repairs. Laundry must be done. Clothes have to be mended and taken to the cleaners. The list could go on and on.

Another important task in home management—one that is easy to overlook—is helping family members to learn to live and work together happily. The quickest or most efficient way to do a job may not be the one that makes the most people in the family happy. For instance, an adult can make preparations for a birthday party faster than can a child. But one of the special joys for children in many families is participation in party preparations. It may be much quicker for a busy mother to dress her nursery-school-age child. But the child's development is related to the satisfaction he derives from dressing himself, even though the process is a slower one for him.

A Definition of Home Management

Home management can be thought of as "an organizational structure within which people function." [1] This is similar to industry's definition of management. However, management in the home differs from management in industry in a very important area: its goals. The major goals of home management for most families are to handle family activities and household work in a way that will contribute to the happiness of the family and the effectiveness of its members. Industry generally seeks more tangible types of goals. The major goals for the management group of an oil refining company might be to produce certain grades and types of oil as cheaply and efficiently as possible and to market them at the best possible prices.

In home management the development of the individual family members is at least as important to most families as the efficiency of the overall management. Thus, families may seek to help their members develop effectiveness by making and carrying out individual decisions as well as through participation in group decisions and activities. Evaluation of the results often is in terms of personal development rather than efficiency of operation as business might define it.

A youngster may be making brownies to use as refreshments for her friends. It might be cheaper and easier to buy them ready-made at the market. Or her mother might be able to make prettier cookies. But the youngster may get a great deal of satisfaction from doing the job, and she may also develop confidence in her ability to manage something on her own. Evaluation of this activity in terms of the family's goals might be to consider it worthwhile, whereas in terms of industry's goals it was not.

The Process of Management

The process of management is the way decisions are translated into action.

---

[1] Barclay, Nancy A., "Organizing: An Action Oriented Concept," in *Actualizing Concepts in Home Management* (Washington, D.C.: American Home Economics Association, 1974), p. 20.

[Effective executives] know that the most time-consuming step is not making the decision but putting it into effect. Unless a decision has "degenerated into work" it is not a decision, it is at best a good intention.[2]

Recently, considerable attention has been focused on how decisions are translated into action. How does one form of action influence other areas? What effect will one decision have on another? This method is sometimes called the *systems approach*.

If we view management as a system for goal directed purposes, there will be sub-systems or sub-processes within it and the managerial system will be related to other relevant systems within which we operate. . . .
    There are other systems with which the managerial system interacts. . . . One . . . is the economic system. A system with which we may not be so familiar is the political system. A third system is the socio-cultural system. . . . Finally, there is the family system of which the managerial system is a part. . . . Management is a system operating within the family and the total family system interacts with the economic, political, and socio-cultural systems to perform its functions. . . . In all of these systems, we need to be aware of the pervasiveness of technology.[3]

Steps in the Management Process

Any process can be broken down into various components, depending upon how detailed one wishes to be. A good description of the steps involved in the home management process is given by Nickell and Dorsey.

First comes *planning* to achieve the objectives; then *organizing* for performance; then *controlling* the plan as it is carried out; and finally *evaluating* the results in light of the goals each family seeks.[4]

Planning.   A plan is made before an activity takes place. One or more people think out what they want to do and how they will do it. In a sense it is an imaginary rehearsal of what will take place.
    Through planning one is able to see the various segments of an activity as part of the whole activity. I am going from New York to Chicago tomorrow because a member of my family is seriously ill. I want

2 Peter F. Drucker, *The Effective Executive* (New York: Harper & Row, 1967), p. 114.
    3 Carole A. Vickers, "Concept Attainment in Home Management," *Proceedings of the Southeastern Regional Conference: Family Economics Home Management* (Tuscaloosa, Ala.: The University of Alabama, 1973), pp. 3–4.
    4 Paulena Nickell and Jean Muir Dorsey, *Management in Family Living* (New York: John Wiley & Sons, Inc., 1967), p. 86.

to be there by noon. Therefore, I need to plan the various parts of my trip to mesh in such a way as to enable me to get there at that time. Perhaps I will need to drive to the airport, take a flight to Chicago, and then make connections from the Chicago airport.

By planning ahead I can make reservations on the plane so that I will be sure to have a seat on the flight that is most convenient. I might need to put gasoline in my car today so that I won't have to stop and do it in the morning when I will be in a hurry. Or I can plan to leave early enough in the morning to have time to put gas in the car.

Planning also enables one to do a job in various parts in such a way that the whole activity meshes smoothly. Suppose I am giving an anniversary party for my parents. Invitations might be sent out several weeks in advance of the occasion. I might do the shopping for food and decorations several days ahead, if my facilities permit. Maybe I'll order a cake a few days before the event. Two days before, I might clean the house, and the day before, do all the cooking.

By planning it is possible to consider how to use various resources most effectively for the purpose one has in mind. It also aids in eliminating time-consuming indecision at each step.

Organizing. Organizing involves making the plans for a particular activity fit into the scheme of other activities that are or will be going on. It may mean dividing responsibilities, rescheduling some activities, deciding what to defer, and how the resources of time, money, and energy might be reapportioned if necessary.

"Organization is the arranging of strategies and resources into patterns appropriate to the value system of the family." [5]

My trip to Chicago, for instance, may mean that I need to defer buying a new spring outfit. Perhaps I will also have to cancel my plans to help at the school fair. It may be necessary for other members of the family to take on the job of caring for the house and preparing meals while I am gone.

Baker mentions that several levels of organizing may be involved in home management.

One level is one person organizing a task. Sometimes this is called work-simplifying. Another level is one person arranging his own efforts for the completion of several tasks he needs to do into a sequence or pattern. A mother employed outside her home is likely to be organizing at this level. A third level is more complicated. It requires that the manager arrange the

[5] Grace Elliott Tasker, "Case Studies of Homemakers' Organization," Master's thesis, Cornell University, 1962, p. 2.

efforts of others who are doing the work into a pattern so that one or more tasks can be completed.[6]

Unless one is living alone, activities of the various family members need to be arranged so as not to conflict with each other. Many times one person cannot do something unless adjustments are made by others. Dinner may need to be delayed because Mary has a choir rehearsal and will be later than usual in getting home, or perhaps because Dad has to work a little later at the factory. John needs someone to drive him back to school so that he can participate in a pep rally the evening before the big school football game.

Coordination of activities also involves sharing work among the various members of the family. Ideally, this should be done according to each person's capabilities, and particularly with the purpose of helping the younger members of the family to develop their feelings of self worth and effectiveness. Maybe it would be better for Janie to make the dinner and have mother clean up afterward. However, sometimes coordination of activities means dividing work according to who is available at certain times.

The sharing of responsibilities as well as the timing and apportioning of tasks within a family need not be limited by how other people handle them, or how the family has done them in the past. In a warm climate it might be better to let the beds air out all day, rather than to make them early in the morning. With the advent of dishwashers many people wash their dishes only once a day or less often. They load the dishwasher after each meal and let the dirty dishes stand there.

Controlling the plan in action. Home management differs greatly from industry in this step of the management process. In the home, control of the plan in action is apt to be fairly casual and often carried on by the same person who is doing the activity. Responsibility for the control of plans may rest on the homemaker, who often is the person carrying on the activity.

Industry, with more manpower and greater specialization of activity, usually plans carefully for control of an operation and also separates the controller from the person who is carrying on the activity that is being controlled. Quality control of a manufactured product may be done both by a machine and by a team that is not the same as the production group.

The success of any plan depends in large part on its being carried out in an effective manner. This means that the people carrying out the activity need certain skills. They either need to know how to do the job

---

6 Georgianne Baker, *Management in Families: Process of Managing.* Michigan State University Cooperative Extension Service Bulletin 455, 1965, p. 8.

they are trying to accomplish or where to get reliable assistance when it is needed. Cookbooks help one learn how to make new dishes. Guidesheets for patterns help one make a garment. Directions on a package of frozen foods tell one how to cook it. Many magazines tell how to make curtains and other articles for the home. Newspaper articles give advice on how to care for the garden.

Often one member of the family will help another learn to carry on an activity. The mother may help her children learn to cook. The father may help with painting or woodworking activities. There is no hard and fast rule. Today many men are excellent cooks. Often the outdoor cooking in a family is done by the father. Many women are very handy with tools and do some of the household repairs.

Flexibility is needed in the control process because activities do not always progress as planned. A change in any aspect of a situation will probably require a change in plans too, if goals are to be accomplished. One may be late in starting dinner. It would take less time to make hamburgers from the ground beef instead of the meat loaf which had been planned. Perhaps it is too expensive to buy a whole new outfit, so Jane decides to use her old purse, but get a new dress and coat. It's too hot to mow the front and back lawn in one morning so Johnny divides the job up and does it in the course of two evenings. Mother doesn't seem to have enough time to work on both the PTA committee and the church bazaar, so she resigns from one group.

Changes in plans are required in many situations. The members of a family may have planned to go on a vacation together. Because of the rising cost of travel they find they do not have enough money for the holiday that they had planned. Perhaps they can go for a shorter period. Or they may decide to go somewhere else that is less expensive.

It is important to keep one's goals in mind when plans are changed. If the family needs to eat at a particular time it may be wiser to change the menu rather than to serve dinner later. There may be small children who cannot wait for a late dinner. Or perhaps Susie has a date at 7:30 and wants to have dinner before she leaves.

"Skillful direction and guidance are needed to help control the plan in operation." [7] Control of plans in home management means that there needs to be a balance between the leadership role of the older, more experienced family members and the younger, less experienced ones. Tact and thoughtfulness are important; so is the belief that all members of the family can contribute something within the limitations of their ability.

Authoritarian, directive guidance by the parents on all matters does not help the young people learn to make decisions and carry out plans independently. There is a place for authoritarian directions by an adult,

[7] Nickell and Dorsey, op. cit., p. 91.

particularly where health and safety are concerned. "Don't play with matches." "It's time to go to bed now." "Don't ride your tricycle in the road." But as youngsters grow in maturity they need to be helped to understand the reasons for rules and begin to assume more of the responsibility for their own behavior. This includes carrying out activities within the home that contribute to the family's welfare. Help and guidance by older people may, of course, be required at certain points, or in some activities.

Evaluating. Evaluation is a technique to help one get increasingly satisfying results from the resources at hand.[8] Examination of the results of past actions can help one make more effective decisions about future behavior. "The XYZ brand of orange juice didn't taste as sweet as the one we usually buy. I won't get it again." "That dessert took too much time to make. It's not worth the bother." "Our car insurance is so expensive. I think I'll get estimates of rates from some other companies."

It is widely recognized that evaluation serves four purposes: (1) to determine what has been accomplished, (2) to be used as the basis for the next plan, (3) to be used to modify the plan, and (4) to help one develop a better understanding of the situation.

Evaluation is closely related to the controlling of an activity. It often takes place in the course of carrying on an activity, and influences the way in which it is continued. "It is taking much too long to iron all these things, and I have so many other things to do. I think that I will let the children use some of their shirts and shorts without ironing them." "I don't think we will put wallpaper in the kitchen. We have already spent so much money fixing up the apartment. It will be much cheaper just to paint."

Evaluation may result in postponing part of the activity. Perhaps the family will decide not to do anything in the kitchen now, and to put up wallpaper in the spring.

Evaluation of long-term goals and plans may result in the making of wholly new plans. A family may have been planning for a long time to send the two children to college. They may even have been putting aside some money regularly for this purpose. However, with the skyrocketing costs of going to college they realize that they are not going to be able to send both youngsters to an out-of-town school for four years. So they begin to reconsider the alternatives. Maybe only one child will go to college. Perhaps they both can go to a local school for two years while they live at home. Maybe Bob can go to a nearby college for four years because the program that he is interested in is available at a school to which he can commute. But Susie wants to specialize in a field that is not offered at a local college. Perhaps she will go away for the full four years. Or she

---

[8] Irma H. Gross and Elizabeth W. Crandall, *Management for Modern Families* (New York: Appleton–Century–Crofts, 1963), p. 109.

might go to a local college for the first two years, then transfer to an out-of-town school for the last two years, which is the period when she will need to specialize.

The Family Life Cycle and Home Management

The activities involved in the management of a home at a particular time will depend on many things. The composition of the family is an important determinant of the types of activities needed at a given period.

A family with children at home has many day-to-day responsibilities for their care and education. An older couple may be much more involved with the need to provide nursing care for one of the family members. A working mother with preschool children may need to select a community facility such as a day-care center or nursery school.

For most families the stages of family life can be roughly divided into four major periods: (1) the single person, (2) the beginning couple, (3) the

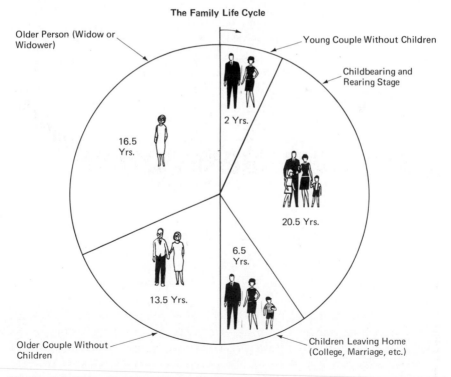

The Family Life Cycle

Older Person (Widow or Widower)

Young Couple Without Children

Childbearing and Rearing Stage

2 Yrs.

16.5 Yrs.

20.5 Yrs.

6.5 Yrs.

13.5 Yrs.

Older Couple Without Children

Children Leaving Home (College, Marriage, etc.)

Figure 1.3. This diagram shows how much time a couple might spend at each stage of life. However, today many young people also maintain independent households before becoming part of a couple.

expanding family, and (4) the contracting family. However, there is no typical life cycle or grouping of stages that describes all families.

Also, although there are many similarities in the activities of families at the same stage of family life, individual needs and tastes often result in great variations. For example, although all parents of preschool children have the job of caring for the children, not all parents will choose to handle it in the same manner. One mother works, even though she has small children. Another mother, who does not work at a paid job, sends her children to a nursery school. Sometimes parents who live near each other have a rotating cooperative play group where several children are cared for. This gives all the mothers more time for other things.

Changes in a parent's job may influence family management. At one point in his life the father may be employed nearby. At another he may have a position that requires a lot of traveling, which means that he is home much less.

One person may be ill for a period of time and need extra care. Suppose the mother is ill. Other members of the family may help her and share in doing some of the work to keep the home going.

Stage 1. The Single Person

A growing number of young adults are living away from their parents' home Many students live in apartments and houses. Some young people establish an independent household when they take their first job. They may move into a city from the suburbs because that is where there are other young people. In the past few years, one-person households have increased largely because young adults want to be on their own.

A variety of group living arrangements have also developed. Many young people, both at school and out of school, share housing with others to cut costs and free money for other things. Generally, at this stage young adults have limited financial assets and want some money available to spend on recreational activities, extra clothing, and extras such as cars, travel, or education.

Many people who share housing still do so with one or more people of the same sex. However, group living arrangements may include both men and women. Some college dormitories have rooms for men or women in the same building. Cooperative and communal groups generally include both men and women.

The largest proportion of people living in group housing arrangements are young unmarried people. However, group living arrangements have been established by childless married couples as well as families with children. Some single parents with children have gotten together to share housing, expenses, and child care. Two or more older people who no longer have spouses or children at home may live together.

More young couples are living together without marrying. The couple may consider this to be a temporary arrangement or as a preliminary to marriage. Whatever the intent of the couple, this practice has become widespread enough to be considered a trend by such people as Margaret Mead, Alvin Toffler, and others.

A number of living groups such as a commune, are organized around a specific purpose. Living arrangements within such a group vary greatly, depending on the purpose and organization of the group. Some of these groups are trying to work out new types of living arrangements to supplant the nuclear family of two parents and their children. Others are designed to meet specific needs—treatment centers for drug addicts or halfway houses for people leaving prisons or mental hospitals.

Generally, young people are leaving home earlier although they may be marrying or establishing families somewhat later. Thus, for many men and women, there is an increasing period when young adults will live away from their parents' home as single people.

If they choose to live with one or more people many of the problems of adjustment and home management that are discussed in the following section, "The Beginning Family," may apply. In any case the single person has to find his or her own way of living. They have to see how much they and others will compromise, cooperate, help, and care for each other. One reason that many of the living arrangements of the young single person are often so temporary is that what appears to be an attractive manner of living often does not work out very well. Faced with the nitty gritty of everyday living, particularly in close quarters, all too often people find it difficult to get along. Someone who is fun for an evening might not be such fun before breakfast. Four people in an apartment may mean that everyone wants the bathroom at the same time and no one wants to clean the kitchen. One argument that has been advanced in favor of group living is that young people are then better prepared for a more permanent type of living arrangement such as marriage.

A growing but still small number of young people are deciding to remain single throughout their lives. A man or woman who lives alone and holds a job has both the responsibilities of the job and the management of the home. In some areas one can find many single men washing sheets and clothes at the laundromat. On the other hand, more single women are taking on the responsibility of financing a house and caring for the yard themselves.

Today there are more alternatives available to people in regard to how and where they will live. Moreover, with the increased mobility of our society, young people often have a greater awareness of alternative life-styles. Even textbooks are being rewritten to illustrate the changing roles of men and women.

Home management for the single person will depend on how and

Figure 1.4. Recreational activities are important to many young people. (Mercury Marine)

where he or she lives, what he or she deems important, and what resources are available, as is the case for families. Moreover, with the present high rate of divorce and a longer life expectancy for women than men, it is likely that more people will have to learn to live as single people at several points in their lives.

Stage 2. The Beginning Couple

This is the period when two people are establishing themselves in a joint household. They may need to make many adjustments to a new situation. Is one person still a student or engaged in some other kind of career preparation that temporarily curtails his earning power? Then they may need to live less expensively than they used to in their parents' homes. Does the husband have a job where he is highly mobile? Then the wife may have to get used to being alone much more frequently than she has been before. Are both members of the couple working? How will they manage the household jobs?

Each individual will probably need to modify his attitudes, values, and habits in order to build a workable relationship. In the early stages of life together the couple must begin to harmonize their differences and work out a way of life that both find acceptable.

Problems of adjustment tend to be fewer if the two people come from very similar backgrounds. But the current mobility of our population increases the probability of marriage between people of widely different backgrounds.

The pattern of behavior that a couple builds during the beginning period will probably remain with them throughout their life together unless there is some major incentive for change. It is a wise couple, therefore, that tries to think out what their values really are, what long-range goals they want to work toward, and how they can reach them.

Stage 3. The Expanding Family

This stage generally extends over a longer period than that of the beginning couple. It lasts from the birth of the first child until the first child leaves home, a time span of about twenty to twenty-three years. There are several subperiods, the childbearing years, the preschool years, the elementary school years, the high school years, and for many families the post-high school or college years. Considerable overlap may exist if there is more than one child in the family. One child may be in elementary school while another is in high school or college. There may be a preschool-age child while the older children are in elementary school.

The period of the expanding family is characterized by activities centered around the children and for the children. During the childbearing years and the preschool period medical care is apt to be a big item. Infants are usually taken to the doctor every month. An illness may call for more frequent visits. Later the doctor's visits may become less frequent but the children will need to be taken regularly to the dentist. They may need to see an eye doctor or some other specialist on occasion.

As the children start school, expenses for clothing and school items rise. By the time they reach high school expenses for food, clothing, and social activities rise very sharply. High school youngsters may spend between ten and fifteen dollars a week on clothing and other items for themselves. This age group constitutes one of the most rapidly expanding consumer markets.

If the youngsters go on to college, expenses mount even more steeply. College, particularly if the student lives away from home, is a tremendous expense for most families. Many mothers have gone back to work just to help meet college expenses. Some college students also work to help finance their education.

Stage 4. The Contracting Family

This is the period that commences when the children start leaving home and continues until just the parents or one parent are left. There are three subperiods. The first is when the children are actually leaving home. Depending on the size of the family and the spacing of the children this may be a brief period or a long one.

Next comes what is commonly called the period of financial recovery, a period in which debts may be paid up. All the children have gone and the family income is still a comfortable one. The father is generally still working, but the mother is much less likely to be employed. Many women stop working once the children leave home because they no longer need so much money. Also the dual task of running a home and holding a job becomes more difficult as they get older and less vigorous.

Many parents give up a large house or apartment and move into smaller quarters. They probably have more money to use for themselves than at any earlier period. Perhaps they refurnish their home, or buy new clothes more freely. They may take more vacations away from home.

Often families use this time to plan for retirement, if they haven't done so earlier. Some families try to save more money. Others cultivate new interests that they can carry over into the retirement period. Many women reduce their work load by simplifying the household as well as by changing their homemaking standards.

Finally comes the retirement period. One of the most striking changes for most families at this time is a sharply reduced income. Very few people have much money other than Social Security payments. Some people do not even have Social Security. They may have other types of assets, however, such as a house without a mortgage, some savings or investments, insurance, or bonds.

The other striking change is that the man, and possibly the woman also, must grow accustomed to filling their time with activities of their own choosing, rather than working at a job. Many older people find this a very difficult adjustment to make.

During the retirement period there may be a sharp increase in health problems. Poor health may make it hard for many retired people to care for themselves. Frequently, this puts additional pressure on an income that is already greatly reduced.

Decreased energy and, possibly, poor health mean that many older people have to learn new ways of caring for themselves and their homes if they are to continue to be independent.

Sharing Responsibility for Home Management

Increasingly, home management is being shared by family members. Among young couples, both of whom are employed, the planning and operation of the household may be shared according to who enjoys what tasks, who is available at certain times, and who has special knowledge and skills.

Many men enjoy cooking. This was first noticed in the 1940s when outdoor cooking grew in popularity. Now there are cookbooks written especially for men and some popular television cooking shows conducted by men.

Families often shop together for food and other articles. On Friday night many men can be seen at the supermarket. On the weekends shopping centers are often filled with families.

Some families are developing lifestyles based on both the husband and wife working continuously at a paid job. Both may hold full-time jobs. In a few situations a husband and wife share a job such as college teaching. Or one may be employed while the other is at school, doing something creative such as writing or painting, or caring for children.

These changes have led to a greater sharing of household responsibilities. Most household work is done by the family members; little is done by anyone outside the family or by commercial services. For example, most people do their laundry at home or in a laundromat.

As more women have taken on paying jobs outside the home, many families have found it necessary to reexamine how the household is managed and cared for. Often standards for housekeeping have been simplified, and other methods used to reduce household work. In many cases husbands and children have taken on greater responsibilities.

The need for younger family members to participate in the manage-

Figure 1.5. More women are taking responsibility for managing their individual and the family's finances. (Burroughs Corp.)

ment of the home can be a source of friction or an opportunity for growth, depending on how it is handled. Young people can learn to take more responsibility or be very resentful that they have to do so. Often their attitude will depend on whether they are being directed to do something, or asked to share in a meaningful fashion in carrying on the functioning of the family.

Even when the young people feel that they are sharing in the family's functioning in an important way there are bound to be some sticky moments. Susie may want to go to the high school basketball game rather than take care of her little sister. John may want to play baseball rather than mow the lawn. But resolving these problems is part of the growing-up process. Dad might prefer to go fishing on a nice spring day instead of going to the office. Mother might want to go to the movies instead of doing the laundry.

If the family feels that both work and play are important they will learn to make adjustments that everyone can live with. They will see that Susie gets to some of the high school basketball games, that she doesn't sit with her sister every Friday, and that John will be able to play baseball with his friends.

The Need for Effective
Home Management

Sometimes managing the home is thought of as a job, to be done in the most effective manner possible, with a great deal of attention being given to controlling the use of resources. On the other hand, for many families the use of resources is left almost entirely to chance, which frequently leads to many problems.

A common cause of family unhappiness is poor management. Sometimes this is the result of having inadequate resources, but often it is caused by not using available resources for important family goals. Recognition of the resources available and effective utilization of them can enable most families to live more happily.

The following case study illustrates some of the management problems encountered by one family. This is a true story about a real family, as told by a counseling agency.

Case Study

Millerstadt–Michigan

Married for about five years and the parents of two preschoolers, Henry and Barbara Millerstadt managed to pile up some $11,000 in miscellaneous debts in less than three years. Before a halt was called, they were living at least $232 beyond Henry's monthly take-home pay of $560 ($6,720 per year) as a finish carpenter. Contributing factors: complete lack of money management know-how; immaturity; marital strife; and the fact that Henry and Barbara made "shopping a hobby."

During the first five years of their marriage, Henry and Barbara Millerstadt had an "obsession" to buy, says a financial counselor who is now working with the family. When they married, neither Mr. nor Mrs. Millerstadt had any real conception of "what money is or what it represents." They made no money management plan, spent without purpose, and incurred debt after debt. When their financial problems turned into marital problems, they looked to divorce as the answer. They probably would have ended up in both the divorce court and the bankruptcy court if an attorney hadn't referred them to a financial counselor. Today, they are embarking on a four-year plan designed to get them out of debt and back on their feet.

Both Barbara and Henry have Midwestern backgrounds, the counselor indicates. Henry was born and raised in an urban Michigan city. His father died about 9 years ago and left Henry, at age 16, to be "man of the house." The counselor feels that is significant. A very slight man, only about 5' 3" tall, Henry is today, at age 25, "immature" and constantly "at war" with much of the world, still trying to be the "man of the house." While the counselor is not sure of the financial circumstances of Henry's background, chances are they were modest. Henry's mother today supports herself on Social Security and part-time domestic work. She lives in an old and modest home and "is amazed at the size of Henry's paychecks and very, very proud of her only son."

Barbara, age 22, was raised in a large city in another Midwestern state, the counselor notes. The couple met when Henry took a trip to Barbara's home city about three years after he graduated from high school. Soon after they met, they married and stayed with Barbara's father, a carpenter, who took Henry on as an apprentice.

Although this seemed an ideal circumstance, particularly for Henry, who up to this point had received no specific job training, the whole situation soon turned sour. Even though Henry's present earning power is a direct result of training which his father-in-law gave him, Henry feels little gratitude, only hostility. He says that he was underpaid by over $1,000 during the time he worked as his father-in-law's assistant, and refers to his father-in-law as "the man who owes me $1,000." In reality, the counselor indicates, Barbara's father is "not too proud of his son-in-law" and this may be at the root of this whole situation. Much of what Henry does—a good portion of the debts he has accumulated—probably relate to Henry's desire to "show his father-in-law what he can do." Henry's hostility towards his father-in-law extends to the point of his refusal to pay a $500 loan co-signed by the father-in-law. "This has given Henry the opportunity to brag about getting part of the money supposedly due him," the counselor reports.

Originally, Henry planned to stay on as his father-in-law's assistant for an indefinite period. However, the assistantship lasted only two years. Henry then packed up his wife and their two young sons and about three years ago moved back to urban Michigan. He had no trouble finding a job. On the basis of his relatively short training with his father-in-law, he was quickly hired as a finish carpenter. Today his monthly take-home pay is $560—more money than he and Barbara "ever expected to see in one place."

With this income as their security, Henry and Barbara soon started on a debt-propelled spending spree that was halted only after they had accumulated more than $11,000 in miscellaneous debts, excluding a home mortgage. Contributing to this shopping spree, the counselor suggests, were the following factors:

- *The Millerstadts had no money management know-how.* On the basis of what they thought was a large income, they soon made shopping "literally a hobby"; they got a home, then furnishings, then whatever they pleased. Buying became an "obsession." The counselor emphasizes that both Henry and Barbara are "completely honest. They have always had every desire to pay every dollar they owe to creditors." But, they were traveling in "unknown surroundings."
- *The Millerstadts' immaturity prodded them on.* Henry wanted to prove himself to his father-in-law and even to his own mother. At the same time, he and his wife began to use "buying" as a means of obtaining satisfaction, the counselor suggests, because their marriage wasn't all they wanted it to be. Eventually, Barbara even used buying as a weapon. At one point, she took the two boys and left home for two weeks. Her intent was to find an attorney and start a divorce action. When she failed to make arrangements —the attorney frightened her away at the statement of fees—she immediately visited a department store and added a $200-plus bill to the family's revolving charge account by buying "stretch pants, perfume, and cosmetics. She then returned to her home and husband."
- *The creditors let it happen.* "Unconcerned, disinterested (and possibly greedy) merchants and creditors played a part in this case," the counselor says. The Millerstadts made a practice of borrowing money for down payments. "This should have been a key" to the creditors. Yet, even though all the family's creditors are ones that report to the credit bureau, evidently none of them ever called to find out what the Millerstadts owed.

The first major debt commitment that the Millerstadts made was for their three-bedroom home, a "sub-division house typical of those built on a mass scale," the counselor says.[9]

Summary

Managing a home today has become a complicated business. Industrialization has revolutionized the life of the American family. People have moved off the farms and into cities and suburbs because that is where the jobs are.

[9] Brenda Dervin, ed., *The Spender Syndrome* (The University of Wisconsin, University Extension: Center for Consumer Affairs, 1965).

The home, which was formerly the center of a great deal of production, has become primarily a consuming unit. Much of the work involved in providing the family with its needs is now done outside the home or with labor-saving equipment.

The management task of the family is to use the available resources to provide the family members with goods, services, and emotional relationships that will enable them to function in the larger society. A family's needs change at different points in the family life cycle.

The process of management is the way decisions are translated into action. The major goals of home management for most families are to handle family activities and household work in a way that will contribute to the happiness of the family and the effectiveness of family members.

Management of the home is a job usually shared by members of the family. But the chief responsibility usually rests on the homemaker, who is generally a woman. As growing numbers of women hold jobs away from home, more family responsibilities are being shared by other members.

One of the most frequent causes of family unhappiness and marital breakup is poor management of family resources. Often this is not the result of having an inadequate income but of using money and other resources unwisely. Effective home management can help families build up a happy life.

CHAPTER FOLLOW-UP

1. What do you think a home should do for the family members? Make a list of priorities. Which would you put as the most important ones? How do you think your ideas would differ from those of your best friend?
2. Look at people that you know. Are there student couples, young families, men and women on their first job, or a wife following a husband in military service? Consider how circumstances can shape the job of home management.
3. Living at college is the first time that many young people are away from home for an extended period. What are some of the management problems of students?
4. Try to project the next ten years for yourself. Where do you expect to live? How much money do you think you might have to live on? Do you think you might marry? Would you welcome children?
5. Do you think the job of family management should be shared between husband and wife? Or do you believe home management is a woman's role? Happy families have used many different methods of management. What do you want to do when you have a home of your own?
6. Do you think a woman should work after marriage? If so, why? If not, why not?
7. In what respects do you think that family life in the United States will

be different when you may be raising a family from the way it was when you were growing up?

SELECTED REFERENCES

Alpenfels, Ethel J. "Emerging Family Forms." *Families of the Future*, Ames, Ia.: The Iowa State University Press, 1972, pp. 134–145.

Baker, Georgianne. *Management in Families: Process of Managing*. Michigan State University Cooperative Extension Service Bulletin No. 455, 1965.

Barclay, Nancy A. "Organizing: An Action-Oriented Concept." *Actualizing Concepts in Home Management*, Washington, D.C.: American Home Economics Association, 1974, pp. 19–23.

Bell, G. Ross. "Changes in Home Environment." *Proceedings of the Southeastern Regional Conference: Family Economics—Home Management*. Tuscaloosa, Ala.: The University of Alabama, 1972, pp. 115–124.

Boulding, Kenneth E. "The Household As Achilles' Heel," *The Journal of Consumer Affairs*, Vol. 6, No. 2 (Winter 1972), pp. 110–119.

Bratton, Esther Crew. "Management Process in Conceptual Framework—Strength or Weakness?" *Conceptual Frameworks: Process in Home Management*. Washington, D.C.: American Home Economics Association, 1964, pp. 37–41.

Crenshaw, Mary A. "Summary of the Conference." *Proceedings of the Southeastern Regional Conference: Family Economics—Home Management*. Tuscaloosa, Ala.: The University of Alabama, 1972, pp. 136–141.

Firebaugh, Francille and Ruth Deacon. *Components of Home Management in Relation to Selected Variables*. Ohio State University Research Bulletin No. 1042, 1970.

Foster, Mary Louise and Caroline Shackleford. "Dialogue on Home Management Residence." *Actualizing Concepts in Home Management*. Washington, D.C.: American Home Economics Association, 1974, pp. 41–43.

Gross, Irma H., Elizabeth W. Crandall, and Marjorie M. Knoll. *Management for Modern Families*. New York: Appleton-Century-Crofts, 1973. Chap. 1, "A Systems Approach to Management."

Hook, Nancy C., and Beatrice Paolucci. "The Family As an Ecosystem." *Journal of Home Economics*, Vol. 62 (1970), pp. 315–318.

Kirkendall, Lester A. "Spectrum of Life Styles: Today and Tomorrow." *Actualizing Concepts in Home Management*. Washington, D.C.: American Home Economics Association, 1974, pp. 73–81.

Knoll, Marjorie, M. "French Lick—Twelve Years Later." *Actualizing Concepts in Home Management*. Washington, D.C.: American Home Economics Association, 1974, pp. 23–31.

Lewin, Kurt. "Group Decision and Social Change." E. E. Maccoby, T. M. Newcomb, and E. L. Hartley, Eds., *Readings in Social Psychology*. New York: Holt, Rinehart, and Winston, 1958, pp. 197–211.

Maloch, Francille, and Ruth E. Deacon. "Proposed Framework for Home Management." *Journal of Home Economics*, Vol. 58 (1966), pp. 31–36.

Minden, Mary Beth. "A Forward Look: Home Management Research." *The*

Family Focus on Management, Washington, D.C.: American Home Economics Association, 1970, pp. 44–54.

Mork, Lucile F. "Young Adults." *Family Economics Review* (1974), pp. 16–18.

Nickell, Paulena, and Jean M. Dorsey. *Management in Family Living.* New York: John Wiley & Sons, Inc., 1967. Chap. 4, "Nature and Role of the Management Process."

Packard, Vance. *A Nation of Strangers.* New York: David McKay Co. Inc., 1972.

Parker, Frances J. "Task Distribution Within the Family." *Journal of Home Economics,* Vol. 58 (1966), pp. 373–375.

Schlater, Jean Davis. "The Management Process and Its Core Concepts." *Journal of Home Economics,* Vol. 59 (1967), pp. 93–98.

Tasker, Grace Elliott. "Case Studies of a Homemakers' Organization." Master's thesis, Cornell University, 1962, p. 2.

Vickers, Carole A. "Concept Attainment in Home Management." *Proceedings of the Southeastern Regional Conference: Family Economics—Home Management.* Tuscaloosa, Ala.: The University of Alabama, 1973, pp. 3–24.

chapter 2

---

values and
home management

All of us have values that we hold dear. Thinking through our values and goals in order to have a clear idea of what we really want out of life is the first step in building a constructive framework for our actions. Biographies of outstanding people show that those with clear-cut goals are most likely to achieve them. A look at some of the happiest people you know would probably suggest that these people know what is important to them. They are willing to do without some things in order to have what they really want.

Selecting goals means putting some things ahead of others or deciding to give up some things in favor of other ones. Going to college means giving up the opportunity to earn money at an early age, or having to work and go to school at the same time.

Many people do not think out what they really want. They go along deciding on this or that as the situation arises. But if one is able to define his or her real values and important goals, he is more likely to achieve them and find happiness.

Marriage and family life complicate the matter of goals. Two or more people must harmonize their ideas, values, and goals. Conflict in marriage often arises because the husband and wife have very different ideas of what is important. When a family is in agreement on basic values and can formulate a priority list for achieving various goals with consideration for all members of the family, family management is much easier and happier. The first step in formulating goals is to examine one's values.

What Are Values?

Values are "normative standards by which human beings are influenced in their choice among . . . alternative courses of action."[1] They are guiding principles for our actions. However inconsistent our actions may appear to others, most people behave in ways that are in harmony with their real values.

Values can be both positive and negative. Human nature is such that people generally act in ways to attain their positive values and avoid their negative ones. Many people even forget that they have negative values at all, because these values are related to unpleasant feelings. Thus they tend to think of values only as positive.

Some individuals go to great lengths in order to avoid the possibility of getting sick. Obviously, they value good health, but they probably also have strong negative feelings about being sick. These lead them to refuse to travel in areas where the health standards are poor, to avoid everyone who might have a cold, and to be very cautious in other ways.

Values are relative. Some are much more important than others in their influence on one's behavior. A girl may value the teachings of her religion and also value attractive clothes. Obviously, these values will have different and perhaps conflicting influences in her personal life.

How Values Develop

We develop values in the growing-up process. From childhood through adolescence most people codify many of their important values. For example, our concepts of what a family is, how to treat other people, the value of religion, and the worth of an education develop fairly early in life.

At first, the values and goals of the parents will be the guiding forces in

---

[1] Francis M. Magrabi, "Investigating Values and Decision," *Journal of Home Economics*, Vol. 58 (1966), p. 795.

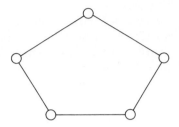

Figure 2.1. Members of a family hold some values in common. (Margaret Jacobson, "Values 1," Extension Bulletin E-647, Michigan State University, 1970.)

the family. Later, as youngsters reach adolescence and the later part of the teens, they may develop goals that are different from those of their parents. In fact, some of these new goals may be, and often are, in conflict with important family values.

Values are very personal. Probably no two people share exactly the same values, even within a family. Schlater's study of the values underlying family decisions seems to bear this out. Some of her conclusions were that "husbands, wives, sons, and daughters tended to have . . . different value profiles," that "family members had more traditional values related to people and more autonomous values related to material possessions," and that "the higher the level of education and income, the more autonomous values an individual held." [2]

People do change their values in response to changing needs, but this is often a difficult and slow process. One illustration of this in society today is that while many of the traditional social lines are breaking down, the majority of people still marry someone from their own race and a fairly similar socioeconomic background. It is still front page news when the son of a millionaire marries a household worker, or when the daughter of a statesman marries someone of another race. The people who are marrying across the traditional lines usually have strong motivation, such as a deep attachment to an individual, and they often face opposition from their families.

A change in values may be effected as a result of a changing social climate. This is particularly evident among young people. Some are rejecting the religious values and social standards with which they have grown up. Whether one agrees or disagrees with this trend, the point is that these young people are adopting new values that they believe are more relevant for today's world.

[2] Jean Davis Schlater, *Investigating Values Underlying Family Decisions*. Michigan Agriculture Station Research Bulletin No. 23 (May 1969), pp. 30–31.

Values Influence Our Behavior

We all have urgent wants, physical and emotional, that we seek to satisfy in order to live and be comfortable. Hunger and thirst are basic physical needs. The desire for self-respect and love are emotional needs. The drive to satisfy these needs motivates much of our actions. How we satisfy them is strongly influenced by our values.

There are various ways of classifying human needs. Maslow describes a hierarchy of needs, starting with the basic physiological needs, hunger, thirst, and sex; going up to safety; love and belongingness; esteem; and, finally, self-actualization.[3] (See Figure 2.1, "Order of Needs.") Self-actualization, the highest rung in this ladder, is "the need to become the most effective person a human being is capable of becoming with the potentialities he has." [4]

Maslow's theory says that we must at least partially satisfy one level of needs before we seek to satisfy the next level. Our basic physiological needs come before everything else.

A starving man is not usually very concerned with whether his work is

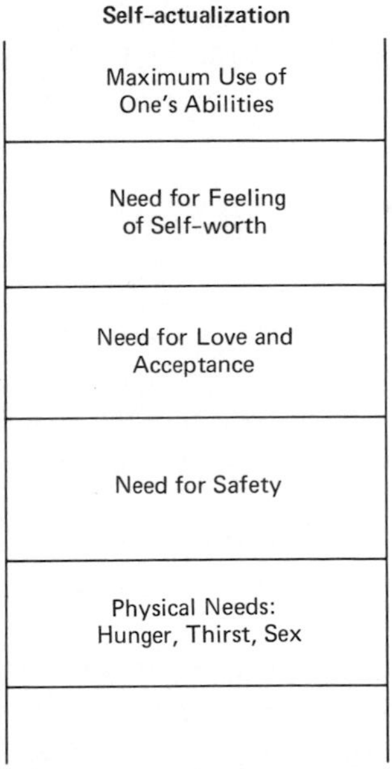

Self-actualization

Maximum Use of One's Abilities
Need for Feeling of Self-worth
Need for Love and Acceptance
Need for Safety
Physical Needs: Hunger, Thirst, Sex

Figure 2.2. Order of needs. (Based on ideas from A. H. Maslow.)

[3] A. H. Maslow (ed.), *New Knowledge in Human Values* (New York: Harper & Row, 1959).

[4] "What Is Self-actualization?" *Forum* (Fall/Winter 1969), p. 4.

interesting. He generally will take any kind of job in order to be able to buy food. In the aftermath of disasters, such as an earthquake or a flood, people are not interested in many levels of needs. Their elementary physical needs are too pressing—survival is primary.

Generally, some of several levels of needs exist at one time. As the lower levels of needs are at least partially fulfilled, then needs on the next level become more compelling.

Most people seek methods of satisfying their needs that are in harmony with their own values. Often another person's behavior may seem incomprehensible to observers who hold different values. Even when starving, followers of the Hindu religion would not kill a cow for food. Cows are sacred objects in the Hindu religion. Many Americans cannot understand the Hindus of India who starve to death while cattle roam the streets.

Values may influence our behavior even when we are not really aware that they are operating. Suppose that a family is looking for a home in a new community. The wife goes to a real estate broker and lists her requirements. She may carefully outline the space that she needs, that she wants a modern kitchen, a family room, and other things. However, she may not mention that she wants to live in an area where the homes have a certain level of elegance. As she looks at houses she may reject a number without even going inside for this reason but be unable to verbalize it beyond saying, "I don't like it."

The Process of Valuing

Many thoughtful people believe that in this era of rapid communication and technological change it is increasingly important for people to develop skill in the *process of valuing*. Increased mobility and improved communications expose us to people and situations where values other than those we grew up with are operating. Changes in where we live, the work we do, and who we interact with often highlight the need for changes in our behavior. People who adapt to new and changing situations most effectively tend to be those who understand themselves, their values, and their needs.

A value is more likely to guide us to constructive action when we are aware that it is operating. For example, a high school student who places great value on further education is more likely to save money than if he or she were uncertain of what to do after high school.

Raths, Harmin, and Simon describe the process of valuing as having seven steps.[5]

[5] Raths, Louis, E., Merrill Harmin, and Sidney B. Simon, *Values and Teaching: Working with Values in the Classroom* (Columbus, Ohio: Charles E. Merrill Publishing Co., 1966), pp. 28–29.

1. Choosing Freely

Young people sharply confront the problem of sorting out their own values when they leave their parents' home, if not before. Going away—to school, to take a job, to enter the armed forces, or even to camp—brings into sharp focus the fact that one must act alone, at a distance from one's family.

A variety of things may complicate the situation—the desire to succeed, the need to get along with other people, the fact that a problem may be unexpected, or many others. Initially, one may be confused and upset when forced to choose. However, eventually most people must make choices in harmony with their values if they are to function effectively in the situation. Some, of course, never get beyond the stage of being mixed up or confused. Still others make choices based on pressures from friends or families.

2. Choosing from Among Alternatives

The process of valuing implies that one can exercise a choice among alternatives. A hiker caught in a snowstorm will generally seek whatever shelter can be found. He or she has no choice. However, a student looking for a place to live at college often does have a certain amount of choice.

Our culture offers the family living above the poverty level a wide range of choices about how they use time, money, and energy. One young couple loves to camp out. Another wants a new car. Their friends may get pleasure from refinishing antique furniture or raising dogs. Still others are interested in changing the political process, or in educating people about inequities in our social system.

A family may need to choose between a birthday party for the children or a night out for the parents. Perhaps they have to decide between new Easter outfits and membership in a swimming club.

It may mean deciding which person gets something new. Does Susie get the skirt she wants or is it more important for Dad to get a new jacket? Shall the family spend more on housing and less on food? Is recreation more important than new clothes? Each family has to decide these things for themselves. No two families will have exactly the same set of priorities.

A working mother may have to choose between not having a birthday cake or buying one at the store, even if she prefers a homemade one. At the Christmas season a busy mother may decide to use frozen dinners for a few nights to give her time to make her Christmas preparations. A retired man living alone may enjoy the companionship and food available in a local restaurant. So he chooses to take many of his evening meals there. Circumstances at a particular time may indicate that one choice is wiser than another.

There are many choices in how to do ordinary household tasks.

Figure 2.3. Most people will not study unless they want to. Learning must be an important value to them. (Bureau of Indian Affairs, U.S. Department of the Interior.)

Personal taste and individual desires influence each family's involvement in the management of its home. One family has furnishings that are sturdy and easy to maintain. Another family gets great pleasure from lovely things that need considerable care.

Members of one family are very fussy about how they maintain their house. They repaint it frequently, are always improving the grounds and keep the whole place in immaculate condition. In another family, the members may not be particularly interested in the grounds around their house. They mow the lawn, but do very little else. Perhaps they are saving their money to send their children to college. Or possibly, they would rather spend their nonworking hours on other kinds of activities, such as tennis, bridge, hiking, or reading.

Sometimes the choices involve the substitution of one resource for another. Often it is possible to spend more time and less money. Some people paint their own homes because it costs less than hiring an outside person to do it. Obviously, this means that they must spend more time and energy on doing the job themselves.

3. Choosing After Thoughtful Consideration of the Alternatives

Sometimes we do things impulsively or on the spur of the moment. Have you ever bought something inexpensive that you really didn't need because you just wanted it at that moment? Perhaps you decided to watch basketball practice because a friend suggested it. These actions didn't really involve the valuing process.

However, your choice of where to go to college or what to do for the summer probably required careful choice and consideration of various alternatives. Can you think of other situations where you had to give careful consideration before deciding on an alternative?

At each step of the way we must make choices. What will I do? How much shall I spend? Should I buy this for Jim or that for me? Where will I go over summer vacation? Shall we have steak or hamburgers for dinner? Who will I room with next semester?

Choosing carefully becomes even more complicated if more than one person is involved. Roommates often disagree over personal values.

Families generally operate within a framework of jointly held values. Choices are usually made within this framework. Let's look at the T's, a young couple who are looking for a place to live.

The T's were married in January. Both were college students at the time and expected to receive their degrees the following summer. They moved into the trailer that Mr. T had shared with a fraternity brother for a year and a half.

After graduation, Mr. T accepted a job as a county extension agent in northern New York State. Since Mrs. T was attending summer school, it was decided that Mr. T would have the task of finding a place for them to live.

Before Mr. T left, they discussed the things they felt were important in the place that would be selected. They decided to rent, rather than buy, because of the uncertainty of making this a permanent home. They expected to stay at least two years, at the end of which they would decide whether to stay, move to another county, enter another field of work, or go back to college for graduate work.

They had also heard that it is very expensive to heat most of the houses available in this section because of the long winters. They decided to take all possible precautions to find a home that would be warm and that would not be likely to have a water system which might freeze. Their trailer had presented this problem, and they hoped to avoid this in their new home.

They agreed that they wanted a large place, so that guests would always feel welcome. Perhaps the confinement of the trailer encouraged this desire. They will probably be quite far from their families (Mr. and Mrs. T are from central New York State and are used to seeing their families at least once a month), and they want to be able to invite them and other friends to visit often. They also want room for a family and for a puppy.

Figure 2.4. A growing number of young people are living in mobile homes. (Mobile Home Manufacturers Association)

They would like to have a nice place, one that they can be proud of. They have decided that it is worthwhile, even if it is more expensive. They are moving into a community where they are complete strangers and plan to do quite a bit of entertaining. Also, because of the nature of Mr. T's business, there will be times when he will want to entertain in his home.

Mrs. T is a graduate of a college of home economics and is anxious to put some of her learning into practice. She probably will not have a full-time job at first, so she will have time to fix up the home they choose.

When the T's finished college, they had two outstanding debts—payments on the trailer and payments on their new car. They sold the trailer and after completing the payments were able to save $700. They also have some money in the bank, which they will leave there to cover unexpected expenses. They have medical and surgical, life, property, and automobile insurance.

Mr. T's weekly income will be about . . . [$200 before] deductions. Besides car payments, the T's major expenses will be for rent, food, clothing, utilities, entertainment, and donations to church.

The T's own very little furniture. The trailer was furnished. If they purchase furniture, they will have to live quite modestly at first or borrow money to pay for the furniture. The couple is not opposed to buying on credit; however, they would prefer to use their credit for more important things. They do have an adequate supply of the smaller things that are needed in the home, such as kitchen equipment, linens, sewing machine, dishes, and silver.

Neither Mr. nor Mrs. T knows much about furniture, but Mrs. T's background in home economics and Mr. T's background in engineering should have prepared them to use their common sense to make satisfactory selections. There are a number of furniture stores in the county seat where they will be living; they can also go to the larger cities about 50 miles away to make their purchases. They would also consider refinishing second-hand furniture if they have space to do it.

At this point, Mr. T has looked at homes in the county for rent and furnished and unfurnished apartments, both in town and in the surrounding country. He feels that it would be better for them to stay in or very near town, even though they would like to have space for a garden. There seem to be too many problems, including heating and plumbing, in the places outside town.

In his last letter to his wife, Mr. T said he thought he had found the ideal place—an apartment in town on a street with many large houses. There are five rooms, recently redecorated, and an extra bedroom of the landlord's that can be used when needed. There is space for an automatic washer, which they would like to have, and there is a large lawn. Mr. T says that, of the places he has seen, it seems to have the greatest number of desirable features. It may be rented unfurnished for [$200] per month.[6]

4. Prizing and Cherishing

Generally, people are proud of their values and hold them in high regard. Sometimes we are faced with difficult choices or situations in which there are no simple answers. Most people look to their values as guidelines at such times.

The issues of school integration has engendered great bitterness on both sides of the question. Some people are very much for one solution; others are very much against it. This has resulted in some people taking public stands based on their values.

5. Affirming

One is generally willing to make known his choice if it is based on his values. One is satisfied with his decision and usually willing to say so. You have probably heard someone say that they are going to act or vote in a particular way because they believe strongly in certain principles or values.

[6] Marjorie Knoll, from "Teaching Home Management," *DHE Topics* No. 19, Department of Home Economics of the National Education Association, 1963. Written by Lorna B. Tallmann, as a class project, "Selection of a Place to Live," at Cornell University, 1961.

6. Acting Upon Choices

A value has to give direction, to form a basis for one's behavior. Our values show up in the way we act, what we do, what we say, and what we don't do. Often it is easier to recognize a person's values from what they do rather than what they say. Can you think of ways in which your behavior reflects your values? Have there been situations in which you learned about someone else's values from their behavior?

7. Repeating

When an idea reaches the stage of becoming a value or guiding principle in someone's life it is likely to result in certain types of behavior being repeated. Values are important in establishing a pattern of behavior. A person who values punctuality is usually on time for appointments. People who place a high value on neatness generally keep themselves and their possessions very tidy. Some people are consistently fair and helpful in dealing with others. Can you think of other examples?

Value Indicators

Values are our strongest guiding principles. However, we may have other guideposts for our behavior that do not meet all the criteria for being a value but are nevertheless important to us—goals, aspirations, attitudes, feelings, and others.

Goals

Most of us try to get or accomplish certain things within the framework of our individual value systems. We have goals—conditions that we are trying to attain. Goals are like markers on a highway—they give a sense of direction to our activities.

One might have the goals of becoming a teacher, going away for the summer, or buying a new car. Someone else might wish to get away from the confining environment of the city and live where the air is cleaner and life is less hectic. This is another type of goal.

We may have both long-term and short-term goals. One's goal for the summer might be to earn enough money to pay his tuition at college in the fall. Completing college is a longer-term goal.

One's individual goals may be at variance with family goals. A youngster may desperately want music lessons, but the family is trying to save for a new house, or perhaps has heavy debts because of the purchase of new furniture. Perhaps the family is saving for the down payment on a car. But they may be willing to postpone getting the car because Susie wants to go to camp this year.

Harmonizing family and individual goals is very important to successful home management and family happiness. The family has only a certain amount of resources, which must be used for everyone. Unless these resources are quite inadequate, as in the case of a family living in poverty, they can often be allocated in ways that will help the individual members of the family as well as the group to reach certain goals.

Research studies as well as the popular literature on the changing roles of women suggest that families may not communicate well about individual goals. Particular attention has been focused on the fact that many women are not happy with the exclusive role of homemaker at all stages of their lives. Many are interested in other activities and goals as well.

Aspirations

Aspirations tend to be less concrete than goals. They point to values but are not as strong a commitment in terms of being guiding principles for behavior. For example, a person may aspire to have more money. The same person, however, might hesitate to apply for a specific job that paid more money because it would mean moving, a long commute, or some weekend work. In this case he would value other things, his leisure time or present living situation, more than the extra income.

Attitudes

An attitude is usually a statement for or against something. Attitudes can and do change. An individual may hold one set of attitudes at one point in his life and a different set at another. Historically, some young people have been very liberal in their views on the social situation in their late teens and early twenties. Many of the same people will have developed much more conservative attitudes by the time they reach their fifties. A young liberal in college may be an arch conservative by the time he is middle-aged.

Many of our important attitudes develop early in life. Studies have shown that attitudes toward the educational process are strongly influenced by one's early experiences. Youngsters who have poor experiences in the elementary grades are not likely to finish school. One of the important stimulants for prekindergarten educational programs for disadvantaged youngsters, was a series of experiments by Dr. Martin Deutsch and a team of associates, which showed how preschool experiences can change a youngster's ability to succeed in school, and as a result his or her attitude toward the possibility of success in school.

Interests

The fact that one is interested in something may indicate a casual or serious interest. It may be more than a passing fancy but not nearly as important as a value. Interest in something may not mean that someone has as strong a commitment as he does to a value. However, a person's interests are often in areas that are related to one's values. A person who enjoys activities with his family may value family life highly.

Feelings

Feelings are expressions of our mood. We may be angry, sad, or gay. These are not values. However, feelings may be responses to situations involving our values. One might be outraged at a person who mistreats a child. In this case the feeling could have been evoked by a sense of outrage at a violation of human dignity, which one values highly.

Feelings may result in some types of behavior but are not a guide to long-term patterns of behavior. For example, if you are angry about something you might say so or you might take some action in regard to the problem. However, your feelings of the moment may not be a guide to your behavior next week.

Beliefs and Convictions

Beliefs and convictions are not necessarily values or even reflections of values, although they may be. For example, one may believe that it will take a long time to build enough decent housing in and around urban areas and yet value the right of everyone to a certain minimum standard of living, which includes adequate housing.

On the other hand, one may believe strongly that even young children should be able to choose their friends, which illustrates one's values in regard to the individuality of people.

Activities

Activities often indicate a person's values. Many people spend a lot of time on activities that are closely related to their important values. The man who works with the Boy Scouts or other service groups may place a high value on helping others.

Cultural Values

Some values are thought to be universal. There is great similarity in many of the principles of the major religions.

Each cultural group has certain principles it values highly. Democratic nations place a high value on the right of each individual to have a say in how he is governed by means of the election process.

The following are some of the values commonly attributed to the culture of the United States.

Activity and work. Americans are generally regarded as active, busy people. They like to be where things are going on, "where the action is." Mobility, particularly in cars, is nationwide as people move about for work and play.

Progress. People tend to look forward rather than backward. Newness is often equated with goodness. Unlike many European countries, America has few old buildings or other objects. Instead people look for continuous improvement in tangible goods.

Material comfort. Most people in the United States enjoy a higher standard of living than the rest of the world. Thus, they have come to expect good food, housing, clothing, medical care, and sanitation as rights. There is a public outcry when unsanitary conditions are found in a food packing plant or a nursing home.

Figure 2.5. Most Americans place a high value on good medical care. (Universal Ophthalmic Products)

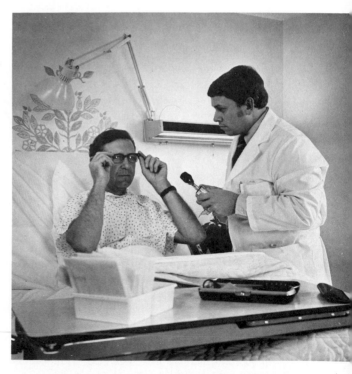

Efficiency.   People often prize "getting things done," finding the most efficient way to do something. This has resulted in many inventions, gadgets, assembly-line methods, and, finally, automation.

Humanitarian ways.   People expect to help the less fortunate. Over a period of years the United States has aided many other less fortunate people and gradually developed increasing benefits for many of the needy within its boundaries.

Value Clarification

People vary in their awareness of their values. One cannot accept without question what people say are their values. It is often evident that values are operating although the individual is not really aware of them.

Values may first come to our awareness when we are faced with a conflict. Suppose we are in a situation where we feel uncertain about what we should do. Should we tell the whole truth or should we not?

As we become aware of values we may also become aware of conflicts among our values. For example, when we must make decisions about such matters as going to school, taking a job, making a purchase, choosing leisure time activities, and many other things.

What's important to you? Consider the following situations[7] and some of the possible solutions.

1. Mr. and Mrs. Smith were married recently and are living in an apartment. Mrs. Smith worked for a few years before marriage and has continued to do so since. She likes her work and they need the money, but now she is pregnant. What should the Smiths do after the baby comes?

2. Mr. Smith's job has been transferred to another state. Therefore, Mr. and Mrs. Smith have to find a place to live in the new location. They have two young children, a boy of three, and a girl one year old. As they think about their move, they realize that their new home must have certain characteristics if it is to be what they want. What should the place they want to find be like?

3. The Smiths had difficulty with their children's behavior on a vacation visiting relatives and friends. The children's ages were two and four. What should the Smiths do about the way their children behave?

4. Next year the plant in the eastern part of the country where Mr. Smith works is moving to another part of the country. He has been offered a job in its new location. The plant in the east is closing, so if

---

[7] Minor modifications have been made in these problems which were developed for a research study by Schlater, op. cit., pp. 34–35.

he stays he will have to find a new job. The Smiths have four children, a boy aged eight, a girl aged six, and another girl and boy who are not yet in school. What should the Smiths do?

5. Mr. Smith this year will have a two-week vacation in the summer. His family is composed of himself, his wife, and their four children—three of whom are in elementary school and one who is four years old. What should the Smiths do on their vacation?

6. At this point the oldest of the Smith children, Bob, is a freshman in high school, the two girls are in elementary school, and the youngest, Jack, is five years old. Next year Jack will be in school, too, and the family is thinking about this new situation when all the children will be in school. What changes should they make in this new situation?

7. The Smith children are now in high school and elementary school and the Smiths have had their living-room furniture since their family was established. It is still usable but scratched and worn looking. What should the family do about the furniture?

8. In the Smith family each youngster thinks his most disliked task is cleaning his room. Bob and Nancy are in high school and Mary and Jack are in elementary school. The children are busy with school work and activities outside school hours. What should the Smiths do about the cleaning?

9. Mr. and Mrs. Smith have an old automobile in the low-priced range. Mr. Smith needs the car to drive to work. Mrs. Smith needs the car for her activities and the oldest of their four school-age children has just obtained his first driver's license. What should the Smiths do about the situation?

10. When Bob was a sophomore in college he fell in love with a classmate at the same college and wanted to marry her. However, his family had only met her once, and did not know her family. What should the Smiths do?

Simon, Howe, and Kirschenbaum suggest a number of other strategies for examining one's values. Here are two. (1) Take three things out of your wallet, pocket, or purse. What do these mean to you? What can these tell you about yourself? (2) List 20 things that you love to do. Code this list as follows.

1. A dollar sign ($) is to be placed beside any item that costs more than $3 . . . (The amount could vary, depending on the group.)

2. The letter A is to be placed beside those items the student really prefers to do *alone*; the letter P next to those activities he prefers to do with other *people*; and the letters A–P next to activities that he enjoys doing equally alone or with other people.

3. The letters PL are to be placed beside those items which require *planning*.

4. The coding N5 is to be placed next to those items which would *not* have been listed *five* years ago.

5. The numbers 1 through 5 are to be placed beside the five most *important* items. The best-loved activity should be numbered 1, the second best 2, and so on.
6. The student is to indicate next to each activity *when* (day, date) it was last engaged in.[8]

Starting out on Your Own

Still another way to look at values is to consider how people set up housekeeping. Two opposite trends seem evident among young people. One is to live very simply with a bare minimum of things. The other is to start housekeeping at a level similar to one's parents.

Following are two lists of home furnishings. The first list was recorded by a single girl from the time she started out in an efficiency apartment until she rented a small house.

Efficiency Apartment

Owned
Record cabinet, two bookcases

Loaned or donated from home
Blankets, pots & pans, casserole

Gifts
Toaster, fry pan, ironing board, iron

Bought
Sofa bed
Dresser
Dining table & four chairs
Stainless steel flatware
China
Rug
Vacuum cleaner
Marble coffee table
Lamp
Chair
Unpainted chest
Sheets, towels
Shower curtain, bath lid, mat
Wash bucket
Tablecloth
Skillet
Pillows

---

[8] Sidney B. Simon, Leland W. Howe, and Howard Kirschenbaum, *Values Clarification: A Handbook of Practical Strategies for Teachers and Students* (New York: Hart Publishing Co., Inc., 1972), pp. 31–32.

One-Bedroom Apartment

Acquired

Double bed (traded for studio couch)
Boudoir chair (old one from home)

Bought

Two occasional chairs
End table
Two lamps
Wall-to-wall carpet
Stereo
Bedspread
Draperies

Small, Two-Bedroom House

Bought

Patio furniture
Washing machine
China cabinet
Sewing machine
Single bed
Unpainted chest
Small rug
Transfer of carpet
Garden equipment
Metal wardrobe
Two air conditioners[9]

Two graduate students furnished a model two-bedroom apartment in a public housing project for a family of four, two adults and two children, in 1972. Here are their selections and the cost of each item.

Furnishings for Two-Bedroom Apartment in a Public Housing Project

Room	Item	Retail Price
Living	Furniture:	($482.29)
room	Chairs (2)	188.00
	Cocktail table	34.95
	Loveseat	169.00
	Side table	34.95
	Storage unit	27.95
		(Cont. overleaf)

---

[9] Reprinted by permission from *Changing Times*, the Kiplinger Magazine (March 1969 issue). Copyright 1969 by The Kiplinger Washington Editors, Inc., 1729 H. Street, N.W., Washington, D.C. 20006.

Furnishings for Two-Bedroom Apartment (Cont.)

Room	Item	Retail Price
Living room (*Cont.*)	Wicker basket	14.95
	Wicker stool	12.49
	Television	89.00
	Pictures, mirror	31.47
	Misc. accessories	62.66
	Window treatments	26.94
		$692.36
Kitchen	Furniture:	($141.75)
	Chairs (4)	71.80
	Table	69.95
	Essential accessories	25.01
	Misc. accessories	36.79
	Window treatments	10.96
		$214.51
Bathroom	Rug and seat cover	1.88
	Shower curtain and hooks	1.87
	Towels and washcloths	4.25
	Misc. accessories	8.81
		$16.81
Master bedroom	Furniture:	($344.90)
	Mattress, box spring	94.90
	Table, chest, dresser, headboard	250.00
	Pictures, mirrors	21.96
	Misc. accessories	67.03
	Window treatments	10.67
		$444.56
Children's bedroom	Furniture:	($272.64)
	Chairs (2)	21.90
	Chests (2)	69.00
	Desks (2)	53.74
	Trundle bed	128.00
	Pictures, mirrors	13.72
	Misc. accessories	49.37
	Window treatments	10.67
		$346.40
	Total	$1,714.64[10]

[10] Study by Virginia Griffin, Ann Camp, and Savannah S. Day. Reported in "A Model Apartment for Public Housing Residents," *Journal of Home Economics*, Vol. 66 (1974), pp. 35–37.

Figure 2.6(A). Home furnishings usually suggest values that are important to people. This attractive living room is in an apartment of a low income housing project. (Courtesy Savannah S. Day; Photographer William V. Griffin)

Summary

Values are standards that influence our choice among alternative courses of action. They may influence our behavior even though we are not aware that they are operating. However, a value is more likely to guide constructive action when one is aware that it is operating. Thinking through our values and goals is the first step in building a constructive framework for our actions.

Harmonizing individual and family goals is very important to successful home management and family happiness. Because goals are generally based on values this is easier if the members share many of the same values.

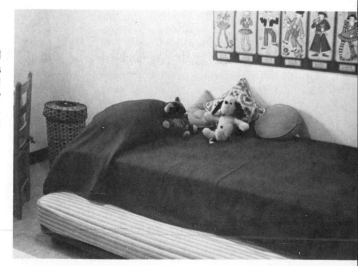

Figure 2.6(B). This small children's bedroom is easy to clean and attractive. (Courtesy Savannah S. Day, Photographer William V. Griffin)

CHAPTER FOLLOW-UP

1. The following example[11] illustrates how a family may eliminate an alternative because of values.

> Assume that two families have similar resources and characteristics. Both households are composed of a self-employed husband age 40, wife 35, and three children, ages 13, 11, and 7. Average annual family income is $15,500. Both families are planning to move to new living quarters. After some investigation, they find there are several houses and apartments available in the neighborhood they desire to live in. Knowing most, if not all, alternatives available, both families begin to sort out relevant alternatives. [Equal rent level is assumed between alternatives and therefore is not a restriction.] Family A would prefer having a front and back yard, but an apartment located conveniently for work and school would also be considered. Family B considers a house out of the question since they do not want to bother with upkeep of the yard nor the house itself. They prefer to spend their leisure time pursuing other activities. Thus, the differences in family preferences would result in family A considering both house and apartment. Family B would eliminate the house as a relevant alternative.

   a. Can you think of other situations where a family may eliminate alternatives because of values?

   b. How did you select a college to attend? You probably applied to a college or several colleges for particular reasons. What alternatives did you eliminate because of your values or preferences?

2. Think about your classmates. What can you conclude about their values from their behavior?

3. What values do you expect to be most important in guiding your life for the first five years after you leave school?

4. What things have caused the greatest problems in your relationship with your family? Is some of the cause of conflict the fact that some of your values differ from those of your family?

5. What changes in values can you see taking place among young people? How are these reflected in their lives?

6. List the equipment and furnishings that you feel you need to have when you start housekeeping. What would you like to add if you could? Why do you want these things? Do they save work or make life pleasanter? How does your list reflect your values?

---

[11] Joseph Gartner, Lee Kolmer, and Ethel B. Jones, *Consumer Decision Making*, Consumer Marketing Bulletin, Cooperative Extension Service, Iowa State University (Nov. 1960), p. 21.

SELECTED REFERENCES

Ater, E. Carolyn, and Ruth E. Deacon. "Interaction of Family Relationship Qualities and Managerial Components." *Journal of Marriage and the Family*, Vol. 34 (1972), pp. 257–263.

Baier, Kurt, and Nicholas Rescher. *Values and the Future*. New York: The Free Press, 1969.

Brown, Marjorie M. "Values in Home Economics." *Journal of Home Economics*, Vol. 59 (1967), pp. 769–775.

Dawson, Judith A. "An Exploratory Study of Long-Range Planning by Families." Master's thesis, The Pennsylvania State University, 1970.

Downer, Donna, Ruth H. Smith, and Mildred T. Lynch. "Values and Housing— A New Dimension." *Journal of Home Economics*, Vol. 60 (1968), pp. 173–176.

East, Marjorie. "Family Life by the Year 2000." *Journal of Home Economics*, Vol. 62 (1970), pp. 13–18.

Edwards, Kay P. "Goal-Oriented Family Behavior." *Journal of Home Economics*, Vol. 62 (1970), pp. 652–655.

Kohlmann, Eleanor L., and Frances Smith. "Assessing Values Related to Home and Family Life." *Journal of Home Economics*, Vol. 62 (1970), pp. 656–660.

Magrabi, Frances M. "Investigating Values and Decision." *Journal of Home Economics*, Vol. 58 (1966), pp. 795–799.

Maloch, Francille, and Ruth E. Deacon. "Proposed Framework for Home Management." *Journal of Home Economics*, Vol. 58 (1966), pp. 31–35.

Mead, Margaret. *Culture and Commitment: A Study of the Generation Gap*. New York: Doubleday & Co., Inc., 1970.

Meeks, Carol B., and Ruth E. Deacon. "Values and Planning in the Selection of a Family Living Environment." *Journal of Home Economics*, Vol. 64 (1972), pp. 11–16.

McKee, William W. "Values in Home Management." *Values and Decision Making*. Washington, D.C.: American Home Economics Association, 1969, pp. 14–20.

Nichols, Addreen, Catherine R. Mumaw, Maryann Paynter, Martha A. Plonk, and Dorothy Z. Price. "Family Management." *Journal of Marriage and the Family*, Vol. 33 (1971), pp. 112–118.

Otto, Herbert A. *The Family in Search of a Future*. New York: Appleton-Century-Crofts, 1970.

Raetzke, Carolyn Perreault. "Family Orientation of 550 Urban Families." Master's thesis, The University of Illinois, 1973.

Raths, Louis E., Merrill Harmin, and Sidney B. Simon. *Values and Teaching*. Columbus, Ohio: Charles E. Merrill Publishing Co., 1966.

Reich, Charles A. *The Greening of America*. New York: Random House, 1970.

Rosen, Bernard C. "Family Structure and Value Transmission." In Marvin Sussman, Ed., *Sourcebook in Marriage and the Family*, 3rd ed. Boston: Houghton Mifflin, 1968, pp. 309–319.

Schlater, Jean Davis. *Investigating Values Underlying Family Decisions*. Michigan State Agriculture Experiment Station Bulletin, No. 23, 1969.

Simon, Sidney B., Leland W. Howe, and Howard Kirschenbaum. *Values Clarification.* New York: Hart Publishing Company, Inc., 1972.

Stoeckeler, Hazel S., and Minoru Hasegawa. "A Technique for Identifying Values As Behavioral Potentials in Making Consumer Housing Decisions." *Home Economics Research Journal,* Vol. 2 (1974), pp. 268–280.

Thomas, Carolyn, and Beatrice Paolucci. "Goals of Young Wives." *Journal of Home Economics,* Vol. 58 (1966), pp. 720–723.

Toffler, Alvin. *Future Shock.* New York: Random House, 1970.

chapter 3

---

decision making

A decision is a "determination or result arrived at after consideration."[1] Decision making is considered the crux of the management process, in the operation of industry as well as in home management. Industry pays its top executives well to keep the company operating effectively. Many people believe that the most important and difficult job of an executive is to make the right decision at the right time.

"Effective executives do not make a great many decisions. They concentrate on the important ones. They try to think through what is strategic . . . , rather than 'solve problems.' "[2] Drucker defines decision making as the development of policy, rather than the type of decision making involved in carrying on day-to-day operations. He

[1] *Webster's New International Dictionary*, 2nd ed. (Springfield, Mass.: G. and C. Merriam Co., 1954), p. 680.
[2] Peter F. Drucker, *The Effective Executive* (New York: Harper & Row, 1967).

considers the decisions involved in daily operations as problem solving or operational decisions.

The decisions involved in home management could be similarly divided into (1) major decisions (sometimes called policy or central decisions) and (2) operational decisions (also called satellite decisions), those that have to be made in order to carry out major decisions.

Suppose a family decides that inflation is cutting into their spendable income so much that they will have to control their food expenses very carefully in order to have enough money left for a summer vacation. The decision to curb food expenses might be considered a major decision. Deciding what to buy, where to buy it and when, whether to eat at home or out on Sunday would be operational decisions. Choosing hamburger versus steak or one brand of peaches versus another brand is an operational decision in this context. The basic decision provided the starting point for all the decisions that followed. The decisions that followed the major decision implemented the major decision.

The division of decision making into two aspects is very useful in large organizations. People at the upper levels, such as the board of directors, make the big policy decisions. Operational decisions are made at lower levels to implement policy decisions.

Families tend to operate much more casually. Decision making in the home often grows out of specific needs. The car breaks down or the

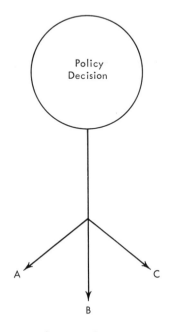

Figure 3.1. A policy decision results in operating decisions.

Policy Decision

A   B   C

Operating Decisions

washing machine needs fixing. Perhaps Susie wants music lessons or Bob wants to go to the game at school. Sometimes the decision is the result of long-range plans. In any case the decision-maker or decision-makers are in close contact with the person who will implement the decision.

College or a first job causes many young people to be faced with making many more decisions independently. They may be living away from home for the first extended period. The use of time and money, the choice of friends, the selection of a place to live, a schedule for meals, work, and sleep, and greater responsibility for planning their work and chores all face them. Some people believe that the high dropout rate of freshmen at college is partly the result of the fact that many students are not prepared to make and carry out these decisions without the help of their families.

Think back over the last few days. What are some of the kinds of decisions you had to make? Which of these are decisions that you would not have had to make before you started college? Looking back, are there some that you might have handled differently for a more satisfactory result?

Increasingly, researchers are recognizing that family management could benefit from some of the techniques used by other social organizations. The development of carefully thought-out long-term plans would direct many subsequent family decisions. This type of process could greatly improve family management in many cases.

Steps in the Decision-Making Process

There is some disagreement as to exactly how many steps there are in the decision-making process. However, there seems to be general agreement that the following are some of the important steps one must go through in reaching a decision.

1. Recognizing that a problem or choice-making situation exists.
2. Weighing the alternatives available.
3. Deciding upon an alternative.
4. Living with the consequences of the decision. (This will probably include some evaluation of the decision.)

Let's consider an actual family situation to illustrate the steps. Mr. and Mrs. Brown have two children, a boy aged seventeen and a girl of fifteen. The washing machine that they have had for seven years breaks down. An estimate of the repair cost, including replacing the motor, is almost $100. The Browns are considering what to do. Step 1, becoming aware of the problem, has already taken place. They know that they will need to make some arrangement to get clothing and household articles washed. The question is what arrangement would be best in their situation.

They could repair their old machine. But that is a sizable amount to spend on an old machine, which might quickly develop another type of problem, which would be expensive to repair. They could purchase a new washing machine. Washing machines vary in price from about $210 for a small machine to $350 or more for a large deluxe model. Or they might try to purchase a used machine in good condition.

Another type of alternative would be not to do the laundry at home. There isn't as much laundry as when the children were younger. Perhaps Mrs. Brown is working and has limited time. They might consider using the local laundromat or sending the clothes to a laundry.

These are the major alternatives available in this situation. The family's decision will depend on their needs, tastes, and pocketbook. Once they decide upon an alternative they will probably act upon it fairly quickly because most people do not possess enough clothes to let them pile up indefinitely. However, it would be possible to postpone a decision for a while by using either a laundromat, an outside laundry, or washing by hand.

Let us assume that the Brown family has decided to buy a new medium-priced washing machine. They will have a wide range of makes and models to choose among. They can choose whether to pay cash or to finance the purchase in various ways.

Once they have actually bought the machine the Browns will have to live with the results of that decision for some time. During this period they will probably evaluate their decision in informal ways, "This washing machine gets the clothes much cleaner," or "The presoak cycle saves the bother of soaking and then going downstairs to start the washing cycle," or "This machine is really not as good as I thought it would be."

The Types of Decisions Families Make

In our various roles as family members, citizens, and wage earners, we are involved with several types of decisions—economic, social, and technical. The line between these types of decisions is somewhat arbitrary, and useful only as a way of examining decision making.

Economic Decisions

We buy many things. These are economic decisions. We use money to obtain many of the things we want. But there are other ways to get them. Some people make or grow the things they want. They spend time and effort instead of money.

The nature and kind of economic decisions that we are able to make

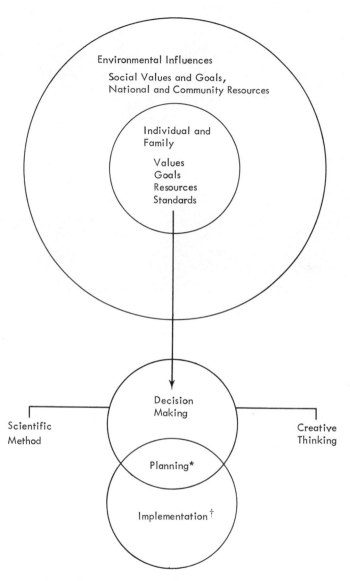

*Planning includes planning, decision-making and planning, and implementation.

† Results in organized family effort for day-to-day activities.

Figure 3.2. The decision-making process. (Many ideas in this diagram have been adapted from Marjorie Knoll, "Teaching Home Management," *DHE Topics*, Washington, D.C.: Department of Home Economics of the National Education Association, 1963; and from Bok Cha Yoon Lee, *College Students' Attainment of Selected Home Management Concepts*, Ph.D. thesis, Pennsylvania State University, 1967.)

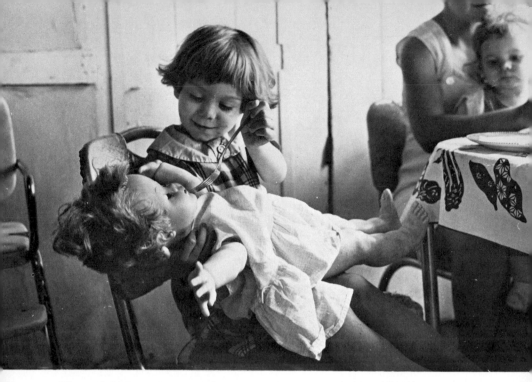

Figure 3.3. Families must decide what is needed most. (USDA)

depend in large part upon how much money we have. A man living on welfare is unable to buy a yacht. Most middle-income families cannot afford to have several homes.

It takes a certain amount of money to be able to have a real choice about its use. At the subsistence level, money tends to go for the basic necessities or, occasionally, for avenues of escape from the problems of living.

The average family in this country is living well above the poverty level and has the opportunity to make many decisions about things other than the basic necessities of life. The spending power of the family has increased tremendously in recent years. In 1936 approximately two thirds of the average family income went for food, clothing, and shelter. Forty years later only about half of the family income was needed for these things.

Economic choices are real choices; if you take one thing you can't have the other. If your boy rides a paper route, he may not have time for the extra homework that might win him a scholarship; if the farmer wants the field for pasture, he can't use it for corn; if the factory accepts a government contract to make signal corps equipment, it won't turn out transistor radios.[3]

[3] *Understanding and Using Economics* (Des Moines, Ia.: Meredith Publishing Co., 1966), p. 1.

Economic decisions may have social implications. If I decide to spend all my money on a new coat I may not have any money to give to the local Community Chest fund. Economic decisions can also have technical implications. If I buy a foreign car I will need to service it at a station that handles this type of car.

Social Decisions

Social decisions are concerned with problems that have broad implications for many people. We may be involved, for instance, in deciding whether our community should provide better after-school play facilities or enlarge its center for senior citizens.

Currently there is considerable agitation in the nation about how social decisions are arrived at, and what social decisions we make. John Gardner, one of the leading critics of the contemporary scene in America, says,

> For our generation there's no such thing as life without trouble. There are only good kinds of trouble and bad kinds of trouble.
>
> The bad kind of trouble stems from apathy, stagnation, the kind of hypocrisy that refuses to admit the existence of problems, the kind of vested interest that prevents institutional change. The good kind of trouble comes from being on the move, from being acutely aware of problems, from the confusion of too many people trying to solve the problem in too many ways all at once, too many critics talking too loudly, too many things changing too rapidly.[4]

Many social issues are creating great dissent throughout the United States: the problems of war abroad and unemployment at home, the treatment of minority groups within the nation, the increasingly crowded cities, and the pollution of our environment, to name only a few.

Gardner goes on to say that as a nation we do very badly at solving social problems, restructuring institutions, or making new human arrangements. We are much more effective in the area of technical change:

> We have learned brilliantly the means of accomplishing scientific and technical advance. But we have a very limited grasp of the art of changing human institutions to serve our purposes in a changing world.
>
> The consequences are familiar. We can build gleaming spires in the hearts of our cities, but we can't redeem the ghettos.
>
> We can keep people alive twenty-five years beyond retirement, but we can't ensure that they can live those years in dignity.
>
> We choke in the air that we ourselves polluted. We live in fear of a

4 John W. Gardner, *No Easy Victories* (New York: Harper & Row, 1968), p. 26.

thermonuclear climax for which we provided the ingredients. We face a population disaster made more probable by our own healing arts.[5]

Social problems are extremely complex. There may be obvious needs, such as a shortage of adequate housing for many people in our urban areas, but a workable solution may be difficult to decide upon. Will the nation's best interests be served by providing housing outside the heart of our cities? Or should we try either to rehabilitate rundown housing or to rebuild on the sites of the debilitated housing? Would it be better to provide free meals at school for children or to see that every family had a minimum income so that they could adequately feed their children themselves? Where should new industries be located—near the population centers, or in less-developed areas where we can build new and better communities?

Part of the problem of bringing about social change is that we are often strongly motivated *not* to change things. We like the old, familiar ways. Any proposal for change is bound to upset some segment of the population.

Individuals and families deal with social problems as well as the larger community. A social decision for the family might be to decide in what community to settle when it moves to a new area. Although there are many economic implications to this decision, it is primarily a decision based on many values, of which the use of money is only one.

Many social decisions involve making changes in areas that are closely related to our value structure. We often feel insecure and threatened at the possibility of such changes. As a result social decisions are often delayed until a crisis arises. But this is not necessarily the most effective way of handling them.

Social decisions have both economic and technical consequences. New public programs will need to be paid for with taxes or fees. Shall motorists subsidize the railroads through higher gasoline taxes? Should the local community swimming pool charge its users a fee or should the costs be paid for by taxes? An illustration of the technical consequence of a social decision is what happens when a new housing project is planned in an area of rundown houses. The occupants of the area must be relocated, at least temporarily, so that the new housing can be built.

Technical Decisions

Technical decisions are concerned with finding the best way to do something, usually in operational situations. How can we turn our

[5] Ibid., p. 27.

inventory over most quickly? Which shoes will wear best on a vigorous growing youngster? What store is the most convenient to shop at? Are the prices cheaper at one supermarket than at another?

Increasingly, business and government are trying to solve technical problems with the use of computers. Computers make it possible to compile and summarize a great deal of information very quickly, and to select among various alternatives based on the data fed into the machine. For example, is space available on a flight next Wednesday at 9:00 A.M. from Chicago to Atlanta? You can usually get the answer in a matter of seconds.

Families can make more effective technical decisions by using as much as possible of the information that is available. In the future more information will probably be assembled for family use with the aid of computers.

Technical decisions have social and economic consequences. If a large company computerizes several of its operations, the people who formerly did these jobs will have to do something else. Perhaps they can be relocated within the same company. Maybe they will be thrown out of work. Or they may be able to learn to run part of the computer operation and earn more than they formerly did.

Factors That Influence Family Decisions

The decisions that one makes are influenced by many factors.

Values

Most major decisions are strongly influenced by one's values. People tend to act in ways that are consistent with their real values. (This was discussed more fully in Chapter 2, "Values and Home Management.")

Considerable differences exist among researchers as to how values influence decision making. Some suggest that there is a direct relationship between values and decisions. Others, such as Braybrooke and Lindblom,[6] feel that, although values are influential in the decision-making process, there is not a simple, direct relationship between a value and a decision. In a choice-making situation where one has to make a decision, alternative A might enhance one value, whereas alternative B might contribute a small amount to the fulfillment of a different value. Is the small amount of the contribution to one value to be preferred to the greater fulfillment of

---

[6] D. Braybrooke and C. E. Lindblom, *A Strategy of Decision* (New York: The Free Press, 1963), pp. 7–8.

Figure 3.4. Where should you live? This is one type of decision that is influenced by one's values. (Agency of Development & Community Affairs, Montpelier, Vermont)

another? Or will the choice be based on whatever value is highest in one's hierarchy of values? Much will depend on the individual situation.

An illustration of the sort of problem raised by Braybrooke and Lindblom might be a college student considering her plans for the summer. She needs money to buy clothes. Her basic school expenses, but not her clothing, are paid by her family. She has been offered two jobs. Should she take a high-paying job as a waitress in her home town or a more interesting one as a tour guide for an international exposition in another part of the country? The tour guide job would mean that she would have to live away from home. Travel to the job and her living expenses there would cut considerably into the already slightly lower salary that she would make in this position. Her final decision may involve weighing the choice of having more money for clothing or having a more interesting summer.

Family Characteristics

The distinctive make-up of a family has decided influence on their decisions. Factors such as the size of the family, the stage of the family life cycle, the parents' occupations and education, the area of residence, and the family's religion may have an important influence on many decisions.

Obviously, the nature and size of many expenditures is related to the stage of the family life cycle. Families with teen-agers need more food per child than families with small children. The market for diapers and cribs is among families with small babies. Expenditures for college are made for youngsters in their late teens and early twenties.

> In a high income economy the stage of the life cycle is probably far more important than income in determining size of total food expenditures. On the other hand, level of income is more significant in determining transportation (automobile) and household equipment expenditures.[7]

Increased education of the parents generally results in their having a higher level of knowledge and the family having a greater number of goals. With greater knowledge, the parents may be aware of more alternatives in making decisions, and also where to go for information in evaluating the alternatives.

The occupation of the wage earners in the family will have a real impact on family decisions. The life style of a professor and a plumber earning the same income may be quite different. The professor may spend a far greater proportion of his income on books and travel. The plumber's wife

---

[7] Joseph Gartner, Lee Kolmer, and Ethel B. Jones, *Consumer Decision Making.* Consumer Marketing Bulletin, Cooperative Extension Service, Iowa State University (Nov. 1960), p. 21.

may need to serve her husband more high-energy foods than if he had a sedentary job.

Families with similar characteristics may make different decisions depending upon where they live. The clothing needs of a person in Florida are different from those of a person in Maine, where winter comes early and stays late. Location can influence the family's way of living. In southern California, where it is mild all year, a backyard swimming pool could be used more often than in the Rocky Mountains, where the swimming season is much briefer.

Family Resources

Families vary in the resources that they possess. One family may have more money, another more knowledge of the possible alternatives. Some families have strong, healthy members, others members in poor health.

One of the current national concerns is how to help families in poverty to improve their situation. Increasingly, we are recognizing that poverty is not only the result of a lack of money, but the result of a lack of many other resources as well.

The mother of a large family on welfare may have poor health as a result of many years of privation. She has little or no income, few assets, if any, and credit is not easily available. She is overwhelmed with household work, which is often done the slow, hard way because she hasn't effective tools, such as a working oven, an automatic washing machine, or even hot running water. Her knowledge of available choices may be very limited. She might not even know where to go for help, if she is isolated in a rural community, ghetto, or suburb.

Middle-income families usually possess many of these resources. Often they can substitute one resource for another.

There are a number of theories about how family resources influence economic decisions. One of the most widely accepted is Katona's theory.

1. Consumers generally follow habitual expenditure patterns. They make many purchases that are similar to ones they have made in the past. The bigger the purchase, the more apt one is to deliberate, to make a real decision rather than to rely on habitual behavior.
2. Food and clothing purchases are generally habitual. We tend to buy similar types of clothing and food over and over again. Some women stick to lots of sweaters and skirts for daily use. A man may wear a sport jacket and slacks in preference to a suit whenever possible. From the tremendous array of food available in modern markets we often select the same kinds for the same occasions every time, such as rice, potatoes, or spaghetti as the staple starchy food for dinner.

3. It is difficult to generalize about the motives of people in making buying decisions. One can more readily identify the motives related to an individual's decision to purchase something specific.[8]

The Roles and Aspirations of the Family Members

Most people assume many different roles in the process of living. A man may be a father, an employee of a corporation, a member of the Lions Club, active in his church, and a member of a golf group. His wife may be a mother, a member of the Parent-Teachers Association of a school, a member of her church's hospitality committee, and an avid gardener.

Each of these roles has an influence on our behavior, including decision making. Mother is not likely to wear the same clothes for gardening and for a PTA meeting. Her husband needs certain equipment to play golf. As an employee of the XYZ Corporation he may be expected to attend the annual employee picnic every spring or to make a small contribution to the fund to send a gift to people who are ill.

One may aspire to belong to a different group. A college boy may want to get on the football team. His parents may want to join the local tennis club. The aspirations influence one's decisions. The aspiring football player may give up cigarette smoking to improve his stamina. His mother may shop more carefully than usual for tennis outfits that she feels will be appropriate for the club. Freshman girls at college are usually particularly anxious to look well so that they will be accepted by the college group. It is well known that freshmen of both sexes tend to arrive on campus with more clothes than upperclassmen.

Reference group standards are important in the purchase of items that have a high degree of visibility—the things that others see. Such standards tend to be much less important in the selection of articles that are largely serviceable, such as soap powder or an alarm clock. Group standards exert a much greater influence in the selection of clothing styles than on the selection of a store in which to buy them, because the styles are much more visible.

The Socioeconomic Setting

The culture suggests certain ways of consuming. Some things are appropriate for breakfast, others for dinner. Americans think of dry cereals as breakfast food, of meat and potatoes as suitable for dinner. From a nutritional point of view these meals could easily be reversed, but that would mean going against our cultural pattern.

---

[8] George Katona, *Psychological Analysis of Economic Behavior* (New York: McGraw-Hill, Inc., 1951).

Cultures vary in their patterns. In England kippered herring is a popular breakfast, whereas in the United States fish is rarely served at breakfast. Most cultures use only a small fraction of the possible sources of nutrition as part of their cultural pattern.

The groups with whom we interact pass on suggestions as to how we should satisfy our needs. "The right solutions suggested by our groups for most of our needs are only a small part of those which could, objectively, satisfy them."[9] Clothing styles are an obvious example.

Our individual reference groups have cultural patterns that influence our decisions. When we select a place to live we may be concerned with getting many features that will make us comfortable, but we are probably also aware of how our housing will look to the people with whom we interact.

Most people belong to several groups which do not overlap very much. The values and cultural patterns of these groups may be different. A college student may come from a home where alcoholic beverages are never used. Away at college she may find herself in a group where everyone drinks beer. Conflicts between cultural standards often arise as we move from one group to another.

The state of the national economy has great impact on the family's decisions. The most important effect of the United States' economy on family decision making has been the long-term trend toward substantially higher real incomes for most families. Real family income is actual purchasing power.

In prosperous periods most people are working and have money to spend. As a result they usually feel optimistic and tend to buy more freely. Studies of buying intentions of families indicate that people buy big ticket items such as cars, houses, and washing machines, more freely when they are optimistic about the future economic situation. They buy less readily when they are concerned about it.[10]

Two major factors are involved in how people view the future economic situation: their evaluation of the national trend and their feelings about their personal financial situation. A family's situation may not be in line with the national picture. While the economy is booming, a man may be unemployed because his trade is no longer in demand. Men who shod horses were thrown out of work when the automobile, train, and trolley displaced horses as a means of transportation. More recently, many agricultural workers have become unemployed as farming has become more mechanized. Computers have taken over certain clerical jobs. A wage earner may also be without work in prosperous times because of ill health,

[9] Chester R. Wasson, Frederick D. Sturdivant, and David H. McConaughy, *Competition and Human Behavior* (New York: Appleton–Century–Crofts, 1968), p. 42.

[10] See the series of studies on buying intentions published by the Survey Research Center, University of Michigan, Ann Arbor, Michigan.

an accident, the relocation of an industry, the changing nature of a productive operation, or many other reasons.

Our Awareness of Things That Are Available

In this era of mass communication we are constantly bombarded with visual and audio messages by television, radio, newspapers, magazines, and billboards. Advertisements and illustrations of new, interesting products and services are all around us. In addition, we can see what is on display at stores, and what our friends and relatives have. All these sources suggest things we might buy, build, make, or do.

Advertising is an important influence on the economic decisions of the family. Often it is the channel through which we learn about new or improved products and services. Even small children are responsive to the lure of advertising. Many a mother has bought a breakfast cereal or cookies because her child heard about them on TV and wanted them.

Advertising can be used in many ways by the family. Some families find that it tempts them to buy many things that they cannot afford, or do not need. Others use it more constructively, such as for comparative shopping. Many homemakers study the newspaper advertisements for food, clothing, and household products before they go shopping.

Ideas of what is attractive and desirable are often suggested by those with whom we interact. It would seem that in many suburban areas backyard pools tend to be clustered in groups. Several families in a row will have pools, and then there will be areas where no one has a pool. Possibly one family has gotten a pool and obviously enjoyed it. This, in turn, gave the people nearby the idea that it would be fun to have a pool.

The Search for Alternatives

Effective consumer decisions require that time and effort be spent looking for information about the relative worth of various choices.

> The most compelling reason for devoting time and effort to the making of better decisions as consumers is that this is an important means of increasing purchasing power. There are two paths by which such increases may be achieved: (1) buying the same (or similar) product at a lower price, or (2), for the same price, buying a better-performing or more durable product.[11]

Suppose that you are planning to buy a portable television set. You have selected the make and model that suits your tastes, needs, and

[11] E. Scott Maynes, "The Payoff for Intelligent Consumer Decision-Making," *Journal of Home Economics*, Vol. 61 (1969), p. 97.

Figure 3.5. These young people are spending time and effort rather than money to have the car washed. (Bethlehem Steel Corporation)

pocket-book. The question of where to buy it may have an important bearing on how satisfied you will be with your selection. Do you want to pay the lowest possible price, which is available at a discount store? Or do you feel that the service on the set which will be provided by a local store might make their slightly higher price a better buy? An older person who has difficulty in lifting heavy things might want to buy from a store that delivers.

The search for alternatives is not limited to the selection of an article and where one buys it. It can also include how you finance it and when you buy. Prices of many goods are lower at sales. Interest rates on home mortgages fluctuate with the economy. These are alternatives that should also be considered.

Most people are willing to put more time and effort into the search for alternatives when the cost of the item is large. They may have to live with the results of a big mistake for a long time. People generally keep their cars at least three years, their washing machines seven or eight years, and their refrigerators even longer. On the other hand, when the cost is small a mistake is not as serious.

One may eliminate an alternative for more than one type of reason. The following example illustrates how a family might eliminate alternatives because of both preferences and resource restrictions.

Assume that because of money restrictions a family sold its car when it moved. After settling in a new home, the family begins to consider means of transportation. Alternatives include new and used cars of American or foreign manufacture, public transportation, bicycles and walking. Because the husband refuses to walk or ride a bicycle, these two alternatives are discarded. Furthermore, upon investigation of the bus schedule, they find that the bus runs too infrequently to meet family requirements. Thus, these three alternative means of transportation are outside the family's relevant range because they are not consistent with family preferences.

The family is now left with the alternatives of a new car or used car of American or foreign manufacture. They eliminate the foreign car because they feel most foreign cars are too small to comfortably seat a family of five, and servicing may be costly. They have now narrowed their alternatives to a new or used American-made car. Because of expenses incurred in moving and a relatively low family income . . . [($5,000)], the family decides against a new car. The new car is eliminated because of limited income. Another family with a higher income may eliminate a new car by preference. The husband may like to work on cars. In this case the new car would have been eliminated because of the family's preferences and not because of its income restrictions.

Deciding on the used car does not end the decision-making process. Remaining possibilities may include different models of cars, methods of financing, color, running condition, choice of a sales agency, and many others.

Having decided on a used car, the family again goes through a process of seeking alternatives. However, this time their search for alternatives is restricted to American-made used cars. They may visit various used car lots, check on used cars in newspaper advertisements, speak to friends, and so on. After a period of investigation, the family may eliminate all but two used cars which they feel satisfy their needs and preferences.[12]

Participation of Family Members in Decision Making

Family decisions may be made by one person, but major decisions often involve more than one person in the decision-making process. The extent of the participation in a decision by the various members will depend both on the type of decision being made and on the attitude of the family members about who should make it. Some families are very authoritarian, and

[12] Gartner, Kolmer, and Jones, op. cit., pp. 7–8.

the husband makes most of the important decisions. Others divide the responsibilities for decision making. In some, the major decisions may be made jointly by the husband and wife but operational decisions involved in the running of the household are made by the wife.

The influence of the children on family decisions varies greatly. A son or daughter who is working and contributing to the family income may have a considerable role in family decisions. Small children are known to exert forces on decisions to buy certain foods. A family may move to another part of the country because Johnnie has asthma and they want to live where the environment is better for him.

Gartner, Kolmer, and Jones also have summarized a partial list of possible interactions among family members in the decision-making process with illustrations of some types of interactions:

1. Decision making for the family by the husband, keeping the family in mind. This involves a certain degree of subtle interaction, since the husband may or may not be aware of family preferences and may or may not care.
2. Decision making for the family by the wife alone with the family in mind. This also is a form of subtle interaction.
3. Decision making by the husband alone and for himself. Although this is, in a sense, individual decision making, it must also be thought of as related to family decision making. Any decision made by an individual within the family, even though it affects him directly, may affect other members of the family and thus be thought of in the context of family decision making.
4. Decision making by the wife alone and for herself. Comments made under 3 are also appropriate here.
5. Decision making by a child alone and for itself. Comments under 3 are also appropriate here.
6. Decision making for the family by the husband and wife, but husband's feelings predominating.
7. Decision making for the family by the husband and wife, but wife's feelings predominating.
8. Decision making by the husband and wife for the family, where both husband and wife have equal voice.
9. Decision making by the husband, wife and children, where all have equal voice.

An example of the first type of interaction might be a husband buying a car. Although the purchase of a car may have been discussed with his wife and other family members, the husband might make the decision by himself.

Food buying may be an example of interaction number 2. The wife does the actual buying of food; however, her purchases will reflect the tastes and preferences of her family and the health and economic situation of the family.

Interactions 3, 4, and 5 probably predominate in buying situations where the items being considered are relatively personal and small in cost. The husband may choose his own brand of tobacco. The wife will choose her own cosmetics, the young child his own candy, and the older child certain items of clothing.

Figure 3.6. Which family member makes the decision on a particular purchase? (American Telephone and Telegraph Co.)

Interactions 6 and 7 might occur in a situation where one member has more technical information about the alternatives than the other, or if the purchasing decision is culturally the role of one member. For example, a woman may assist in choosing the family car though the final choice is made by the husband.

An evening's entertainment may be an example of interaction 8. Both husband and wife may have equal voice in choosing what to do on a night out. If preferences are similar, then the choice will satisfy both. If preference differences do exist and each has equal voice, an impasse may be reached. If, however, one ultimately predominates over the other, the pattern of interaction may shift from No. 8 to another type of interaction. The final choice in this case will not be mutually satisfactory to both individuals.

Interaction 9 may occur in choosing the site of the family vacation. In this type of decision making, all family members except very small children may participate in (1) determining what alternatives are available, (2) determining the relevant alternatives, (3) appraising the relevant alternatives, and (4) making the final choice of a vacation place.[13]

Decision-Making Styles

People approach making a decision in different ways An individual's manner of making decisions is referred to as his style. It is not yet clear whether each person has only one manner of approaching decision

[13] Ibid., pp. 14–15.

making, or whether their style changes with the type of decision confronting them.

A decision-making style has three elements. The *mode* is the manner of stating the problem. "Maybe this will happen if I do thus and so." I believe in the value of this, therefore, I will do the following." The *time reference* refers to the time period for action that is under consideration. The third element of style, *the decision rule*, describes the way in which an individual arrives at the final choice of an alternative. Three different decision rules are: (a) preferential ranking . . . of alternatives from best to worst; (b) objective elimination, in which the advantages and disadvantages of each alternative are weighed and action is changed if the situation calls for it, and (c) immediate closure in which one or more alternatives . . . are immediately discarded and attention is focused on one alternative.[14]

The extent of the participation of various family members in a decision will depend both on the type of decision being made and on the attitude of the family members about who should make the decision.

Case Studies[15]

The A Family

GENERAL CHARACTERISTICS

Age: Mr. 43, Mrs. 41, son 20 (overseas), daughters 15 and 4. Married 22 years. Both spouses graduated from high school. Occupations: Mr. is a public transit operator. Mrs. has worked outside the home for several periods during her marriage, the last in an electronics manufacturing plant prior to the birth of the youngest child.... Organizations: Mr., American Legion, Transit Union, church; Mrs., church, and church women's chairman. Housing: own their two-story home, seven years in the house, thirteen in the neighborhood. Living room furnished with couch and easy chair, built-in bookcases well filled with books, magazines. Dining room suite. Rugs both rooms. Furnishings worn.

The fifteen-year-old daughter wants to join a social club at school. Her father is against it because "he doesn't like the smoking that goes on at the parties." Mrs. A. feels that if the girl "is going to smoke, she is going to smoke." Early in the school year Mr. A. had restricted the daughter to no dances or games until she brought her grades up. Now that the grades have improved, the restrictions are off. The daughter must have certain grades before she can get into the club, and must maintain her grades. Mrs. A. thinks that if they don't let the girl join the club, "she may let her grades drop." Mrs. A. concluded, "When the time comes, I'll have him talked into it. I told her not to worry about it."

---

[14] Irma H. Gross, Elizabeth Walbert Crandall, and Marjorie M. Knoll, *Management for Modern Families* (New York: Appleton–Century–Crofts, 1973), p. 232.

[15] From Reta R. Lancaster, "Case Studies of the Decision-Making of Ten Non-College Educated Homemakers," Master's thesis, University of Kansas, 1966.

At the time of the interview, Mrs. A. was still thinking about where she should work. She said that they had had to buy a new car the previous month. Her husband decided that their nine-year-old car wasn't worth fixing and bought a new car. Mrs. A. said her job would pay for the car, for dentures for her husband, and for having their house exterior painted.

Mrs. A. has made application at a government ordnance plant outside the city. Two problems with working at this job are (1) it is shift work and (2) she must find a ride. Mrs. A. had done some looking for a ride, but was not successful because the people she knew who worked at the plant were on regular hours. Mrs. A. does not drive and did not mention learning to drive as a possible alternative. She did say that if she knew how to drive she could take the car to work while her husband took the bus. She has talked with her family about the possibility of her working. The fifteen-year-old daughter is going to do the ironing at ten cents a piece. A niece on the next block will care for the four-year-old daughter. Mrs. A. will be working nights part of the time and is afraid that her husband, who sleeps soundly, may not wake up "when the fifteen-year-old comes in from dates to check her curfew." Mrs. A. said she plans to sleep on the back porch when she comes in after working the night shift in order to be able to sleep undisturbed in the mornings while the family is getting up. She said Mr. A. wants her to work at the ordnance plant where she can "make more quicker and get it over with." Mrs. A. said she would be getting a "good salary" and "could save up twice as fast." A friend who has worked at the ordnance plant for six months "has been [given a raise] —more money that Mr. A. makes." When the interviewer inquired how Mr. A. felt about that, Mrs. A. said it would not cause problems because they put their money in the bank and "it isn't my money or his money, but our money."

In response to a question about how she felt about this decision, Mrs. A. replied that "what has to be, has to be" and added that she "can do it." She likes to be at home and "do for the home" and she feels "a mother's place is at home." Before, when she worked, the two children were in school and the "only consideration was finances." She said that she felt "more uncertain" about this than any decision she has "ever made." She is "not sure how it will all work out, especially shift work and getting a ride." In conclusion, Mrs. A. said in a confidential tone, "to be honest with you, I put in my application" at the ordnance plant and "if it's the Lord's will, I'll get on there, and if it isn't, I won't, and will look elsewhere." The electronics plant where Mrs. A. worked five years ago is closed now. She has the name of a plant "run by one of the men" where she previously worked, but she hasn't called there yet. She said she would have to start "at the bottom" of the wage scale ... if she "went back to electronics." Mrs. A. said she had considered baby-sitting and taking in ironing for extra money, but "children make me nervous" so she had decided against it.

The F Family

GENERAL CHARACTERISTICS

Age: Mr. 30, Mrs. 28, son 3, daughters 9, 6. Married ten years. Both spouses high school graduates. Occupations: Mr. is a truck driver, Mrs. has been a bookkeeper two years since marriage. . . . Organizations: the family attends church on Sunday but "that is all we do." Mrs. F. is preschool president. Housing: own their small house, four years in the house, both spouses have lived in the area "all our lives," both sets of parents "live within ten blocks." Both exterior and interior of the house appeared to be in need of repair, e.g., boards on the porch were worn, a pane was missing from an interior door. The small living room contained a couch, coffee table, two lounge chairs, an easy chair and end table, a portable record player, console television and two guitars. The furniture was worn.

Mrs. F. began by saying, "Do you want a nice, juicy problem with lots of strife and struggle?" Then, with some pause, she told of a decision over what kind of cabinets to put in the new camper her husband is building. She said, "It's a major decision, really." Mr. F. is building the camper from "scratch." He started it four months ago. At that time they had a "rough idea" of what the inside would be like, but when it "came to actually doing it, his ideas were different from mine." "It really became a problem" for them three weeks prior to the interview, Mrs. F. reported. First it was a matter of how much space would be devoted to cabinets, then the problem also included what should go where and what type of finish should be used on the cabinets. Mrs. F. repeated several times that really this should be only a minor problem, but when "two people have different ideas, it doesn't come out so minor." They have now reached a compromise by purchasing the "icebox and the stove" for the camper. They decided that choosing the appliances would "simplify things." Mrs. F. reported that the appliances are the cheapest available. Now the cabinets will be built to fit around the icebox and the stove. She said, "You don't realize how many things you have to decide on something as simple as this until you really start. It seems like a simple matter, but it isn't." In an attempt to clarify her statement, the interviewer asked if she was saying that, had they known, they would not have started building the camper. Mrs. F. agreed, adding "either that or I would have said 'You build it and it will be just fine.' " Mrs. F. said she "made the mistake of offering a few simple suggestions."

In describing her feeling about this decision, Mrs. F. said she had the feeling of "frustration." She said there was a "relief at reaching a decision, but a terrible feeling at what's left to decide yet." She commented that when they bought their present house she had much the same feeling. She said the house was very small and there was the problem of whether they should put money into it, or go on paying rent. Mrs. F. said that after the papers were all signed it was a "relief to know something had been decided, even though it might not have the best solution."

The previous Sunday, Mr. and Mrs. F., while house-hunting, had looked at a large house which had "many of the things we want" in a house, but also "a lot we don't care about." Mrs. F. said they were undecided about whether to take the house or wait until fall in hopes of finding a better house in the meantime. She added that perhaps they will have saved more money by then, too. Mrs. F. said that they had lived in a small house so long that she doesn't know what to think about a "huge" house. The house has six rooms on the second floor and four on the main floor. Mrs. F. mentioned a concern over the disadvantages of the cost of heating a large house, the problem of keeping the house clean, and keeping track of the children in such a big place.

Prior to looking at houses Mr. and Mrs. F. decided on "a price range and how much a month" they could pay. They also had agreed on the general area in which they wanted to live because "this is important to us." In addition, they decided they would like to have a basement and a garage. Mrs. F. said these decisions were made by "mutual consent." She added that they agreed not to look at "more than we can afford" because "it's depressing." She and her husband have tried to "stick strictly to where if we like it, we can afford to buy it." Mrs. F. regretted they couldn't afford more because all the things they'd "like to have are difficult to find" in their price range. The F.'s have been hunting for a house for two months. Prior to that they "just talked about it."

With a baby due in three weeks, Mrs. F. said they needed a chest of drawers. Mr. F. wants to get a small chest to match the children's bedroom set, but Mrs. F. wants a double dresser which would give her more drawer space. She wants to get an unfinished chest and stain it to match the dining room set. Mr. F.'s "objection" is to the price of the double dresser. The F.'s haven't "quite worked it out" but Mrs. F. has "a feeling I'm going to win." Mr. F. "usually holds out a while, then he gets tired of arguing and gives in. I hold out a bit longer," she said. Mrs. F. said that her husband "doesn't really care, it's only that he'd rather spend [less]." She observed that they are going to have to "hurry up and decide." The chest, if small, will be for the baby. If they get the double dresser, the other things stored around the house will have to be "shuffled to make room for the baby's things" in the children's room. Mrs. F. said that since the baby is expected in three weeks, the dresser "may have to go unstained for a while." She said that finishing the double dresser was the "only disadvantage."

Summary

Decision making is considered the crux of the management process. Decisions involved in home management can be divided into two parts, major or policy decisions, and operational decisions, which are made to carry out major decisions.

Decision making is the process of making a determination after deliberation. Some of the important steps involved in making a decision are

1. Recognizing that a problem or choice-making situation exists.
2. Weighing the alternatives available.
3. Deciding upon an alternative.
4. Living with the consequences of the decision.

Families are involved with several types of decisions—economic, social, and technical. Economic decisions generally involve the use of money. Social decisions are concerned with problems that have broad implications for many people. Technical decisions are concerned with finding the best way to do something, usually in operational situations.

A wide variety of factors influence family decisions: the family characteristics, the nature and extent of family resources, the roles and aspirations of family members, the socioeconomic setting within which the family operates, and its awareness of things that are available, among others.

Effective consumer decisions require that time and effort be spent looking for information about the relative worth of the various choices. In economic decisions most people are willing to put more time and effort into the search for alternatives when the cost of the item is large.

CHAPTER FOLLOW-UP

1. You probably bought some new clothing this season. Why did you select the things that you purchased? In the process of making your final decision, what alternatives did you consider and eliminate? Why did you eliminate these alternatives?
2. Are there situations that you can remember where your decision was changed because of the influence of some other person or group of people?
3. Can you think of some decisions where you have invested a lot of time and effort considering the various alternatives. Are there other situations where it didn't seem worthwhile for you to weigh your choices so carefully?
4. Most people change their behavior somewhat when they join new groups. Can you think of any ways in which your behavior and thus your decision making changed when you entered college?
5. If you are living away from home have you changed your handling of money? What prompted these changes? How did you decide on new methods of managing money?

SELECTED REFERENCES

Aldous, Joan. "A Framework for the Analysis of Family Problem Solving." Aldous et al., *Family Problem Solving*. Hinsdale, Ill.: Dryden, 1970, pp. 265–281.

Baker, Georgianne. *Management in Families: Decision-Making*. Michigan State University Cooperative Extension Bulletin No. 453, 1964.

Bean, Nancy McLain. "Decision Class, Linkage and Sequence in One Central-Satellite Decision Complex." Master's thesis, Michigan State University, 1968.

Boharic, Kathleen Kane. "Wife's Perception of Husband–Wife Roles in Major Decisions." Master's thesis, University of Illinois, 1973.

Carbaugh, Katherine Anne. "Self-Actualization and Selected Aspects of Family Interaction in Decision-Making." Master's thesis, Washington State University, 1970.

Cavanaugh, Catherine, and Dorothy Z. Price. "Teaching Decision-Making to the Disadvantaged." *Journal of Home Economics*, Vol. 60 (1968), pp. 337–343.

Cox, Pamela. "The Relationship of Job Autonomy and Social Class to Self-Actualization and Conjugal Power in Family Decision-Making." Master's thesis, Washington State University, 1970.

Dale, Verda. *Managerial Decision-Making and the Homemaker.* University of Massachusetts Cooperative Extension Service Special Circular No. 286, not dated.

Drucker, Peter F. *The Effective Executive.* New York: Harper & Row, 1967.

Edwards, Kay P. "Goal-Oriented Family Behavior." *Journal of Home Economics,* Vol. 62 (1970), pp. 652–655.

Eigsti, Marilyn Hostetler. *Interrelationships of Value Orientation, Decision-Making Mode and Decision-Implementing Style of Selected Low Socio-Economic Status Black Homemakers.* Ph.D. thesis, Michigan State University, 1973.

Firebaugh, Francille Maloch, Nancy E. Johnson, and Frances M. Magrabi. "Computer Use in Household Decision Making." Report for the Subcommittee on Computer Use in Household and Family Decision Making with Evelyn P. Quesenberry and Robert L. Rizek. The land-grant universities and the U.S. Department of Agriculture, 1972.

Freed, V. H. "The Influence of the Physical Environment on Decision-Making." "Decision Making: How and What." Proceedings: 1968 Western Regional Workshop, College Teachers of Home Management, Corvallis, Ore.: Oregon State University, 1968, p. 42.

Gartner, Joseph, Lee Kolmer, and Ethel B. Jones. *Consumer Decision Making.* Consumer Marketing Bulletin, Cooperative Extension Service, Iowa State University (November 1960).

Gross, Irma H., Elizabeth Walbert Crandall, and Marjorie M. Knoll. *Management for Modern Families.* New York: Appleton-Century-Crofts, 1973, Chapter 6, "Decision Making."

Harter, Charlotte T. "The Economy's Effect on Decision-Making in Home Management." "Decision Making: How and What." Proceedings: 1968 Western Regional Workshop, College Teachers of Home Management, Corvallis, Ore.: Oregon State University, 1968, pp. 31–41.

Hendrix, Susan J. "Self-Actualization and Social Perception in Family Decision-Making." Master's thesis, Washington State University, 1970.

Knoll, Marjorie, M. "Toward a Conceptual Framework in Home Management Decision-Making Organization Process." *Journal of Home Economics,* Vol. 55 (1963), pp. 335–339.

Keenan, Maxine K. "Models for Decision-Making." Long Beach, Calif.: Department of Home Economics, California State College, 1969.

Lancaster, Reta R. "Case Studies of the Decision-Making of Ten Non-College Educated Homemakers." Master's thesis, University of Kansas, 1966.

Lau, Lana S. "Families' Decision-Making Process and Their Knowledge in the Purchase of Life Insurance." Master's thesis, Southern Illinois University, 1973.

Magee, John F. "Decision Trees for Decision Making." *Harvard Business Review,* Vol. 42 (1964), pp. 126–138.

Magrabi, Frances M. "Investigating Values and Decisions: Some Questions of Methodology." *Journal of Home Economics,* Vol. 58 (1966), pp. 795–799.

_____and LUCILLE MORK. "Computer-Assisted Problem Solving: Budgeting for Retirement." *Actualizing Concepts in Home Management.* Washington, D.C.: American Home Economics Association, 1973, pp. 63–66.

McCann, Duska Leone. "Values and Other Factors Which Influence Consumer Choice of a Portable Lamp." Master's thesis, The University of North Carolina at Greensboro, 1972.

Nichols, Addreen, Catherine R. Mumaw, Maryann Paynter, Martha A. Plonk, and Dorothy Z. Price. "Family Management." *Journal of Marriage and the Family.* Vol. 33 (1971), pp. 112–118.

Noyes, Marilyn B. "Difficulty of Decision-Making by Widows." Master's thesis, Utah State University, 1971.

Plonk, Martha A. "Exploring Interrelationships in a Central-Satellite Decision Complex." *Journal of Home Economics,* Vol. 60 (1968), pp. 789–792.

Poulson, Jenniev. "Selected Factors to Consider in Teaching Decision-Making." "Decision Making: How and What." Proceedings: 1968 Western Regional Workshop, College Teachers of Home Management, Corvallis, Ore.: Oregon State University, 1968, pp. 43–48.

Price, Dorothy Z. "Actualizing Concepts in Home Management: Decision Making." *Actualizing Concepts in Home Management.* Washington, D.C.: American Home Economics Association, 1974, pp. 1–3.

_____ "Social Decision Making." *The Family: Focus on Management.* Washington, D.C.: American Home Economics Association, 1970, pp. 14–20.

Reese, Alice Sue. "Attitudes of Parents and Their Sons Toward Independence in Decision-Making Situations." Master's thesis, Louisiana State University, 1970.

Schlater, Jean Davis. "The Management Process and Its Core Concepts." *Journal of Home Economics,* Vol. 59 (1967), pp. 93–98.

Taubin, Sara. "Community Resources to Implement New Concepts of Home Management." *Actualizing Concepts in Home Management.* Washington, D.C.: American Home Economics Association, 1974, pp. 44–47.

Thompson, Mary C. "An Adaptation of the In-Basket Technique for Use in a Simulated Managerial Situation." Master's thesis, Michigan State University, 1967.

Tribble, Mildred F. "Relationships Among Five Dimensions of Twenty-Five Home and Family Decisions." Master's thesis, Louisiana State University, 1970.

Weber, Janice M. "An Exploratory Study of Two Decision-Making Approaches." Master's thesis, Washington State University, 1970.

Wood, Sharon Foltman. "Day to Day Decision-Making of College Educated Homemakers." Master's thesis, Pennsylvania State University, 1966.

part two
the
use of
resources

The management of resources is one of the most challenging aspects of home management. One is constantly faced with decisions as to how to allocate resources. How much time shall be used for this? How much money can you afford to spend for that? Should you cut down here to have time, money or energy for something else?

Individuals and families have a variety of resources that may be used to satisfy their needs and desires. These are: (1) human resources, such as time, energy, knowledge and skills, and interests; (2) economic resources, such as money, credit, and other material assets; and (3) environmental resources, such as community facilities and natural resources.

Resources are limited. But there are ways of getting the most from them. Often one can substitute one or more resources for another—use time and energy to save money, or spend money to save time or energy. Community resources can be used for recreation to cut costs. You can make needed repairs yourself, instead of calling in a painter, plumber, or carpenter. Or one can spend more on services such as restaurant meals, a car wash, dry cleaning, and so on to save time and energy.

chapter 4

human resources

The effective use of time and energy is of particular concern in the management of the home. Today many people are anxious to spend as little time as possible on household work so that they may have time for other things, a job, more creative activities, recreation, or other things. Energy management is of particular concern to homemakers with heavy work loads, older people, or those with physical handicaps.

Using Time Effectively

Long-term trends in paid employment have reduced the number of hours worked per week, and the number of workweeks in the year. However, the time spent on homemaking has not decreased in spite of automatic equipment and convenience foods. In fact the trend seems to be for homemaking to take slightly more time. (See Figure 4.1.)

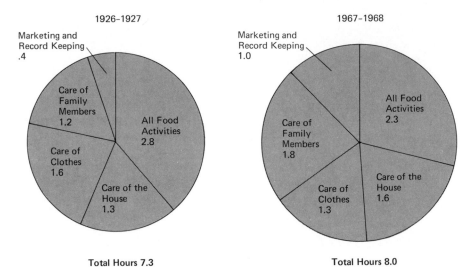

Figure 4.1. Comparison of Time Used for Household Work by Urban Home-makers. (Source: Kathryn E. Walker, "Homemaking Still Takes Time," *Journal of Home Economics*, Vol. 61 (October 1969), p. 622. 1926-27 data from Wilson, *Use of Time by Oregon Farm Homemakers.* Oregon State College, Agricultural Experiment Station Bulletin No. 256, 1929.)

Factors Influencing the Time Spent on Household Work

The amount of time spent on household work in a family depends on a number of things.

The family situation. Most important of all are the size of the family and the age of the children. Families with young children and many people have the most work. Small families can live in more compact, easy-to-care-for houses, apartments, or mobile homes, whereas big families generally want more space. Young children require considerable care and attention. Figure 4.2 indicates how the demands on a homemaker's time change at various stages of the life cycle.

Whether the homemaker is employed. Working women put in a long day, thanks to the combination of outside employment and homemaking activities. A multi-national study indicates that the working mother, in both socialist countries and capitalist societies, has less free time than her husband.[1]

---

[1] Alexander Szalai, "The Multinational Comparative Time Budget Research Project," Geneva, Switzerland: International Social Council and UNESCO, 1966.

In families where the homemaker was employed, the number of hours spent in household work decreased as the hours of employment increased. (See Table 4.1.) This reduction of hours probably indicates, in part, better use of time and also a willingness to simplify some household tasks. But it also reflects the fact that most employed homemakers do not have as many children, and particularly small children, at home. However, as job opportunities for women increase and more women feel compelled to work to maintain the families' standard of living, the number of homemakers with small children may increase.

TABLE 4.1
Hours per Day Spent on Household Work

Item	Hours	Item	Hours
All homemakers	7.3	*Age of youngest child*	
		Under 1 year	9.3
Number of children		1 year	8.3
0	4.8	2 to 5 years	7.7
1	6.8	6 to 11 years	7.1
2	7.8	12 to 17 years	6.0
3	7.7		
4	8.2	*Paid employment per week*	
5 or 6	8.5	None	8.1
7 to 9	9.2	1 to 14 hours	7.3
		15 to 29 hours	6.3
		30 hours of more	4.8

SOURCE: "Time Spent in Household Work by Homemakers," *Family Economics Review* (Sept. 1969), p. 5. Based on a study conducted by Kathryn E. Walker, Department of Consumer Economics and Public Policy, New York State College of Human Ecology, Cornell University.

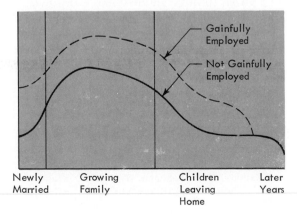

Figure 4.2. Demands on a homemaker's time at different stages.

The standard of living. A higher standard of living has also increased the need to use time for household work. Homes are larger and contain more things. More rooms need to be cleaned, more equipment has to be kept in repair, more clothes need to be laundered, mended, and sorted. Shopping has become more complex. With the increasing number of products on the market, and variations of foods and other goods, it takes more time to shop, particularly to shop wisely.

> There have been changes in the nature of the family's work over the years. While some of these changes have freed time, others simply have changed our way of using time.
>
> If the community provides all kinds of child care and educational services, the family still needs to "chauffeur" children to the day-care center, the library, the swimming pool or the baseball diamond. If industry provides ready prepared foods, someone in the family must use time to choose from the ever-changing market shelves, wait in line at the checkout counter and at the traffic light and then find a place to store foods for "instant use." Many labor-saving devices commonly used today lighten the work load, but they require time for service, maintenance and repair. Some changes in the family's work have made it physically easier to do, and many people mistake "easier" for "less time consuming."[2]

Housekeeping standards. Housekeeping standards also influence the amount of time used for household activities. The very fussy housekeeper who wants everything "just so" will spend more time than the more casual housekeeper. Families that expect assistance from the children generally have to accept a somewhat less meticulous job.

Whether new products or commercial products are used instead of home-produced ones is a matter that is also affected by standards. Some people wouldn't dream of using a prepared frozen dinner. However, the volume of sales of these products indicates that many people are more flexible in their standards of what to serve. Or, one's standards might be that frozen dinners are acceptable in some situations, but not others. A family may use them when they are pressed for time or if a child must make his own dinner but never for guests.

An interesting related development is the rapid increase in the use of frozen prepared main dishes by restaurants. Often the customer is unaware that the meal had been frozen because it is served on a regular plate.

Furnishings and equipment. The house and its furnishings make a difference in how much work and time are needed for upkeep. Carved furniture and little china knickknacks take time to keep clean. However,

---

[2] Kathryn E. Walker and William H. Gauger, "The Dollar Value of Household Work," Cornell University Cooperative Extension Service Information Bulletin 60, 1973, p. 3.

to some people the extra time and work are worthwhile because they get enjoyment from these objects. Other people couldn't be bothered with the extra work these require.

The availability and organization of supplies and equipment influence the time spent on housekeeping. It takes far less time and effort to do the family laundry with good equipment located conveniently. Preparing family meals is easier and faster in a well-arranged kitchen. Most people are aware of this, and a big selling point in new houses is an attractive modern kitchen.

Location. Where the home is located makes a difference, too. The gap between the amount of the time spent by farm and urban homemakers on household activities has narrowed because farm families are buying much more of their food and household goods. However, in general, farm homemakers still spend more time on household work, particularly food preparation activities, than urban homemakers.

The presence of a person with a handicap. Housekeeping takes more time if the homemaker has a physical handicap or needs to care for someone with a handicap. Often people with various types of handicaps can carry on many activities if they take more time, and if tools and equipment are arranged to fit their needs.

Pets. Pets add to the work load, and the time needed for household activities. In many urban areas dogs must be walked on a leash. Pets must be fed and groomed. Their food needs to be prepared and the utensils washed. Also, like people they tend to track in dirt from the outside. However, the growing number of household pets in the United States suggests that many people feel that the extra work they generate is worthwhile.

Attitude toward the task. There has been a growing recognition of the influence of psychological factors on physical activities. Various studies seem to suggest that there is a relationship between one's attitude and the amount of time spent on an activity. People who dislike sewing usually will buy most of their clothes if possible. People who get great pleasure out of cooking are often willing to spend a lot of time on meal preparation, at least for special occasions. Can you think of other examples?

Time Spent on Household Activities by Family Members

Homemaking is still largely a woman's job. While about 40 per cent of the married women in the United States are holding paid jobs, approximately 60 per cent are full-time homemakers. In addition, single women of all ages maintain their own households.

In many families the homemaker is someone other than the mother. Perhaps it is a grandmother or other female relative. Some homemakers are men. Sometimes the father is responsible for managing the household. A widowed man, one with custody of his children, or the father in a family

TABLE 4.2

Household Activities Performed by Family Members	Hours per Week of Wife's Employment Outside the Home			
	0 hours	1–14 hours	15–29 hours	30+ hours
	Hours/day			
Food-related Activities				
Wife	2.3	2.2	1.9	1.5
Husband	.1	.1	.2	.2
Children	.3	.4	.4	.4
Other Helpers	*	*	*	*
All Workers	2.7	2.7	2.5	2.2
House-care Activities				
Wife	1.6	1.4	1.3	1.1
Husband	.6	.7	.6	.6
Children	.4	.4	.4	.4
Other Helpers	.1	.1	.1	.1
All Workers	2.7	2.6	2.4	2.2
Clothing-care Activities				
Wife	1.3	1.3	1.1	.8
Husband	*	*	*	*
Children	.1	.1	.1	.1
Other Helpers	*	*	*	*
All Workers	1.4	1.4	1.3	.9
Family-care Activities				
Wife	1.9	1.4	1.1	.6
Husband	.4	.3	.4	.3
Children	.1	.2	.1	.1
Other Helpers	.2	.2	.5	.2
All Workers	2.6	2.1	2.1	1.2
Marketing, Management and Recreation				
Wife	1.0	1.0	.9	.8
Husband	.4	.4	.4	.4
Children	.2	.3	.3	.2
Other Helpers	*	*	*	*
All Workers	1.7	1.7	1.6	1.7

* Less than .1 hour.

SOURCE: Kathryn E. Walker, "Time-Use Patterns for Household Work Related to Home-maker's Employment." Talk at the 1970 National Agricultural Outlook Conference, Washington, D.C., February 18, 1970, p. 6.

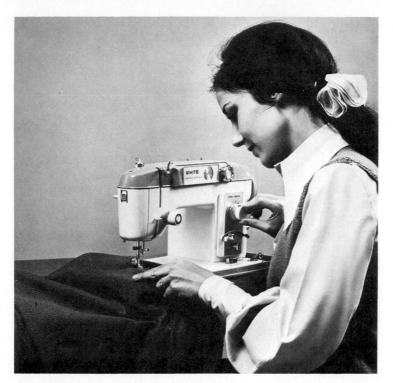

Figure 4.3. The use of time varies with one's interests. People who enjoy sewing generally spend more time making clothes than people who dislike sewing. (White Sewing Machine Company)

where the woman is the principal wage earner might be the homemaker. A man living alone has to take care of the operation of the household or arrange for someone else to do so. In the case of a retired couple the husband may be in charge of the household because the wife is physically unable to do so.

Table 4.2 shows how the various family members contributed time to household activities in a study of almost 1,300 families in the Syracuse, New York, area.

> What is most clearly seen. . . is who contributes the giant share of household work. . . the wife! This is true whether or not she is employed. In addition the figures do not show that husbands increase their work contribution if their wives are employed. This points to an interesting conclusion. While one social convention—that against mothers working—has broken down, another social convention—one that labels most of household tasks "women's work"—leaves her with a disproportionate share of the household tacks. One can only speculate about how long it will take society to change its perception of household work responsibilities in order that there might be a more equitable sharing of household tasks.[3]

[3] Walker and Gauger, op. cit., p. 5.

Today many young women are considering whether they want to hold a paid job for most of their lives and how this would affect family responsibilities if they decide to marry.

> It seems appropriate, at a time when more and more women are choosing employment, to encourage families to examine the employment cost-benefit ratio for the mother of the family, to look closely at the stages in the family cycle when benefits can outweigh costs, and to consciously decide what each member of the family is willing to pay in time to reach the goals that they have."[4]

Many young couples are considering this together. Evidence of some approaches are occasional newspaper articles about couples who are employed by the same organization and some who share a single job.

Controlling the Use of Time

The homemaker faces the same problems in the use of time that an executive in the business world does. There are constant interruptions and many people and jobs that demand attention. In addition, there is continual pressure to use time in unproductive ways.

One way for the homemaker to increase her effectiveness is to plan time rather than tasks. Usually there will be more things to do than one can manage within the limited span of a day, week, or lifetime. By planning time, one can allocate a place for the important and urgent things.

> Most discussions of the executive's task start with the advice to plan one's work. This sounds eminently plausible. The only thing wrong with it is that it rarely works. Effective executives know that time is the limiting factor.[5]

Many executives use a three-step process in planning time. First, they try to find out where their time is really being spent. Then they try to organize their time and to cut out unproductive uses of time. "Finally they consolidate their 'discretionary' time into the largest possible continuing units." [6]

This type of planning is applicable to homemaking. Many homemaking activities require a block of time to be able to do a meaningful segment of the task.

---

[4] Kathryn E. Walker, "Household Work Times: Its Implication for Family Decisions," *Journal of Home Economics,* Vol. 65 (1973), p. 11.
[5] Peter F. Drucker, *The Effective Executive* (New York: Harper & Row, 1967), p. 25.
[6] Ibid.

Planning the Use of Time

Plans for use of time involve anticipating certain future events and planning the way in which they will fit into the time schedule.

The timing of household activities is frequently determined by conditions outside the home, as well as within it. The decision as to when dinner shall be served will be influenced by whether the family wishes to eat together, when the various members can get home, possibly by the age of the children, and by the facilities available. The working hours of the wage earners, or the presence of very young children who function best with a very early dinner hour, may preclude having everyone eat together, particularly during the week. If the dining facilities or eating equipment are inadequate, then some family members may have to eat at different times.

Some jobs require more than one person, such as moving a heavy piece of furniture. The timing would be dependent on when two people are available who can do this.

The timing of work also depends on the allocation of tasks within the family. If Bob, who is in high school, is going to mow the lawn, then it must be timed around his school hours, and possibly other activities.

The weather may be an important influence. If it is raining one would not schedule a picnic, mow the lawn, wash the outside of the windows, or take the children out for a walk.

There are a number of techniques that people use to manage their time.

Routines. One common technique is to work out a routine or rhythm in one's activities. Routines reduce the need to plan constantly the time and work sequence for each activity, particularly those which are repeated at intervals.

Most people eat meals at fairly regular intervals. Some other household activities that many people routinize are: when to do laundry, on which day to market, how to clean the house, where they put groceries, and the procedure in the daily care of children.

Balancing the work load. Balancing the work load reduces pressure and frees time at peak periods. There are periods in one's life when the work load is particularly heavy, when the children are small, when someone is ill, or if the homemaker is trying to do a job in addition to homemaking. At these times in life the most that is possible is to eliminate unnecessary jobs, simplify and streamline activities, share the work load with other family members if this can be arranged, and use as much as possible of the help afforded by good tools and equipment, out-

Figure 4.4. A family member shares in household work. (Cooperative Extension Service, Washington State University)

side services, and possibly outside help. However, the size of the job will only be eased by these procedures; the work load will still be heavy.

At other times it is possible to balance the work load more evenly through the planning of time and work. A young homemaker who is just starting out might use some of her free time to plan and organize her furnishings and equipment, with the thought in mind that her time may be more limited in the future. This is particularly effective if she and her husband are in a place where they intend to stay for a few years.

On a short-term basis one can often plan time ahead. The busy home-maker may prepare in advance for a party by shopping early, and by pre-paring, and then freezing some of the foods. The working mother might buy seasonal clothing for herself and the children two or three times a year, rather than one item at a time if money is available. There are many ways to plan ahead in homemaking.

Reducing the warm-up and clean-up involved in activities. Some jobs require considerable time in getting ready to do the job or in cleaning up afterward. These tasks are most efficiently done if one can schedule them at a time when most or all of the job can be done at once, thus eliminating the need for repeated get ready and clean-up activities. Cutting out a pattern is an example of this type of job. Ironing may be, if the equipment is put away each time. Vacuuming is another. It may be more efficient to vacuum the whole house or a sizable portion of it at one time, rather than to clean each room in turn from top to bottom.

Dovetailing jobs. There are many jobs that can effectively be com-bined: emptying the dishwasher and setting the table, taking clothes out of the dryer and folding them, washing kitchen cabinets after a party be-cause the shelves are empty, taking sheets out of the dryer or off the line and putting them back on the beds without having to fold them.

Influences on Time Plans

Attitude toward the task. Attitude is an important influence on the success or failure of plans, and how long they take. Many people keep postponing jobs they dislike, such as doing the ironing or cleaning the kitchen fan. Even if they have planned to do the task, there always seem to be plenty of excuses for postponing it.

Research suggests that homemakers often report that it takes less time to do jobs they dislike.[7] This raises a number of questions:

Do disliked tasks actually take less time than liked tasks because home-makers have learned time- or work-saving methods, use more adequate equip-ment and supplies, or have quality-quantity standards that are comparatively lower than for liked tasks? Or do homemakers have greater unity within dis-

[7] Dulce Maria de Fonseca, "Analysis of Dishwashing Time in Selected Indiana Families," Master's thesis, Purdue University, 1964.

Nancy Carol Hook, "Use of Time in Regular Care of the House in Selected Indiana Families," Master's thesis, Purdue University, 1963.

Francille Maloch, "Characteristics of Most and Least Liked Household Tasks," Ph.D. thesis, Cornell University, 1962.

liked tasks and, therefore, perceive time as less? Or is their motivation greater to complete a disliked task than a liked task? [8]

The handling of interruptions. The way that interruptions are handled has an important influence on whether plans are carried out. The homemaker has considerable autonomy in the management of her time and work, if she chooses to exercise it. Generally she can decide within the framework of certain obligations when to do various tasks, or whether she wishes to take a nap, read, or visit with friends.

Interruptions can be handled in many ways. Some need immediate attention, such as the baby who is crying because he is hungry, Susie, who needs a Band-Aid because she fell off her bike and scraped her knee, or mopping up the floor because something has overflowed. Many others can be postponed or the time devoted to them greatly reduced.

> Telephone calls, unexpected visits, arrival of delivery men or inspectors or salesmen, calls from Johnny or Mary to help them find this or that can successfully break up your day. You may find that it takes you two hours to do an hour's ironing because you haven't the courage to disregard the telephone or the doorbell.[9]

People feel differently about interruptions. Some people enjoy a break in their regular work. Others feel that they are really needed when family members and friends keep calling on them for various things. Many people just do not know how to handle some of the unwanted interruptions.

Evaluating the Use of Time

A useful technique for evaluating the use of time spent in homemaking is through the use of homemaking work units. A homemaking work unit is the amount of work done in one hour under average conditions by one worker.[10] To see how these work, let us assume that you are a homemaker who is trying to improve her use of time.

> Do you think it takes you more time than it should to do your household work?

[8] Rose E. Steidl and Esther Crew Bratton, *Work in the Home* (New York: John Wiley & Sons, Inc., 1968), p. 99.

[9] Lillian M. Gilbreth, Orpha Mae Thomas, and Eleanor Clymer, *Management in the Home* (New York: Dodd, Mead & Company, 1960), p. 31.

[10] This definition and the excerpt discussion on work units is from Kathryn E. Walker, "New York State Homemaking Work Units," Cooperative Extension Service, New York State College of Home Economics at Cornell University and the U.S. Department of Agriculture.

Are you sometimes torn between doing community work and completing a homemaking job?

Do you wonder if you could or should help the family financially by working away from home in addition to working at home?

Are you interested in comparing the time spent on work in your home with the average time used in other homes to do a comparable amount of work?

... Homemaking work units provide a tool for helping you make choices in the use of time. As a basis for comparison, homemaking work units point up similarities and differences; they do not provide patterns for imitation. Because families differ, no one can say how much time should be used for the work of the home. What is right for other families may not help you attain the kind of home you want, but by comparing your use of time with that of others you may see where you want to change your present situation, or where you want to continue it unchanged. . . .

Work units have been established for the six most time-consuming homemaking tasks—meal preparation, dishwashing, physical care of family members, washing, ironing, and regular care of the house. These six homemaking tasks take more than three-fourths of the total homemaking time in the average household. Time used to do household work in 250 New York State farm and city homes was the basis for the units.

HOW TO USE THE WORK UNITS

... The use of the work units will be presented step by step. . . .

To compare the time you use for your household work with the average time used in other households for the same amount of work, you need to note the particular situations in your home that may affect your work load. Use column 1 of the work sheet (p. 100) to record general information about your family.

You also need to know the amount of time that is used in your household to do the work. Recall the amount of time that you and your family members and other helpers used on any *weekday* for the *first three of the tasks* listed above. It may be easiest to think of the time used yesterday. You need only estimated time, not clock-watched time. [The following pages tell you] what to include and what not to include. Record this time in columns 2 and 3 of the work sheet. . . . For washing, ironing, and regular care of the house recall the time used during an entire *week*.

After adding your time and that of helpers, use the table on page 101 to change your minutes to tenths of an hour. . . . Record it in column 4.

DISHWASHING TIME

Include:
Clearing the table
Putting food away
Scraping, stacking, washing, rinsing, drying dishes
Putting dishes away
Cleaning counter, range, and sink

Do not include:
> Sweeping the kitchen or doing other regular cleaning jobs that you do after washing dishes

If the dishes are air-dried and put away at the time of preparing the next meal, include this time in dishwashing and not in meal preparation time. If the dishes are put back on the table, this table-setting time should be included as preparation time for the next meal.

MEAL PREPARATION TIME

Include:
> Preparing food for meals
> Setting the table
> Serving the food

Do not include:
> Preparing food for snacks
> Packing lunches
> Preparing food for future use
>> quantity baking
>> freezing or canning foods

When food is prepared during one part of the day to be served at a meal later in the same day, the time for its preparation should be included with that of the meal at which it is served. In the case of leftovers, include only the time used to prepare them for serving.

TIME FOR PHYSICAL CARE OF FAMILY MEMBERS

Include:
> Bathing, dressing, feeding, putting children to bed
> Taking children to and from school or the doctor's office
> Helping children with lessons
> Preparing a formula for a baby and special food for small children
> Caring for a sick family member

Do not include:
> Taking care of children at the same time that you are doing something else
> Reading to or playing with children

TIME FOR WASHING CLOTHES

Include:
> Gathering soiled clothing and household linens
> Preparing equipment for use
> Sorting, spotting, washing, rinsing, starching, hanging up or taking down clothes
> Putting clothes into and removing them from a dryer

Do not include:
> Washing clothes by hand
> Washing blankets, curtains, and other special items

IRONING TIME

Include:
    Sprinkling and ironing personal clothing and household linens
    Putting clothes away
Do not include:
    Ironing of unusual pieces such as ruffled curtains
    Pressing of wool suits

Note that most pieces are considered as one piece; exceptions are handkerchiefs, napkins, and towels.

TIME FOR REGULAR CARE OF THE HOUSE

Include such daily or weekly tasks as:
    Bedmaking
    Mopping
    Sweeping
    Dusting
    Picking up clothes
    Putting rooms in order
    Vacuum cleaning
    Caring for house plants
    Caring for the furnace or stove
Do not include tasks usually done less frequently than once a week in your home. These may be:
    Washing windows
    Cleaning bed springs
    Seasonal cleaning
    Special cleaning

Regular care of the house must be checked on a weekly rather than a daily basis because families have different cleaning patterns. Some do most of their cleaning on one day and "pick up" on other days of the week; some have two or three cleaning days; others divide the cleaning time fairly evenly throughout the week.

OTHER HOMEMAKING TIME

You probably spend much time for homemaking activities in addition to the six for which there are work units. You may wish to total this time.
    Include any work which you consider a part of your homemaking job:
    Baking
    Canning and freezing
    Gardening
    Washing clothes by hand
    Sewing and mending
    Pressing clothes
    Marketing

Keeping accounts
Entertaining
Special and seasonal cleaning
Other

WORK OTHER THAN HOMEMAKING

In addition to working at home you may use time in working away from home.

Include as "other work":
    Part-time or full-time employment
    Work done to help a relative or friend
    Work done for the farm or other family business
Include as "community work":
    Any work that is done as a community service

WORK LOAD FOR YOUR HOUSEHOLD

When you have recorded the time used in your home for household work, you will want to compare this time with that used in other households for the same task or tasks.

Since a work unit is the amount of work done in one hour, you can estimate the work load in your home for each of the 6 work-unit tasks by using the work sheet . . . as follows: Identify your family situation in column 5; note the work units established for it in column 6; and record this number in column 7. This will give your work load in units of work.

Dishwashing—the work load is determined by the number of persons in your household.

Meal preparation—examine your menus to determine their type according to the [classification of meal types on p. 102]. Total the work units (or parts of a unit) for all meals served in a day to determine your work load in meal preparation.

Physical care of family members—start with the youngest child to determine the work load. Add to this the work units required for the care of the second and third child. Although the units for the second and third child decrease, this does not mean that these children require only this number of units of work; but the time for the youngest child is reduced somewhat when there is more than one child. Note that no units are allowed for family members who are 11 years of age or over. Units have not been established for families with more than three children under 11 years of age.

Washing clothes—determine the work load in washing by multiplying the number of tubfuls of clothes washed by the work unit per tubful.

Ironing clothes—the work load in ironing is determined by the number of pieces ironed during each ironing period. After determining the number of work units for each time ironing is done, add them to determine the work load for the week. The total number of pieces ironed in the week cannot be combined, because the time is dependent upon the number of pieces ironed during a single ironing period. The unit-per-piece ironed decreases with the number of pieces ironed at one time; the picture is incorrect if all pieces are added together.

Regular care of the house—the work load in regular cleaning is dependent on whether or not there are children in the family. Although there are other factors that affect time used in cleaning, the presence of children makes the greatest difference in the amount of time used for the task.

Now, compare the work load in work units for your household (column 7) with the time you used (column 4) to do this amount of work. Remember that one work unit is the amount of work done in one hour under average conditions.

USE OF SUMMARY SHEET

If you wish to calculate your total homemaking work load for a week, you can record the approximate time you used for each day's activities and the appropriate work units on the summary sheet. . . .

ANALYSIS OF YOUR USE OF TIME

Perhaps by looking at your use of time in relation to the way others use their time, you may be able to see where you want to change and where you want to continue without changing.

Have you used more time than the average to do some of your household tasks? Less time to do other tasks? [The following] is a list that may help you determine why you spend more or less time. Are you satisfied with the results? Would a change in your standards be desirable? Could a change in method help? Does the equipment you have give you the kind of help you need?

Is yours a heavy work load? Is it light? How have you adjusted your work load in order to do all the work you do? Are you satisfied with the way you use your time?

You may spend more than average time in your household to do the work of the home if you:

—Have no pressures to get the work done.

With little work to do and much time to do it, there may be no need for reducing the work time.

—Have inexperienced help with your work.

If a young son or daughter does a job, it may take longer than if you do it, but you may be more interested in his learning to work than in getting the job done quickly. You may need the help and not be concerned that it takes longer.

—Have little or no automatic equipment.

For example, washing clothes in a wringer-type washer takes more time than using an automatic washer.

—Are past middle age.

We all slow down, some sooner than others, as we grow older.

—Have high standards of work.

Possibly you do not mind working a long time at a job, because a job "well done" gives you a strong feeling of satisfaction.

Work Sheet for Recording the Homemaking Time Used in Your Home

General Information (col. 1)	Homemaking Activity	Approximate† Time Used in Your Household by		
		Homemaker (col. 2)	Helpers (col. 3)	All Workers (hrs) (col. 4)
Number in household _____		Yesterday		
	Dishwashing			
Ages of children				
Youngest _____				
Second youngest _____				
Third youngest _____				
Menu served:				
Morning	Meal preparation			
	Morning	_____	_____	_____
	Noon	_____	_____	_____
	Evening	_____	_____	_____
			Total _____	
Noon	Physical care of family members			
	Total time used yesterday			
		Last week		
Evening	Washing clothes			
	Ironing clothes			
	First ironing	_____	_____	_____
	Second Ironing	_____	_____	_____
	Third ironing	_____	_____	_____
			Total _____	
	Regular care of house			
Tubfuls of clothes washed last week _____	Other homemaking			
	Baking			
Pieces of clothes ironed each ironing period*	Sewing and mending			
	Marketing			
1 _____	Gardening			
2 _____	Preserving food			
3 _____	Entertaining			
	Other			
	Other work			
	Community work			

Work Sheet for Estimating the Work Load in Your Home

Basic of Work Units (col. 5)	Work Units (Col. 6)	Work Load (in Work Units) for Your Household (col. 7)
Number of persons for whom dishes were washed		
2 persons	0.9 unit/day	
3 persons	1.0 unit/day	
4 persons	1.2 units/day	
5 persons	1.5 units/day	
6 or more persons	1.6 units/day	_____
Types of meals served (See following page)		
Type 1 meal	0.3 unit/meal	Morning _____
Type 2 meal	0.5 unit/meal	Noon _____
Type 3 meal	0.8 unit/meal	Evening _____
Type 4 meal	1.0 unit/meal	Total _____
Age of family members cared for daily		
Youngest member under 2 years	2.0 units/day	Youngest child _____
Youngest member 2 to 5 years	1.0 unit/day	Second child _____
Youngest member 6 to 10 years	0.6 unit/day	Third child _____
Second member under 6 years	0.5 unit/day	Total _____
Second member 6 to 10 years	0.3 unit/day	
Third member under 6 years	0.2 unit/day	
	Total units—daily tasks	
Number of tubs of clothes washed	0.5 unit/tubful	
Number of pieces ironed per ironing period		First ironing _____
1 to 9 pieces	0.2 unit/piece	Second ironing _____
10 to 29 pieces	0.1 unit/piece	Third ironing _____
30 or more pieces	0.07 unit/piece	Total _____
Family composition		
All-adult households	4.0 units/week	
Households with children under 18 years	7.0 units/week	_____

* Each piece = 1, except: 2 towels or napkins = 1 piece, 6 handkerchiefs = 1 piece

† Table for changing minutes to nearest tenths of an hour

Minutes	Hours	Minutes	Hours	Minutes	Hours
5	0.1	25	0.4	45	0.8
10	0.2	30	0.5	50	0.8
15	0.3	35	0.6	55	0.9
20	0.3	40	0.7	60	1.0

Meal Types

Breakfast types
Type 1
  Any number of easily prepared foods
  or

  1 or 2 items requiring some preparation plus any number of easily prepared foods

Examples of easily prepared breakfast dishes:
  cold cereal, fruit juice,
    toast, beverage
Example of dishes requiring some preparation:
  hot cereal, cooked friut,
    eggs, bacon, sausage

Type 2
  3 dishes requiring some preparation plus any number of easily prepared foods
  or
  1 time-consuming dish plus any number of easily prepared foods

Examples of time-consuming breakfast dishes:
  waffles, potatoes, hot breads

Noon and Evening Meal Types
Type 1
  Any number of already prepared or quickly prepared foods

Examples of already prepared foods:
  packaged foods, canned fruits, ready-to-serve leftovers, bakery products

Type 2
  Leftovers somewhat changed in form plus Type 1
  or
  1 time-consuming dish plus 1 to 4 already or quickly prepared foods

Examples of quickly prepared foods:
  reheated leftovers, frozen or canned foods, hot sandwiches, canned soups, eggs, baked potatoes, weiners

Type 3
  1 time-consuming dish plus 5 or more already or quickly prepared foods
  or
  2 or 3 time-consuming dishes plus Type 1

Examples of time-consuming dishes:
  fresh vegetables, meats (chops, roasts), home-baked pies and cakes, puddings, creatively used leftovers, some salads

Type 4
  4 or more time-consuming dishes plus Type 1

—Like the work.

You may spend more time doing those jobs that you like. This may be because you want to prolong the pleasure of the job, or because you have a high standard for the job.

—Have a health problem in your family.

In addition to the time you spend for physical care of the person who is ill, you may need more time for many homemaking tasks.

—Have many interruptions in your work.

It takes time to start and stop a job.

You may spend less than average time in your household to do the work if you:

—Have good equipment.

This is especially true if you have automatic equipment.

—Plan your work.

Time saved by planning ahead can be applied to getting the work done.

—Have no help with your work from family members or others.

If there is much work to do, and no one to help, you may have found ways to make the work easier.

—Dislike the work.

You may have found a way to get the job done more quickly because you do not enjoy it, or you may be less concerned with doing the work as thoroughly as others do.

—Are relatively young, yet an experienced worker.

The heavy work load usually comes at the time when children are small and the homemaker is young.

—Have time pressures.

When there is much to do in a day, you may have found ways of doing work efficiently, or have accepted its being done less thoroughly or its being left undone.

—Have relaxed your standards of work.

Possibly you have found that by being less "fussy" you can save time to spend with the family, work away from home, or take part in community activities.

—Have simplified your work.

Time saved by changing your methods of doing routine tasks may have freed time for doing things you want to do.

The Dollar Value of Household Work Time

Recently attention has been focused on the dollar value of the homemaker's work in the household. Household services take time. If the homemaker did not perform them, they would take time from someone else.

If for one reason or another, the family members do not take care of their own house repairs, lawn mowing, meal preparation, and laundry care, then someone else usually does and is customarily paid in dollars and cents. When

Activity	Time Used in Your Home								Your Work Load in Work Units							
	M	T	W	Th	F	S	Sun	Total	M	T	W	Th	F	S	Sun	Total
Washing dishes																
Preparing meals																
Physical care of family																
Washing clothes																
Ironing clothes										X				X	X	
Regular care of house									X	X	X	X	X	X	X	
Total time for the above tasks																
Other homemaking																
Other work																
Community work																
Total work time																

Figure 4.5. Summary of homemaking time and work load for one week. (Kathryn E. Walker, *New York State Homemaking Work Units*, Cooperative Extension Service, Cornell University)

the household services are turned over to someone else to produce, they have a money value—the value of the time spent by the worker. The same services are just as valuable when provided by a family member. Consequently, a money value can be given by valuing the time the family spends on household work at the wage rates that would be paid to others for the same services.[11]

The Management of Energy

It is much more difficult to manage energy than to manage time. Time has definite boundaries—there are so many hours in a day, week, or month. Energy, on the other hand, is harder to gauge and much more difficult to apportion.

The Amount of Energy Available to an Individual

People vary in the amount of energy that they have. Age, physical heritage, and state of health all influence how much energy one has. Moreover, one's energy varies from day to day and during the night. An individual may be vary tired after a long trip or a late night. As the day goes on, energy tends to decrease.

People's attitude and emotions also influence their energy. The girl who is too tired to do anything suddenly gets all charged up when she is invited out by someone she finds special. In times of great excitement, a person may be very stimulated and draw upon energy reserves that he didn't know he had.

Reducing Fatigue

Some time ago industry learned that there were two major types of fatigue, physical and psychological. They found that it was possible to arrange working conditions and schedule rest periods in a way that would reduce both types of fatigue and increase the effectiveness of the worker.

Many of industry's methods can be applied in the home. Attractive surroundings help a person enjoy his work more. Many people keep the radio on while they do housework. Others enjoy sewing or ironing in front of the TV.

Rest periods reduce physiological fatigue. A lunch break or a short rest will often enable one to "snap back" and go on with a tiring job. Homemakers are particularly fortunate in that they often can schedule their coffee breaks or rest periods when they feel that they need them most.

A change of pace is helpful in reducing fatigue. Break up long, heavy

[11] Kathryn E. Walker and William H. Gauger, "Time and Its Dollar Value in Household Work," *Family Economics Review* (Fall 1973), p. 9.

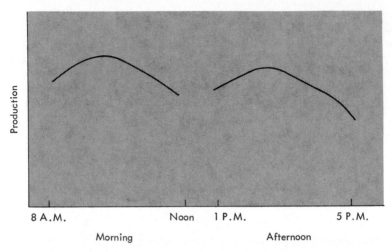

Figure 4.6. Production curve for heavy work. This diagram shows how an individual might be expected to perform when doing heavy work. The upward rise of the curve represents the warm-up period, then the worker reaches a plateau, and finally becomes less productive as fatigue sets in. A lunch break gives a boost, although generally productivity in the afternoon does not tend to reach as high a level as in the morning. Short breaks for coffee or relaxation may also boost the productivity curve.

jobs with smaller, lighter ones. Clean the kitchen thoroughly but only dust the living room. Take the children to the park. Then sit and mend or iron when you get home, or relax by reading or chatting with a friend on the telephone.

Tuck in a few things that are fun or pleasant. Be sure to plan for some moments when you can be with another adult if your family is at the small-child stage. Many homemakers find that they are refreshed by a chance to spend a little time with another adult during the day. Others welcome a visit from a friend or relative, or a break in the everyday routine such as helping at school, church, or a community activity.

The Energy Required for Household Tasks

It is possible to measure the energy used by household tasks. One method is to measure the oxygen intake or carbon dioxide output when an individual is performing various activities. From this the calories per minute that are used for each type of activity can be determined. The calories burned up in each type of activity will vary with the size and weight of an individual.

A recent approach to the measurement of light work has been done by

TABLE 4.3
Approximate Amount of Energy Required in Various Household Tasks

Use/Minute		
Light *1–2 Calories*	*Moderate* *2–3 Calories*	*Heavy* *3–4 Calories*
Knitting or crocheting	Using the vacuum cleaner	Scrubbing the floor
Hand sewing	Using the carpet sweeper	Waxing the floor
Machine sewing	Polishing furniture	Lifting heavy baskets of wet clothes
Preparing meals	Hanging clothes from a laundry cart	Lifting young children
Washing dishes	Marketing	Carrying bags of groceries
Dusting furniture	Bathing and dressing a young child	

measuring heartbeat rates. There is a close relationship between these two approaches. Table 4.3 groups some common household tasks according to the amount of energy needed for them.

For most houschold work, energy expenditure is not the primary cause of fatigue. Generally, women of moderate size must expend energy at the rate of 4 calories a minute or more to cause physical fatigue.

Recently concern has been expressed over the fact that many home-makers are not getting enough activity to maintain their physical fitness. Also, a lack of physical exertion adds to the problem of weight control, and obesity is a health problem for many people.

The Contribution of Knowledge and Skills

Family members possess certain knowledge and skills that can facilitate home management. For example, the need of family members, what community resources are available, where to go for information, and the range of alternatives available for management of a problem are just a few of the kinds of things it helps to know in managing a home.

There are useful skills in carrying on home activities. Some people are very good at planning and controlling the use of money. Another person may be an excellent cook. Still another may be skillful in furnishing a home attractively on a limited budget. Others are skillful in maintenance or repair activities. One person may be very effective in working with young children. All of these skills can contribute to successful home management.

Knowledge and skills can also be used instead of other resources. The person who has the skill to do small plumbing repairs doesn't have to hire a plumber for these jobs. The individual who knows where there are free campsites doesn't have to spend time looking up this information or money paying for a campsite that charges a fee.

Case Studies

Bob Markam is a twenty-four year old engineer. He lives in a one-room apartment in a small city and works for a construction company that builds factories.

He has lots of friends and a steady girl, Sue. He likes to eat out and go places with his friends but often cooks a simple supper at home to cut costs.

He didn't have much money saved when he finished college so he furnished his apartment largely with leftovers from family and friends. However, he did buy a comfortable new bed with one of his first paychecks. One of his present projects is fixing up the apartment a bit—painting it, building a desk, and hunting for some inexpensive dishes and glasses.

He is a fairly neat housekeeper but sometimes likes to sleep late. On those days he doesn't get much done before he goes to work.

Some days he goes to the office first, other days he goes directly to the construction site. In order to be able to get around easily he drives his car to work.

Bob's home management activities are really very similar to those of many young men and women living alone. Here is his early morning schedule for one day.

Bob Markham's Early-Morning Schedule

Activity	Time					
	7:45	8:00	8:15	8.30	8.45	9:00
Shower and shave						
Dress						
Call Sue						
Eat breakfast and read newspaper						
Straighten up						
Drive to the office						

Mrs. Pat Morris[12]

Pat is a petite, attractive, thirty-year-old homemaker. She and her husband both graduated from a [large] midwestern university where she was an elementary education major. They were married soon after their graduation. Mr. Morris received his Ph.D. from the same university last year and is presently employed by the U.S.D.A. They have four children: a son, aged eight; a son, six; a daughter, five; and a son, three.

THE HOUSE

The Morrises are buying a fairly new home. They are furnishing it a little at a time with contemporary furniture.

"When my husband was a graduate student we lived on a limited income and looked forward to a little more money," she commented. "Now that he's working we still don't find ourselves any better off because the house and furnishings are so expensive. We would rather have fewer good things and look forward to adding more as we can afford them."

The house is quite satisfactory except for the kitchen, which Pat feels is too small. Storage space in the rest of the house is very adequate. Most of their meals are eaten in the dining room alcove. The children sometimes have snacks and breakfast at the card table in the kitchen. Pat likes having a laundry area close to the kitchen. The extra space in the laundry area is handy as a mudroom for children's boots.

... A walk-in storage closet houses all the downstairs cleaning supplies as well as coats and children's outdoor garments. All of the bedrooms have large closets for clothes and for toys. Extra storage is provided upstairs under the eaves.

HOMEMAKING EXPERIENCE

Mrs. Morris' experience with homemaking before marriage was quite limited. She said she didn't like to go into the kitchen.

> Before I became a homemaker I thought homemaking must be terribly boring but I did like children and looked forward to having children. Now I find I enjoy homemaking very much.
>
> Even though I didn't help out in my mother's home very much, I guess I picked up a lot of habits from her. She used to write down meal plans and jobs to be done. I do much the same now.

GENERAL WORK PATTERN

In regard to the way she plans her work, she said,

> When I was first married I would sit down and try to think of the jobs that Mother had done and write them down. Sometimes I would write out a week's jobs at a time. I would write out the jobs to be done and the

---

[12] This and the following case study are from Grace Elliott Tasker, "Case Studies of Homemakers' Organization," Master's thesis, Cornell University, 1962.

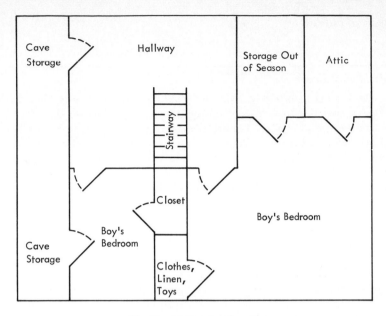

The Morris' Upstairs Floor Plan

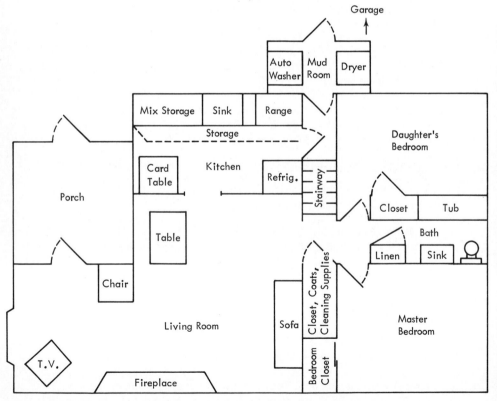

The Morris' Downstairs Floor Plan

Figure 4.7. The Morris' floor plan. (Grace Elliott Tasker, "Case Studies of Homemakers' Organization")

time to do them. When I had one child I really didn't need to plan very much, but when the second and third child arrived I had to plan quite often. I used to sit down in the morning and write out everything I planned to do that day. Now I pretty much outline in my head the things I have to do unless I'm having company. If I am giving a dinner party or planning for extra company I usually plan three or four days ahead of time.

Pat said,

I usually try to do one big job a day. I find that with so many interruptions it is impossible to accomplish more than one big job a day, other than the daily child care and meal preparation.

When the four children were tiny, my brother-in-law stayed with us. I found I had to leave things or decide what things were absolutely essential and take time to relax. I tried to relax and read while the children took their naps. I learned that that was the only way I could enjoy homemaking.

A brief sketch of [part of] Pat's weekday morning as recorded by her is shown on the following page.

On Monday Mrs. Morris's one big job is doing all the washing that has to be ironed. She also tries to clean up the house a little. On Tuesdays she does all the ironing. Ironing is not a favorite activity of hers.

I have to force myself to do the ironing so I plan to do it every Tuesday. . . . I iron very little especially since we purchased a dryer. On Wednesdays I wash again but only things that don't have to be ironed; that way I don't have ironing sitting around. I dislike to see it because then I have to do it. I also try to do a little cleaning on Wednesday. Sometimes on Wednesdays and Thursdays, my major item is sewing. Lately I've been doing a lot of baking on Thursdays because my children seem to enjoy it so much. Friday is the big cleaning day. By "big" cleaning I mean getting out the vacuum cleaner with all its attachments and really giving the place a good cleaning. On Saturdays I change the bedding and buy the groceries.

I plan menus before going to the market, I usually sit down just before shopping and plan the menus. By this I mean I plan the meat, the salad and the dessert for each day. I plan lunches by deciding what kind of soup or a salad and sandwich I will serve. Breakfasts are rather standardized so I just buy the same things every week. My other menus are somewhat standardized in that I plan from a variety of about fifteen different menus. I take the menu list and transfer it to the grocery list before going to the store. I have to do this because we are on a limited budget. I need to plan carefully in order to get the things my family needs and still be in a price range we can afford.

Mrs. Morris manages to participate in community activities because she feels this is important to her well-being.

Pat Morris' Early-Morning Schedule

Activity	7:00	7:15	7:30	7:45	8:00	8:15	8:30	8:45	9:00
Fix husband's lunch & breakfast	-----								
Fix children's breakfast		-----							
Get check book for husband									
Children and I eat			-----						
Get dressed									
Get scissors out of couch for boy									
Do dishes				----------					
Start washing machine					.				
Cut out picture for child						.			
Make beds downstairs							---.		
Make beds upstairs								..---.	
Dress youngest							.		
Pick up toys upstairs							.		
Dress two for outdoors								...	
Check on school bus								.	
Put clothes in dryer								.	
Clean playdough off table								.	
Dampen clothes									---.---
Fix daughter's hat									.
Hang up children's coats									.

"I enjoy getting out and doing things," she said, "otherwise I'm afraid I'd get that 'cabined-in' feeling."

"My husband and I take turns going out," she said. "We can't really afford a sitter so we take turns; then one of us is always at home."

"My husband and I belong to a once-a-month dinner club which sometimes meets at our house. Once in a while my husband brings home a guest for dinner. Other than that we do very little meal time entertaining."

Being organized means to Pat for one thing having a place for things and having things in their place; second, it means to her having an idea when to do the main jobs, and third, allowing time to do the things you want to do.

"I get very upset when I have to hunt all over the house for a shoe or a pair of scissors," she said, "I like to have things in their place."

"I enjoy homemaking," she concluded, "it is challenging and rewarding."

Mrs. Connie Ryan

Mrs. Connie Ryan was recommended by her husband, Charlie.

"My wife's a good manager," he said. "She looks after my four boys and still has time to help me when I need her." When I called her, she commented, "When Charlie told me about you, I said 'Now Charlie, I don't know whether I can help her or not.' " I hold her that no one knew better than her husband what kind of a manager she was. I made an appointment to visit her the next day.

When I knocked Connie came to the door in a neat house dress looking very trim and pretty. She graciously invited me in and took my boots out to the back porch. We set down in the living room. We talked about Charlie a few minutes. She said she was glad he was taking the community course and hoped it would help him learn a little about public relations. He has had some difficulty in controlling his workmen, largely because he is so easygoing, she thought.

Charlie owns and operates a fleet of trucks. He has seven men working for him. They haul salt to New York and other places. He also does some plumbing and carpentry work on the side.

"I've known Charlie since we were both nine and rode the school bus together," said Connie. "I was very shy, but Charlie used to come over and visit my mother. He still thinks my mother's the greatest cook around. He moved away after that and I didn't see much of him until he came out of the service. When he first came over I ran up the stairs. He came to the bottom of the stairs and said, 'Are you going to come down or shall I come up?' We started going together in March and were married in June. We have been married sixteen years. The first two years were the roughest. Sometimes little things cause you to eat your heart out but you just keep right on living. After a while you see how silly it was to worry."

Mrs. Ryan is thirty-eight years old. She is the mother of four boys aged 15, 9, 8, and 3.

THE HOUSE

The Ryans own their home. They tried at one time to sell it as it is in need of repair, but were unable to do so. They have more or less resigned themselves to fixing it up a little at a time as the money comes in.

"The living room really needs a coat of paint," she said. "The boys and I laid tiles on the floor last fall. The boys also tiled the bathroom one night while I was out and surprised me when I got home."

The furniture was well worn. The two chairs and sofa were placed facing a large TV in the corner. From the living room one entered a good-looking kitchen with new plywood cabinets which Connie's father had made. Connie had used pegboard to hang pots and pans over the range. In the kitchen was an electric dishwasher, a refrigerator, a range, and a large table.

A hallway extends on one end of the kitchen to two bedrooms and a bath. The bathroom, freshly tiled by the boys, houses a tub, toilet, sink, and a floor-to-ceiling storage closet where Connie stores toiletries and linens.

The baby's crib and a large bureau fill one of the bedrooms. In the bureau, Connie, Charlie, and the baby keep their clothes. Connie and Charlie sleep on the living room sofa. Three single beds, three bureaus, and one closet fill the other bedroom. Each of the three boys has a separate bureau for his clothes. The closet is shared by everyone.

The house has a second floor which is unfinished. Connie has high hopes of remodeling it this summer.

A room at one end of the kitchen serves as a combination of office, laundry, and storage for food. On one side of the room is a big desk where Charlie can talk to the men without interfering with the rest of the house. At the other end of the room is an automatic washer and dryer, a freezer, and a cupboard for canned food storage.

GENERAL WORK PATTERN

Part of Connie's weekday morning was recorded by her as follows.

> I usually get up at 7 A.M., get dressed and make up the bed. I call the 15-year-old boy at 7:15 A.M. By the time he gets dressed I have his breakfast ready. The other boys get up around 8 A.M. I get their breakfast at that time. Charlie and I don't eat breakfast. We do drink coffee but not right away. As soon as the boys are up and I've fixed their breakfast, I make beds. Some women like to clean up the kitchen first but I like to start with the bedrooms and work out. When I make the beds I usually sweep under the beds and around the floor. With the boys this is necessary every day. I then gather up the clothes. I do a full tub of white clothes every day.
>
> Charlie and the boys are very independent. They help me and help themselves. Charlie likes to cook. He helps me do what needs to be done. He likes to help. He just slips in knowing what to do without being told. He is in and out a lot during the day. Some women can't do anything when their husbands are at home but Charlie doesn't bother me at all. I'd rather let my work go and sit down and talk to him if he comes in.

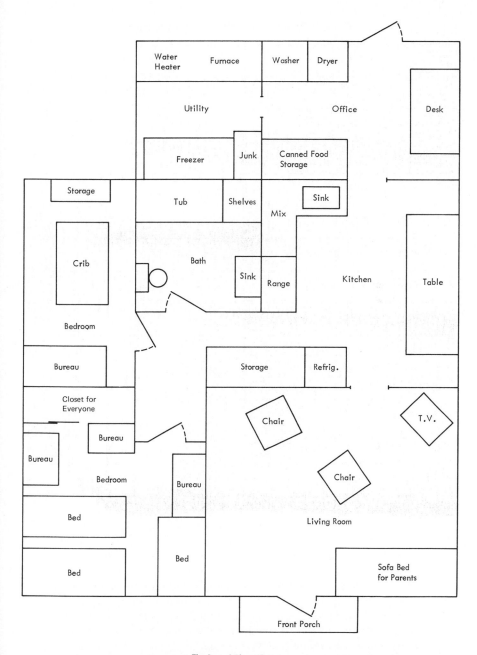

The Ryans' Floor Plan

Figure 4.8. The Ryans' floor plan. (Grace Elliott Tasker, "Case Studies of Homemakers' Organization")

Connie Ryan's Early-Morning Schedule

Activity	Time								
	7:15	7:30	7:45	8:00	8:15	8:30	8:45	9:00	9:15
Get up and dress	.----.								
Breakfast for son	.----.								
Telephone and coffee		.----.							
Make our bed and son's			.----.						
Get younger boys up and fed				.-----					
Make up beds, pick up clothes					.----.				
Clear table, tidy kitchen						.----.			
Sort and wash clothes							.----.------..		
Meat from freezer								.---..	
Stir up donuts								.---..	
Yesterday's clothes from dryer,									.
fold and put away									.-----

My work bothered me so when I had only one child. Now I think I get as much if not more done with the four. You get to an age when you have so much to do that you don't let it bother you. You just get up and do it.

You wanted to know if I had any plan to my work. . . . Well, when you have children, the telephone always ringing, and your husband coming in wanting you to do things, you don't plan; you just do things as they come up. When I was first married and the children were small I used to write things down that I had to do or else I would forget them. Now I know pretty much in my mind what has to be done.

I usually plan in general at night what has to be done the next day. I decide in the morning what kind of meat I'm going to serve at night and get it out of the freezer. I decide what else to fix in the afternoon. Most of the planning I do is in my head.

I shop for groceries just once a week. When you're from a farm you learn to do your shopping once a week because when I lived at home with my parents we only went to town once a week. I keep a list of things I need at the grocery store. We have a lot of things in the freezer so I don't have to plan too far ahead.

I would be lost without a garden. When spring comes I just don't feel right unless I can start working the ground. Last summer I froze strawberries, rhubarb, peppers, and cherries. I like to can most of the vegetables, green and yellow beans, tomatoes, beets, and pickles.

I don't have any special time to do the ironing or cleaning; I do things as they need doing.

Being organized means to Connie getting everything done in one day that is the most important. Nothing makes her feel more disorganized than to start several different jobs and not have time to finish any of them. To avoid this, she tries to finish one job before starting another.

She believes that a certain amount of overall routine helps her to keep her family going and helps her to get things done.

She thinks she learned most of her housekeeping patterns from her mother.

"I remember Mother warning me many times that when I got something out to put it away as soon as I finished with it," Connie laughed.

"You know the secret to my management," she offered, "is to get dressed as soon as I get up in the morning. A lot of my friends go around half the morning in a bathrobe. No wonder they don't feel like working. I just get dressed and I'm ready for work."

Summary

One way for the homemaker to increase effectiveness is to plan time rather than tasks. Plans for the use of time involve anticipating future events and planning for their place in the time schedule. By planning time one can allocate a place for important and urgent things.

Homemaking still takes time. Homemakers with young children and large families have a particularly heavy load. Working women also put in a long day. Other things that influence how much time is spent on homemaking are: the standard of living, housekeeping standards, the type of furnishings and equipment, whether the family lives in the city or on a farm, the presence of a person with a handicap, whether there is a pet, and the attitude of family members toward various tasks.

Most household work is done by family members, the bulk of it by women. The working mother has a disproportionately heavy work load.

The timing of various activities is frequently determined by conditions outside the home, as well as within it. Some jobs require more than one person. Others must wait until the person who is to do it is available. Some may be dependent on the weather.

A number of factors need to be considered in making time plans. Routines aid in the control of time. The work load need to be balanced, if possible. Time and work can be saved by devotailing jobs.

It is much more difficult to manage energy that to manage time. Time has definite boundaries—there are so many hours in a day, week, or month. One's energy is harder to gauge and apportion.

People vary in the amount of energy that they have. Moreover, one's energy varies from day to day and during the day. Attitudes and emotions influence how much energy each one of us seems to have at a particular moment.

Family members possess certain knowledge and skills that can facilitate home management. Sometimes these skills can be used instead of other resources.

CHAPTER FOLLOW-UP

1. Make a time plan for yourself for a week. Then try and operate on it. When you are using your plans, make a note of where they work well, and when they seem to fall apart. Consider how you might be able to make them function better.
2. Reread the case studies in this chapter. How do you think that you might improve on the time schedules of these homemakers? Try planning a new schedule for one of these homemakers.
3. Have several students do the same activity for an equal length of time, vacuuming, dusting furniture, or any other activities that you decide upon. Have each person record when they got tired. Compare the differences. Consider whether the fatigue was physical or psychological. How might it be possible to reduce fatigue in each of these activities? Repeat these activities using one or more methods of reducing fatigue, to determine if it is possible for each person to continue for a longer period before they begin to feel tired.
4. Keep a record for a week of the times when you feel tired. Make a note as to whether you think this is physiological or psychological. Is there any regular pattern to indicate when you might expect to be tired tomorrow? Many people have low points in the day that are fairly regular. By recognizing your own pattern you can plan to do some of the less tiring activities at your low points, and squeeze in time for rest and relaxation.

SELECTED REFERENCES

Agan, Tessie, Stephan Konz, and Lucy Tormey. "Extra Heart Beats As a Measurement of Work Cost." *Home Economics Research Journal*, Vol. 1 (1972), pp. 28–33.

Bartley, S. Howard. *Fatigue: Mechanism and Management.* Springfield, Ill.: Charles C. Thomas, Publisher, 1965.

Bates, Louise. "Home Management and Single-Parent Families." *Actualizing Concepts in Home Management,* Washington, D.C.: American Home Economics Association, 1973, pp. 85–87.

Chisenhall, Sarah Cawthon. "Home Management Practice of Twenty-five Homemakers Employed with Rotating Work Hours." Master's thesis, The University of North Carolina at Greensboro, 1972.

De Fonseca, Dulce Maria. "Analysis of Dishwashing Time in Selected Indiana Families." Master's thesis. Purdue University, 1964.

De Grazia, Sebastian. *Of Time, Work and Leisure.* New York: Twentieth Century Fund, 1962.

Drucker, Peter. *The Effective Executive.* New York: Harper & Row, 1967.

Elliot, Doris E., Mary B. Patton, and Mary E. Singer. *Energy Expenditures of Women Performing Household Tasks.* Ohio Agriculture Experiment Station Research Bulletin No. 939, 1963.

Gauger, William H. "Household Work: Can We Add It to GNP?" *Journal of Home Economics,* Vol. 65 (1973), pp. 12–15.

Gitobu, Juliana Kathuni. "Use of Time for Household Activities by Employed and Nonemployed Rural Homemakers." Master's thesis, Cornell University, 1972.

Goetz, Helen Margarete. "Examination of Selected Social and Economic Influences on the Performance of Certain Household Tasks." Ph.D. thesis, Purdue University, 1965.

———, Eldena Purcell, Sarah L. Manning, and Cleo Fitzsimmons.. "Quantity and Quality Measures for Homemaking Work Units." Research Progress Report 217. Agricultural Experiment Station, Purdue University, 1966.

Hall, Florence Turnbull, and Marguerite Paulsen Schroeder. "Effects of Family and Housing Characteristics on Time Spent in Household Tasks." *Journal of Home Economics,* Vol. 62 (1970), pp. 23–29.

Hook, Nancy Carol, "Use of Time in Regular Care of the House in Selected Indiana Families." Master's thesis, Purdue University, 1963.

Hoopes, Johnnie Ray, and Mary Brown Patton. "Energy Expenditures of Homemakers Performing Floor-Care Activities and an Evaluation of Floor Appearance." Ohio Agriculture Experiment Station Research Bulletin No. 946, 1963.

Jarmon, Carolyn. "Relationship Between Homemaker's Attitudes Toward Specific Household Tasks and Family Composition, Other Situational Variables and Time Allocation." Master's thesis, Cornell University, 1972.

Kinder, Faye. *Meal Management.* New York: Macmillan, 1973.

Krassa, Lucie G., and Emma G. Holmes. "Research on Time Spent in Homemaking: Annotated List of References." Agricultural Research Service Bulletin No. 62–15, U.S. Department of Agriculture, 1967.

Linder, Staffan Burenstam. *The Harried Leisure Class.* New York: Columbia University Press, 1970.

Magrabi, Frances M., Beatrice Paolucci, and Marjorie E. Heifner. "Framework for Studying Family Activity Patterns." *Journal of Home Economics,* Vol. 59 (1967) pp. 714–719.

Manning, Sarah L. "Time Use in Household Tasks by Indiana Families," Purdue Agriculture Experiment Station Research Bulletin No. 837, 1968.

Parker, Frances J. "Task Distribution Within the Family." *Journal of Home Economics.* Vol. 58 (1966), pp. 373–375.

Purcell, Clara E. "Development of an Indiana Homemaking Work Unit for Washing Clothes." Master's thesis, Purdue University, 1965.

Richardson, Martha. "Energy Expenditure of Women for Cleaning Carpets with Three Types of Vacuum Cleaners," *Journal of Home Economics*, Vol. 58 (1966), pp. 182–186.

————, and Earl C. McCracken, "Energy Expenditures of Women Performing Selected Activities." Home Economics Research Report No. 11, Agr. Research Services, U.S. Department of Agriculture, 1960.

————, and ————. "Work Surface Levels for Laundry Tasks in Relation to Human Energy Expenditures." *Journal of Home Economics*, Vol. 58 (1966), pp. 662–668.

Ronald, Patricia Y., Mary E. Singer, and Francille Maloch Firebaugh, "Rating Scale for Household Tasks." *Journal of Home Economics*, Vol. 63 (1971), pp. 177–179.

Steidl, Rose E., and Esther Crew Bratton. *Work in the Home.* New York: John Wiley & Sons, Inc., 1968. Chap. 4, "The Temporal Component," and Chap. 7, "The Physical Component: Energy Expenditure."

Tasker, Grace E. "Case Studies of Homemakers' Organization." Master's thesis, Cornell University, 1962.

Walker, Kathryn E., "Homemaking Still Takes Time." *Journal of Home Economics*, Vol. 61, (1969), pp. 621–624.

————. "Household Work Time—Its Implications for Family Decisions." *Journal of Home Economics,* Vol. 65 (1973), pp. 7–11.

————, and William H. Gauger. "The Dollar Value of Household Work." Information Bulletin No. 60, New York State College of Human Ecology, Cornell University, 1973.

————, and ————. "Time and Its Monetary Values in Household Work." *Family Economics Review* (Fall 1973), pp. 8–13.

Whitman, Frankie. "The Market Value of a Housewife." Master's thesis, Cornell University, 1972.

chapter 5

---

economic resources

Many economic resources are used by individuals and families. Income obviously is an important economic resource. Assets, the things we already own, such as clothes, a typewriter, or savings, are also economic resources. Earning power or potential income is another economic resource. People often get goods and services through the use of credit. This is still another economic resource, and so are fringe benefits from a job, and government benefits.

Types of Resources

Income

Some people think only of money income—a salary, paycheck, or pension—when considering income. However, economists define *real income* as the whole flow of goods and services available for the satisfaction of human wants and needs over a period of time.

Money income is a form of *direct income*. A gift of homegrown vegetables from a friend is another type of direct income. Did you get a gift certificate for Christmas? This is direct income, too.

However, if a grandparent or a friend babysits without charge, their service replaces something that would otherwise be paid for with money. This is a less direct form of income, sometimes called *indirect income*.

It is now widely recognized that the services contributed to the family by its members are a form of income to the family. In most cases the services of family members are not paid for directly and might be considered indirect income. However, sometimes these services are paid for directly, such as when a housekeeper is hired or a youngster is paid for doing extra tasks.

Assets

Some of the important assets that a family may own are a house or other real estate, an automobile, a savings account, life insurance that has a cash value, household equipment, and stocks and bonds.

Many of these assets can be turned directly into cash. A house can be sold; savings can be withdrawn from the bank or credit union, a life insurance policy can be surrendered for its cash value, stocks and bonds can be sold.

Often these assets can be used as collateral for a loan, another way of getting purchasing power. A house mortgage and a car loan are used by many people. One can also borrow against the cash value of a life insurance policy, savings accounts, stocks, and bonds.

Ownership of real estate and other durable goods can also contribute indirectly to usable income. The individual or family that owns a house or washing machine can use these instead of spending money for rent or laundry services.

Estimating the indirect value of a house or durable goods can be quite tricky. Generally, the operating expenses of durable goods are less than equivalent services. However, the cost of buying a house or other major equipment plus operating expenses may not be less expensive than other alternatives over a short period. For example, buying a washing machine, particularly on the installment plan, plus operating costs may be more expensive than doing the wash at a laundromat.

The value of an asset, however, can change when considered over a long period of time. The life expectancy of a washing machine is generally about eight years. After that, the repair costs tend to be very high. If it is purchased on installments and paid for during the first three years of use, then for the next five years it will be possible to launder at home less expensively than elsewhere. The same is true of other major household assets. Many people pay for a house during their working years with the hope that they will be able to live there less expensively during retirement.

Earning Power

Potential earning power is an important asset. Education and job skills have generally increased the amount of money one can earn. Generally, the more education or training one has, the higher one's income is apt to be. A 1972 survey by the Census Bureau showed that if the head of the household had completed four or more years of college, family income was 59 per cent higher than the average household. However, if the head of the household had only eight years of school, family income was 42 per cent lower than the average for all households. This doesn't mean that more education or training in any field will increase your earning power. Some fields are overcrowded or the demand for certain skills is decreasing.

Banks and other lending institutions recognize earning power as an important asset. Generally, they are willing to lend more to people who can earn more.

Earning power is an asset even if it is not being used currently. In periods of need many families count on the earning power of a woman who is not regularly employed outside the home. Some women enter and leave the work force in response to family needs. They may work to help their husbands through school or for a few weeks before Christmas. Other women take full-time jobs to help pay for their children's education. Of course, many are also regularly employed.

Credit

Credit can be used instead of income to get goods and services and, thus, is an economic resource. The ability to get a loan or installment credit at reasonable rates when needed is important to most people. Whether credit is available when needed depends both on economic conditions (whether lenders have money to lend) and one's credit rating. Are you a good credit risk? The checklist in Table 5.1 is used by one bank. Try it and see.

Fringe Benefits

A growing number of jobs provide various benefits to employees and their families. Most regular time workers are covered by the federal Social Security program (OASDI). Employees and employers contribute to the fund for these benefits. You have probably seen an item listed as

Figure 5.1. Television sets and other durable goods are often purchased with credit. (Zenith Radio Corporation)

FICA on a paycheck. This is the deduction for Social Security. The principal benefits are retirement income, income if the worker becomes disabled, and hospital insurance after age 65 (Medicare Part A). In addition, there are educational benefits for children of insured workers in the event of the death of the worker (Medicare Part B) and a low-cost doctor's insurance plan for retired workers and their families.

Many workers are also covered by unemployment insurance and workman's compensation insurance for job-related injuries. A growing number of employers now pay for all or part of the health insurance for workers and their families. Many have pension plans (generally the worker must contribute as well as the employer) to supplement Social Security, sick leave with pay, and vacations with pay. Since about 1960 labor unions have placed greater emphasis on the importance of good fringe benefits to workers in negotiating contracts.

Government Benefits

Since the devastating depression of the 1930s the United States has developed a growing number of programs to help people maintain a minimal standard of living. Through various programs funds are available for many people without any income or with very low incomes as well as a variety of other services. Many of these are financed jointly by the federal and state governments but administered by each state. Most benefits vary depending on the state plan.

TABLE 5.1
What's Your Credit Rating?

			Points
Previous Loans with Same Bank	No previous loan— No points given or deducted	Satisfactory loan —40 points	Unsatisfactory loan— Subtract 40
Residence	Less than a year— No points given or deducted	1–4 years—15 points 5 or more—25 points	
Telephone	Home telephone— No points given or deducted		No phone— Subtract 25 points
Job	Less than a year— No points given or deducted	1–4 years—15 points 5 or more—25 points	
Salary (gross monthly)	0–249—No points given or deducted	$250–$499— 10 points $500–$749—20 points Above $750—30 points	
Bank Accounts		Special checking —20 points Regular checking —30 points Savings account —20 points	
Purpose of Loan		Car—25 points (No points given for anything else)	

Total Points

40 points or less—Applicant is a poor risk. (If loan is granted at all applicant must have a co-signer to guarantee the loan.

41–79 points—Applicant is considered.

Over 80 points—Loan is granted except in unusual situations.

Distribution of Income

Currently, middle income is between $7,000 and $15,000 a year for a family in the United States. Forty-seven per cent of all families have incomes in this range. Almost one fourth of all families have incomes over $15,000, and a little more than one fourth have incomes below $7,000.

Projections are that family income will increase in the coming decades. "By 1990, families with incomes exceeding $15,000 (in 1971 dollars) will number well over 40 million and account for close to 60 per cent of all families."[1] (See Figure 5.2.) Poverty is likely to still be with us although fewer families will be in this category.

Family Spending

Back in 1874–1875 the first studies of family expenditures in the United States were made. At that time "about 94 per cent of the total

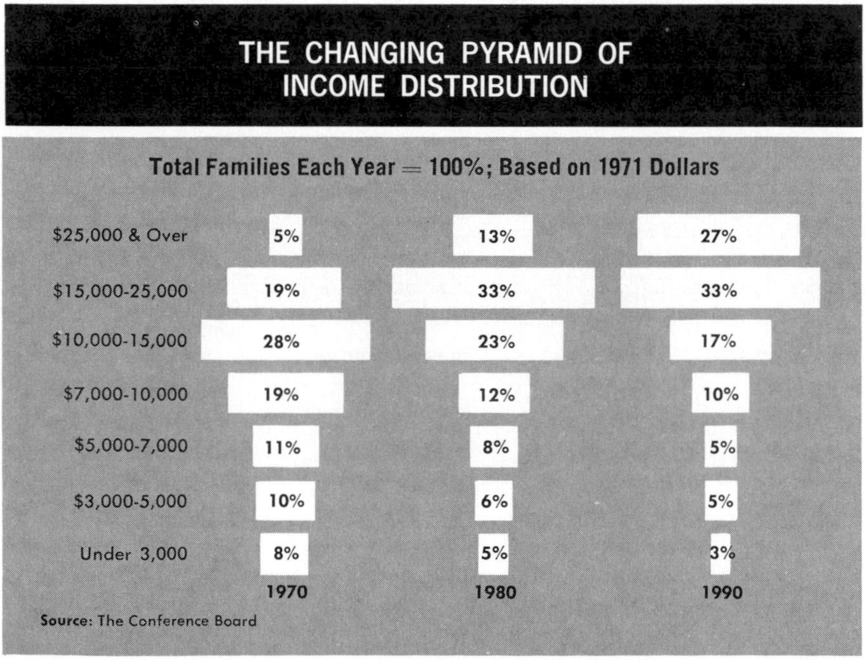

THE CHANGING PYRAMID OF INCOME DISTRIBUTION

Total Families Each Year = 100%; Based on 1971 Dollars

	1970	1980	1990
$25,000 & Over	5%	13%	27%
$15,000-25,000	19%	33%	33%
$10,000-15,000	28%	23%	17%
$7,000-10,000	19%	12%	10%
$5,000-7,000	11%	8%	5%
$3,000-5,000	10%	6%	5%
Under 3,000	8%	5%	3%

Source: The Conference Board

Figure 5.2. The Changing Pyramid of Income Distribution. (Source: The Conference Board; illustration lent by The National Consumer Finance Association)

[1] Fabian Linden, *The U.S. Economy in 1990* (New York: The Conference Board, 1972), p. 12.

family spending went for food, shelter, fuel and clothing."[2] By 1973 these items accounted for less than 50 per cent of the family's spending.

Much of this change was made possible by an increase in family income. Because projections for the future indicate that this long-term trend will continue, we can expect a greater proportion of family spending to be for things other than food, clothing, and shelter.

"As a family moves up in the earning scale, each dollar of additional income is spent differently—relatively less goes for necessities, more becomes available for other things. For example, consumer outlays for food and for footwear increased by about 2.5 per cent a year, on average between 1955 and 1970, whereas consumer spending for foreign travel and for higher education grew more than 6 per cent."[3]

Family Spending Over the Life Cycle

Family spending tends to change over the life cycle. A young couple, newly married, may have only themselves to care for. As children come into the family, income is reapportioned to accommodate their needs and wants.

As every parent knows there are many expenses involved in raising a child, Children need food, clothing, shelter, medical care, and transportation to school. In addition, many parents try to provide activities for various aspects of their children's development, such as music or dancing lessons, or college.

Teen-age youngsters generally have ravenous appetites as well as expanding needs and wants for other foods and services. Consequently, family food bills increase along with an increase in other budget categories when children reach the teen years. Also, at this age youngsters usually want more money for recreation, extra clothing, radios, and many other things.

Expenditures tend to increase as a child grows older, High school-age youngsters are more costly than toddlers (except in unusual situations). And the expense of sending a child to college can be staggering. "Although costs vary considerably according to where the child lives, during the first 18 years costs per child took from 14 to 17 per cent of family income."[4]

As children leave home the parents may use money for things that they could not afford when they had children at home. In the later years, medical expenses may take a large segment of a reduced income.

[2] "Changing Consumption Patterns," Bureau of Labor Statistics Report No. 238–11 (Washington, D.C.: U.S. Department of Labor, 1965), p. 4.

[3] Ibid.

[4] Jean L. Pennock, "Cost of Raising a Child," *Family Economics Review* (March 1970), pp. 14–15.

Living Costs at Different Income Levels

The family's cost of living depends on the manner of living, the number, ages, and sex of the people in the family, and where they live.

As a guideline the Bureau of Labor Statistics of the United States Department of Labor has worked out budgets that are revised annually for various standards of living for a family composed of a thirty-eight-year-old husband, employed full time, a wife who is not employed outside the home, a boy of thirteen, and a girl of eight. The assumptions are made that the family has been married about fifteen years, and are therefore fairly well established in the middle stage of the family life cycle; that the husband is an experienced worker; and that they have an average inventory of clothing, home furnishings, large equipment, and other goods.

There are also budgets for an urban retired couple.

Cost estimates for the budgets are given for each of 39 metropolitan areas and for a sample of nonmetropolitan areas with population of 2,500 to 50,000 in each of the four regions. BLS has also developed a scale that can be used to estimate for families of other sizes and types the cost of a budget comparable to that for the four-person family at a moderate standard of living.

The BLS budgets are useful as guides for social and legislative programs on wages, prices, credit, public assistance, and taxes, for evaluating adequacy of incomes of groups of families; and for measuring differences in living costs among cities and areas. The budget quantities and pricing specifications can be used to estimate costs for areas not in the BLS list.

Figure 5.3. Composition of family used for the Bureau of Labor Statistics' family budgets.

These budgets are not meant to show how families should spend their money or to be used as patterns of spending by families.[5]

Regional Differences in Living Costs

Where one lives influences living costs. Honolulu, Hawaii, is the most expensive place in the United States to live. There, food costs 19 per cent more than average costs elsewhere in the United States. Most things have to be brought to this island, far from the major growing areas. Housing in Hawaii is even more expensive. Building sites are scarce and costly, and most building materials have to be imported.

Many companies take living costs into consideration when they transfer their employees. Often they will pay a cost-of-living differential when transferring a family into a high-cost area.

Farm Family Spending

The most dramatic change in farm family spending since 1940 has been that it now is much closer to the spending pattern of the urban family. With greater mechanization in farming it became increasingly profitable in most cases to reduce the variety of crops grown and concentrate instead on producing one or a limited number of crops. In this way, the farmer can utilize mechanical tools and the natural endowments of the land to the fullest extent. Today many of our most productive farms and ranches are large and highly specialized. Increasingly, small-scale farmers and families who farmed poor land have been forced off their farms because they could not compete.

As a result most farm families do not try to raise all their own food. It is much more efficient to buy many things. With the reduction in production for home use, farmers now sell most of their crops for cash. So, like workers in other occupations, they have money to spend and some choice about how they wish to use it.

However, there are still many poor farm families. A large number live in impoverished areas or work poor tracts of land. Some are seasonal workers for farm owners. Many are older couples.

The Effect of Inflation

The value of the dollar is not always the same. During a period of rapidly increasing inflation money buys less and less. Price rises outpace rises in income, so that the average person finds himself unable to buy as much as he could before the inflation started.

[5] Emma G. Holmes, *Family Economics Review* (Sept. 1969), p. 12.

Families try to cope with inflation in various ways. They buy less. Perhaps they decide not to buy a new car or new clothes for Easter. They cut down on toys for Christmas, presents, contributions, and many other things. They switch from high-priced goods to cheaper ones. They might buy more hamburger meat instead of steaks or roasts, watch TV instead of going to the movies, repair things instead of replacing them. They tend to shop more carefully. Many women compare prices of individual food items much more carefully when they feel pinched by rising prices.

Inflation not only raises the cost of goods for the individual and the family, but also for public improvements, such as roads, bridges, and services such as garbage collection, electricity, and schools. The increased cost for public facilities is borne by individual families through the raising of taxes.

Inflation is hard on people in all walks of life. It is hardest on people with fixed incomes, such as retired families living on Social Security, or low-income families on welfare. These groups usually had very little to begin with and inflation cuts into this little bit very hard.

Historically, the end result of galloping inflation has been economic depression. When people are unable to buy, companies have to stop producing, people are thrown out of work, and unemployment rises.

Planning Family Spending

Families generally use money soon after they get it. According to one study, families go on a spending spree within a day or two after they get their paychecks.[6] Families who received paychecks more often than once a month tend to spend on the day they are paid, according to a two-year pilot study of the spending patterns of a small group of families in Ohio. Generally, they spent 25 per cent of their money within one or two days after they got it.

The same pattern is observable in supermarkets on Friday nights and Saturdays. The stores stay open late so that people can buy when their pockets are jingling. Many families gear their big food buying to when they get money. Often they buy food first, then pay some bills, and finally buy other things.

Our society exerts great pressure on the family to spend. The economy functions on the basis of a high demand for consumer goods. Buying by the individual consumer accounts for much of our gross national product. Hence there is a great push to keep the production-consumption cycle going.

[6] Francille Maloch and C. R. Weaver, "Orientation to Day of Pay," *The Journal of Consumer Affairs*, Vol. 3 (Winter 1969), pp. 137–144.

Critics of this cycle feel that the result has been an overemphasis on production of goods for individual use and inadequate provision for the public goods and services that benefit everyone. One complaint is that we have built too many disposal units, but not enough sewage treatment facilities to handle the increased sewage resulting from use of this type of equipment.

The idea of planning expenditures carefully in advance does not appeal to some people. But it is an important way of making money a useful tool to help us get the things we want.

Other groups in society that handle money feel that planning is important in directing the use of funds. Business organizations make out annual plans for expenditures in great detail. Individual departments have their own subplans. Town and city governments, school boards, recreation committees, transit authorities, and almost every important group that one can think of operates with an expenditure plan in order to make their outlays and income balance.

If a family wants to keep a rein on its spending and channel it in certain directions, it, too, needs to plan. Just using income as it comes in usually doesn't enable the family to get the things it really wants.

Most of us have more ideas about how to use money than we can afford to put into practice. So the only solution is to make choices, buy one thing, and forget about another; get less of something, or a less expensive version, so we have money for something else. A spending plan can help us see each purchase in relationship to all the other things we want and need for ourselves and the rest of the family.

A spending plan need not involve pages of voluminous detail. In fact, this is where many spending plans bog down. But it does need to be sufficiently thoroughly worked out to be useful as a way of evaluating possible expenditures and keeping a brake on spending.

Steps in Financial Planning

Set goals. There is no ideal financial plan to fit everyone. Each family needs to make a plan that fits their needs, goals, and income. One family may choose to spend a great deal on a handsome home, another will be more interested in having a new car every few years, or fashionable clothes, vacation trips, or other things.

A spending plan needs to be built around both immediate needs and longer-term goals. Ann and Bill are a newly married couple. They want to furnish their apartment as attractively as possible. In addition, they still have payments to make on their car. They hope to start a family in a year or two and to be able to buy a home of their own in a few years.

Mr. and Mrs. Smith are in their late forties. Their children are all through school and living away from home. They have only themselves to care for. They might want to move to a smaller house or an apartment. Perhaps they would also like to do some traveling. They also feel that they should begin to plan some savings for the retirement years. Their spending plan would be quite different from Ann and Bill's because they have very different goals.

Estimate income. The next step is to estimate family income for a specific period. Some people make a yearly income and spending plan. They like a broad picture, which they get from such a plan. This is particularly useful for people who have an income that fluctuates during the year, such as a farmer, a family where the wife works part of the year, or a self-employed professional.

Other people prefer to work with the pay period—a week, two weeks, or a month. This works reasonably well for people with a fairly regular income each pay period. Many families receive the same amount of money at regular intervals for the entire year.

Other families get their money less regularly. The husband may get a raise midway through the year. Or perhaps he gets a bonus at Christmas. A farm family might get a crop loan in the spring and payment for their crops in the fall. Self-employed professionals often receive money irregularly. Figure 5.4 shows some of these different patterns.

The lifetime income pattern also varies greatly from family to family. In one family the husband may be the only wage earner over all the years of family life. He may have a steadily increasing income pattern, or a period when he is ill and unable to work. Or perhaps he is laid off because the

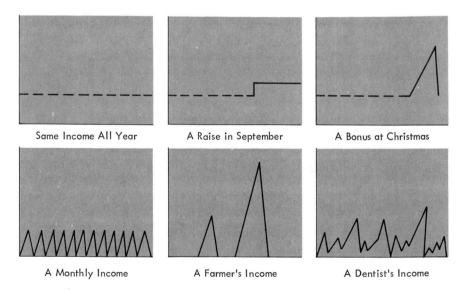

Same Income All Year A Raise in September A Bonus at Christmas

A Monthly Income A Farmer's Income A Dentist's Income

Figure 5.4. Variations in income patterns.

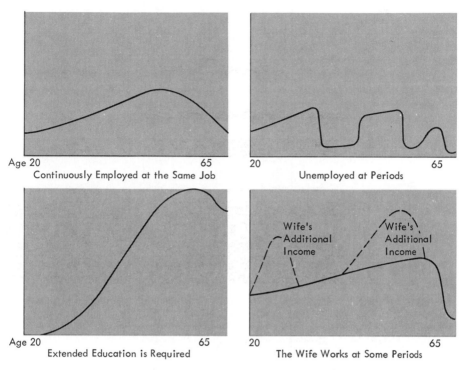

Age 20   65   20   65
Continuously Employed at the Same Job   Unemployed at Periods

Age 20   65   20   65
Extended Education is Required   The Wife Works at Some Periods

Wife's Additional Income

Wife's Additional Income

Figure 5.5. Profiles of family income over a lifetime.

company for whom he was working has lost a portion of their business. Maybe part way through the working years the husband decides to go back to school for further training. Perhaps the wife will work at some periods. Some of these variations in lifetime patterns are shown in Figure 5.5.

There are so many variables that will influence a family's income over the life cycle that it is hard to say with certainty what the pattern will be for any individual family. But we do know that certain types of occupations are in great demand and will continue to be so for some time to come. Medical personnel is in short supply. The computer industry is expected to be one of the fastest-growing industries. We can hypothesize that some jobs will be replaced gradually by machines, more office operations will be carried on by computers, the harvesting of more crops will be done mechanically.

Sue and Dave Moretti have a fairly easy income to estimate. Sue is a transportation coordinator for a public school district employed on a ten-month basis. Dave is a young engineer employed year round by a large aircraft company. In addition they have a small savings account that earns interest.

TABLE 5.2
Sue and Dave Moretti's Estimated Yearly Income

19—

Income from	Jan.	Feb.	March	April	May	June	July	Aug.	Sept.	Oct.	Nov.	Dec.	Total
Husband's job	$850	$850	$850	$850	$850	$850	$850	$850	$850	$850	$850	$850	$10,200
Wife's job	$700	$700	$700	$700	$700	$700			$700	$700	$700	$700	$7,000
Interest	$15			$15.15			$15.30			$15.45			$60.90
Monthly totals	$1,565	$1,550	$1,550	$1,565.15	$1,550	$1,550	$865.30	$850	$1,550	$1,565.45	$1,550	$1,550	$17,260.90

Make a spending plan.   The following examples show how families
with different types of income patterns and amounts of money plan their
spending.

Sue and Dave Moretti's Plan.   Sue and Dave made up a careful outline
for their plans based on a monthly income. (See Table 5.3.) Both are paid
by check each month. Income tax deductions and social security payments
are taken out of their checks by their employers. In addition Dave's employer also takes out $50 a month, which is deposited directly in their joint
savings account, and $16 a month for health insurance that covers them
both.

Sue and Dave deposit their monthly checks in their joint checking
account and draw checks as needed. Any funds that are not used for expenses during the month are put in their savings account. However, they
like to keep a minimum of $200 in the checking account for emergencies.
When they have big expenditures, such as insurance, clothing, car repairs,

Figure 5.6. Many people use personal and bank checks to pay their bills.
(Chase Manhattan Bank)

TABLE 5.3
Outline for Sue and Dave Moretti's Spending Plan

19—

Item	Jan.	Feb.	Mar.	April	May	June	July	Aug.	Sept.	Oct.	Nov.	Dec.
Total money income												
Fixed expenses												
Taxes												
Income												
Social security												
Rent												
Insurance												
Life												
Health												
Automobile (2 cars)												
Installment payment												
Total												
Flexible expenses*												
Food and beverages												
At home												
Away from home												
House operation												
House furnishings												
Clothing												
Dave												
Sue												
Personal allowances												
Transportation												
Medical care												
Recreation and education												
Gifts and contributions												

* Many of these are planned on a month-to-month basis.

furniture, or other items, they transfer money from their savings account to their checking account.

Mary Gallagher[7]

Mary Gallagher (25 years old). Denver, Colorado.

Employment: Teaches English in a secondary school. Has been teaching here two years. Before coming to Denver she taught in Chicago for two years.

Background: Mary grew up around Chicago but went to college in Colorado. Decided to leave the Chicago area after two years of teaching and join friends in Colorado. Her father is an industrial worker—he is from Ireland. Mother works in local retail store—grew up in Chicago. Parents did not want Mary to leave home, but she felt it would be more fun in Colorado—plus she likes to ski.

- Feels most of her money goes for clothes and food.
- Has charges at local department stores. Felt she wanted to buy nice gifts for her family this past Christmas and is paying off a $150 bill in one store on a monthly basis. [This is included under entertainment.]
- Wants to buy a $400 stereo for the apartment in next few months. Not sure how she will buy it. Parents never used credit—always cash. She's worried and feels she should pay off her other bills first.
- Problem she has with money is that she feels she lives from paycheck to paycheck. Is paid twice a month—first check goes for rent and bills; second check to enjoy.
- Does not have a savings plan—keeps saying she will start the next month.

TABLE 5.4
Mary Gallagher's Spending Plan

Income: Around $8,200 before taxes. Take home pay $6,233.
Monthly Expenses:

Housing	$120	(Shares new apartment with another girl—rent includes utilities)
Food	80	(Eats out a couple of times a week)
Clothing	100	(Varies, but this is average for dress, slacks, shoes)
Car or Transportation	50	(Auto expenses—gas—insurance)
Entertainment	50	(Approximately)
Insurance	10	
Medical	5	
Savings	0	
Household Help	20	
Drycleaning and Laundry	12	
Other	20	(Sends to younger sister who is in college)

[7] Source: "Managing Resources: Some Family Case Studies," *Penney's Forum* (published by the J. C. Penney Co.), (Fall/Winter 1969), pp. 6–7.

- Skis in the winter and shares ski house with friends. Pays $120 for the season plus $6 per weekend for food. Has her own equipment and spends $100 for season tow ticket.
- Has a very small life insurance policy.
- Family is important to her. She is helping a sister who is in college. Also, having fun is important to her.
- In future—would like to be married soon. Dating a young engineer now, but not sure if they will marry. She may go to graduate school.
- Flies home twice a year. Parents came to visit her last summer so will fly home only once this year.

Jane Smith's Plan. Jane and her three children live in a small apartment in the middle of a large city. Sarah is six and in kindergarten. Bobbie is three and Myra is only one. Her husband is not living with them and doesn't help her financially. Jane gets a welfare check for $249 every two weeks from the government.

Jane has a hard time making her money stretch to cover the necessities. Her rent is high in relation to her income, $30 a week, but she couldn't find anything decent that was less expensive. Also, she has no major household equipment to ease her job and very little in the way of extra clothing or other assets. She generally has to buy everything she needs when she needs it. She never has enough money to take advantage of end-of-season sales, or stock up at food specials.

Usually, she pays her big bills every two weeks when she gets her check, and buys food for two weeks at that time. What's left has to stretch to cover everything else. She would like to buy a washing machine but has been unable to accumulate enough money for a down payment. Also, she would have a hard time meeting time payments.

TABLE 5.5
Jane Smith's Spending Plan

Income: A welfare check for $249 every two weeks	
Monthly Expenses	*Expenses Paid Every Two Weeks*
	Rent $60
Gas and Electric $20	⎱ Pay Gas and Electric Bill or
Furniture Payments $25	⎰ Furniture Payment $20 or $25
	Food $65
	Total $145 or $150

Other Expenses: These vary from week to week, and are paid out of what is left, $94 or $99. They are clothing, carfare, cleaning supplies, household linens, telephone, laundry, cleaning, shoe repair, TV repair, haircuts, and everything else.

Evaluate Your Money Management Plan

1. Does it meet long-term goals?
2. Does it meet short-term goals?
3. Do expenditures balance with income?
4. Are necessary expenditures, such as food, clothing, shelter planned?
5. Is there flexibility to meet changing needs or emergency expenses?
6. Has money been allocated for savings?
7. Is the plan easy enough to be manageable?

Control of family spending. Money has a way of dribbling away on lots of things unless we really work at controlling spending. Making a spending plan doesn't guarantee that it will be used as an operational tool. A design for controlling the actual use of money is also needed.

Families have different ways of putting a brake on spending. Sometimes one adult is much less prone to spend than the other. The person who is less free in spending money might take most of the responsibility for handling much of the family's money.

Some families take their income and immediately divide it into envelopes for rent, food, clothing, and so on, so that they know just how much is left. Many people have their employers deposit a regular sum in their savings account. Others have deductions made for government bonds or other investments.

Often families deposit their money in a checking account and write checks as needed. In this way they don't have a lot of money in hand all the time and they also have a record of how they spend their money.

Many people carry only as much money as they know they will need for one day. By not having extra money in their purse or pocket they find that they are less apt to overspend.

Other families divide the responsibility for family spending. They plan for spending and control of spending as a family. By becoming aware that they are working on a plan for the whole group, the members may be more apt to consider how they use money in relationship to others' needs. Each member has some money to use for his personal needs as he wishes. This should take into consideration the family's income and the age and needs of the individual.

Younger members of the family can be helped to grow in the ability to manage money. Youngsters might start off in elementary school with a small amount for minor needs. As they get older they might take over responsibility for buying their school supplies, some of their own clothing, paying for their transportation, recreation, and other things. By the time they finish high school they should be aware of what things cost, how money can be used constructively, and how to keep a rein on their own spending.

Records are a very useful tool in controlling family expenditure and in revising plans for spending. They need not be very detailed, but it is very helpful to keep a list of daily expenditures for at least one pay period. Such a record enables one to look at each expenditure and see where the money really is going. This is very important in evaluating the effectiveness of a plan.

Records also are needed for tax purposes. For example, suppose you buy a house for $20,000 and over a period of 15 years spend an additional $5,000 fixing the porch and improving the kitchen, Later you sell the house for $30,000. The federal government will tax you on the whole $10,000 difference between the purchase price and the sale price—unless you have records to prove that some of the difference has been spent on improving the building rather than just on maintaining it or unless you buy a house within a year that costs more than the sale price of the first one.

Credit. Control of family spending is often complicated by the fact that many things can be bought on credit. Some people are tempted by their needs or desires to acquire more than they can pay for. The result can be a very unhappy family situation.

Credit can be a very useful tool. Most families would be unable to buy a home without financing through a mortgage. New cars are generally bought on the installment plan. But credit buying needs to be kept at a level that the family can afford. Fifteen per cent of after tax income is usually recommended as a safe limit for the amount of credit. A spending plan can help guide the family in deciding how much credit it can handle at any one time. What is available after necessities and existing contracts are paid? What can be reallocated from other areas to finance a new purchase?

The widespread use of credit cards has made it very easy for many people to "buy now, pay later." There is a trend in the United States to encourage people to buy more freely through the use of various forms of credit.

Many families are not aware of the fact that they can shop for credit as well as for the article that they are buying. This is even true in the mortgage market. The rate of interest and fees charged may often differ slightly from one bank to another, or from a bank and an insurance company. Credit is available at varying prices. For instance, a bank may charge less for a personal loan than an automobile sales finance company does for car financing. A personal loan may be cheaper than buying a television set on the installment plan.

There are several recent laws dealing with consumer credit. The following are the most important provisions of these laws.

1. Women applying for credit must be considered on the same basis as men—on their income and other qualifications.

2. If a customer notifies a creditor about a computer error in the statement of his account, the creditor must reply in 30 days and resolve the matter in 90 days.
3. A consumer may sue the purchaser of an installment loan or contract (the holder in due course) if the contract violates the Truth in Lending Act. Until now it was possible for the contract to be sold to a third party, leaving the consumer with no recourse.
4. If a customer purchases an item at a store on a credit card, both the store and the credit card company may be held responsible for faulty merchandise. This means that the customer may withhold payment if the item is faulty if: (a) the item costs more than $50; (b) the store is within 100 miles of the customer's home; and (c) if the customer makes a good-faith attempt to get the store to resolve the matter.
5. Anyone purchasing a home must be given the amount of the closing costs when the creditor makes the mortgage commitment.
6. The monthly bills for a charge account must identify each transaction separately.

What Is Spending? What Is Investing?

Recently, it has become increasingly difficult to draw a line between spending and saving. At one time it was very easy to make this distinction, because saving was quite distinct from the other things that one spent money for. Today, however, with amortized mortgages, life insurance plans with built-in savings, Social Security coverage, health insurance, and other spending–savings combinations, it is more difficult to separate savings entirely from spending. Payments of the Social Security tax are in large part contributions to a pension plan from which the contributor expects to benefit eventually. Ordinary or straight life insurance has a built-in savings feature that can be used by the policyholder as a source of loans or cash. Home owners, in this period of rising values for homes, often feel that the part of their monthly mortgage payments that reduces the amount they owe represents a form of saving. Prepayment of medical expenses through group health insurance plans might also be construed as a form of saving.

Then there is the question of whether an investment in equipment that can be used over a long period of time is just spending or is really a capital investment. A family may purchase a washer and dryer with the expectation that they will be able to use them with only a modest outlay for electricity and repairs for the next seven years or so. Industry would consider this type of investment as a capital outlay and write off its cost over the period of its expected usefulness.

Expenditures for education raise a similar type of question. Because there is a relationship between the amount of education a person has and his probable lifetime income, is an expenditure for education an investment or just an outlay?

Then there is the type of situation where the family both saves and borrows at the same time. A family may use a payroll deduction plan for the purchase of bonds, stocks, or savings in a credit union. At the same time they may contract to buy something on the installment plan. Many people feel that they will meet installment-plan payments, but if they use their savings for the purchase they will not replace the savings. So they choose not to use their savings to buy things such as household equipment that they can finance with an installment contract. Technically, the only real savings to the family would be if they made more money on their stocks, bonds, or savings after allowing for the income tax and subtracting whatever they were paying for the installment credit minus income tax deductions for interest on the loan. But installment credit is generally offered at a higher rate of interest than most investments earn, which means that most families have a net loss with this type of situation. Credit buying costs them more than their savings earn.

Summary

Many economic resources are used by individuals and families, such as income, assets, earning power, credit, fringe benefits, and government benefits. Some people think only of money when considering income. However, economists define real income as including the whole flow of goods and services available for the satisfaction of wants and needs.

Family income has increased over the past 100 years, and projections indicate that it will continue to do so. As family income increases money is used differently, less for necessities, and more for other items.

A family's cost of living depends on the manner of living, the number and age of the people in the family, and the place where they live. In recent years, farm family spending has more closely approached the spending pattern of the urban family.

Most people have more ideas of how to spend money than they can afford to implement. One of the ways to keep spending in line with income is to plan family spending carefully. The steps involved in planning expenditures are setting goals, estimating income, making a spending plan, and controlling family spending.

Credit can be a very useful resource. However, its use must be kept at a level that the family can afford.

CHAPTER FOLLOW-UP

1. Money means different things to people. What are some of the ways in which you see this evidenced?
2. One way to get more mileage out of your money is to substitute other resources for money? How do families substitute one resource for another?
3. What are some of the ways in which families accommodate fluctuations in income?
4. If your income or allowance was sharply cut for a brief period, where would you cut down on your spending?
5. Assume that you have inherited $5,000. What would you do with this money? Would your closest friends be likely to do the same things? How would their ideas differ from yours?
6. Now imagine that you are 15 years older and received the same inheritance. How might you use this money at this point in your life?
7. Marriage counselors feel that differences about the use of money is one of the chief causes of marital discord. What are some of the important attitudes about money that you would like your spouse to have?

SELECTED REFERENCES

Blackman, Myra M. "A Study of the Real Income of Selected Households in Williamson County, Illinois." Master's thesis, Southern Illinois University, 1970.

Boyd, Virginia, and Beatrice Paolucci. "Changing Patterns in Rural Michigan Families." *The Rural Community and the Rural Family in 1985,* Research Report 193, Agricultural Experiment Station and Cooperative Extension Service, Michigan State University, 1973, pp. 3–8.

Bymers, Gwen J., and Marjorie Galenson. "Time Horizons in Family Spending." *Journal of Home Economics,* Vol. 60 (1968), pp. 709–716.

Hafstrom, Jeanne L., and Marilyn M. Dunsing. "Level of Living: Factors Influencing the Homemakers' Satisfaction." *Home Economics Research Journal,* Vol. 2 (1973), pp. 119–132.

Holmes, Emma G. "Budget Guides." *Family Economics Review* (Sept. 1969), pp. 12–14.

Linden, Fabian, ed. *Expenditure Patterns of the American Family.* Prepared by the National Industrial Conference Board, based on a survey conducted by the U.S. Department of Labor. New York: Industrial Conference, 1965.

Maloch, Francille, and C. R. Weaver. "Orientation to Day of Pay." *The Journal of Consumer Affairs,* Vol. 3 (Winter 1969), pp. 137–144.

McAfee, Linda. "Consumer Credit and Family Budgets." Master's thesis, Colorado State University, 1973.

Melson, Patricia B. "Family Financial Decision-Making: A Comparison of Lower and Middle Class Families Formed Before and After World War II." Ph.D. thesis, Purdue University, 1970.

Mork, Lucile F., and Jean L. Pennock. "Expenditures and Value of Consumption of Farm and Rural Nonfarm Families in North Carolina." *Family Economics Review* (Sept. 1970), pp. 5–9.

Pennock, Jean L. "Cost of Raising a Child." *Family Economics Review* (March 1970), pp. 14–15.

————, and Lucile Mork. "Expenditures and Value of Consumption As Measures of Level of Living." *Family Economics Review* (June 1970), pp. 3–8.

Rudd, Nancy. "Financial Assets: The Changing Family Portfolio." *Family Economics Review* (Summer 1973), pp. 15–17.

Smith, Carlton, Richard Putnam Pratt, and the Editors of Time-Life Books. *The Time-Life Book of Family Finance*. New York: Time-Life Books, 1969.

Williams, Flora L., and Sarah L. Manning. "Net Worth Change of Selected Families." *Home Economics Research Journal* (Dec. 1972), Vol. 1, pp. 104–113.

chapter 6

---

environmental resources

Environmental resources are very important to individuals and families. The two general types of environmental resources are community facilities, which are usually manmade, and natural resources.

Community Facilities

A wide range of community facilities is often available in the United States—schools, libraries, water supplies, sewage treatment plants, health services, recreational programs and facilities, public transportation, and many others. Many of these are publicly owned and supported by tax dollars. Others, such as some transportation systems, are privately owned and supported by the fees they charge.

These facilities are important resources because they often replace services that the individual or family would have to pay for directly out of personal income. Public water supplies and sewage disposal eliminate the need for private wells, springs, and septic systems. Moreover, they are often better facilities than the individual householder could provide. Most families rely on public schools for their children's education. Public libraries reduce the need for individuals to buy books, and make them available to many more people. Can you think of other examples?

Some kinds of public facilities are much more efficient than the ones that an individual family can provide. Public transportation systems generally use less energy per rider than individual cars, and cost less to the user than driving a private car.

Community facilities often supplement the services provided by an individual or family. Recreational facilities are an example. Some communities have a wide range of recreational facilities and programs—after-school programs for children, public swimming pools, baseball fields, tennis courts, golf courses, "Y" and youth center programs, centers for senior citizens, and other facilities.

In addition to public facilities there are many privately owned community facilities that are widely used—bowling alleys, sports arenas, skating rinks, movies, theatres, concert halls, and others.

Community facilities are considered important by many people. A growing number of young people have gravitated to places like Colorado, Oregon, and Vermont, in large part because these areas have recreational opportunities and a less developed, more natural environment. Many families look for school and recreational facilities before buying a home. Public transportation is often desired by people who must commute to work, even if they own an automobile. The car may need to be serviced, the weather may be inclement, or they may need to share the car with other members of the family. The presence of a public water supply and its connection to a public sewage system usually increases the value of a house in an urban area.

Community facilities tend to be concentrated in urban areas, cities and suburbs. Fewer are available in most rural areas. Kindergartens are an example. In most urban communities public kindergartens and often transportation to kindergarten are available. However, many rural areas have no kindergartens. Sometimes there are private kindergartens for which the parents must pay tuition and also provide transportation to and from the school. The same is true of many other facilities.

Widespread concern with the availability, quality, and cost of community facilities is shown by the heated debate that often accompanies plans for changing them or building new ones. Often there is a conflict between groups who expect to use a community facility heavily and those who do not. Retired persons may be worried that they will not be able to afford increased taxes for new schools and bike paths. Younger families

Figure 6.1. Many people enjoy using this path along the Chesapeake and Ohio Canal. (National Park Service, Department of the Interior)

may think that recreational facilities and health care programs for older people are not the most urgent needs in the community.

Natural Resources

There has been a growing recognition of the need to conserve natural resources so that there will be enough for present and future generations. Concern has focused around these areas—population pressure, land use, water supplies, air pollution, the use of energy, rising noise levels, and the use of publicly owned resources.

Population

Population growth is a worldwide concern at present. The world population is growing very rapidly, with 70 million people being added each year. At this rate the population of the world will double every 30 to 35 years.

From the beginning of the history of man, population growth has been held in check by limited food supplies, epidemics of virulent diseases, war, and other disasters. Now, however, modern medicine and technology, coupled with programs of improved sanitation, have given people in the industrialized world a much longer life expectancy. People of the non-industrialized nations do not have nearly as long a life expectancy, but it is better than it formerly was. Infant mortality has been greatly reduced in many poor countries, and there are fewer epidemics of the dreaded diseases such as typhus and cholera.

However, the poorer, less industrialized nations are increasing their population very rapidly. Egypt spent ten years constructing the Aswan Dam to make it possible to irrigate one third more land. However, during the construction period the population increased more than one half. By the time the dam was opened there was less arable land to feed each person than before it was started. One projection is that Egypt will need four more Aswan Dams in the next 24 years just to maintain its present ratio of arable land to people if the population continues to grow at its present rate.

The World Health Organization has estimated that even in years when there are no major agricultural disasters, such as droughts and crop failures, 10,000 people starve to death every day, and approximately one third to one half of the world's population is undernourished. Better agricultural methods in some countries and more effective distribution systems within and between nations would help. However, these approaches will not supply enough food for the world's population in the foreseeable future without a decrease in population growth.

Population concentration is also a problem. People are distributed unevenly across land areas. In the United States most people live in cities and suburbs because that is where they can find employment. Eighty per cent of the people live on less than 10 per cent of the land. One can fly across miles and miles of open, sparsely populated land in the United States.

Other parts of the world have the same situation. Politics, wars, and other problems have accentuated this. Hong Kong and Calcutta are teeming with people. They have among the highest population densities of the world. But countries like Australia and Canada still have big open areas of arable land.

Demographers project that in the next 20 years urban "corridors" of the United States will have an even greater population density. Some of these areas are from Chicago to Pittsburgh, Boston to Washington, and San Francisco to Los Angeles.

Population concentration in the United States has been a mixed blessing. Generally, workers in urban areas enjoy higher incomes, women can more readily find employment outside the home if they want it, fewer people live in substandard housing, and access to medical and educational facilities is better than in rural areas.

However, fewer people in urban areas own their own homes, the crime rate is higher, and environmental problems (particularly air and noise pollution) are aggravated by the difficulties of providing adequate safe water and disposing of sewage and solid waste.

Because of these problems many industries have moved out of the cities to suburbs and more rural areas. But this has thrown city dwellers, who depended on these industries for jobs, out of work. Some community planners feel that it is best to build new cities on open land for a mix of industry, homes, and shopping facilities. Reston, Virginia, is a community designed this way. It is still too soon to know how Reston will work out over a long period of time. Initially, there seem to be a number of attractive features. Many people can work near their homes. Provision for open spaces, recreation, schools, and even safe bicycling for children has been made in the plan.

The Use of Land

Recently, in the United States greater attention has been focused on the way land is used. There is great opposition to the further development of government-owned land—forests, beaches, scenic areas, and other open spaces—for commercial purposes. Many people are anxious to keep existing open spaces and recreational land as undeveloped as possible.

There is also a growing push for the federal government to acquire additional land, particularly scenic areas, seashores, mountain tops, and so on. In addition, many local communities and states have passed bond issues to match federal funding for the acquisition of smaller open areas.

A closely related concern is the need for planning for the use of privately owned land. The larger cities have high-rise buildings with little or no open land around them. Suburbs, on the other hand, usually have people spread out in individual homes surrounded by grass. As the suburban population increases and ages, there is growing pressure to build multifamily dwellings and clusters of homes.

Zoning regulations, which control private land use, have become very controversial. There is often disagreement over the best use of land and an individual's right to use their own property as they wish. Also, there is much debate about zoning regulations that require large lots for each home because such zoning keeps out people who cannot afford so much land. More communities and some states have zoning regulations designed to control the disposal of sewage. Many communities require that all new homes must be connected to central sewers. In addition, the owners of many existing homes are being forced to hook into central sewage systems

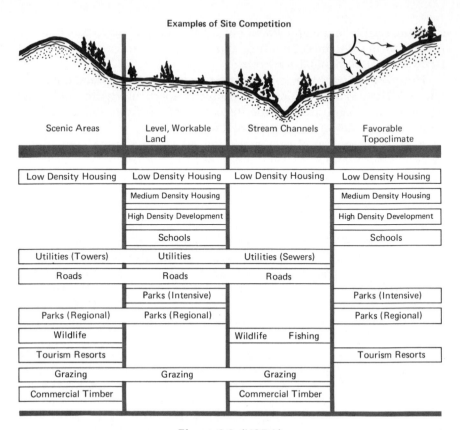

Figure 6.2. (USDA)

in suburban areas. This means that the homeowner must help pay for the sewage line and his individual connection, which often runs to several thousand dollars.

Even rural areas are concerned about sewage. The state of Vermont has passed regulations requiring approval of the septic system of new homes built on small lots. In areas of poor percolation, where the ground absorbs moisture slowly, greater space is needed between homes to insure that individual septic systems do not overflow and water supplies are not contaminated by sewage.

Water

The United States is generally free of the major waterborne diseases that still ravage many less-developed nations. In Thailand, where only 10 per cent of the people have piped water supplies, 40 per cent of all deaths are caused by waterborne diseases.

However, in the United States there is growing concern over the fact

Figure 6.3. The house above was built in a flood plain. Zoning regulations can prevent this by requiring that streams be contained as shown below, or that no building be allowed in such areas. (USDA; Soil Conservation Service)

that drinking water may contain harmful or undesirable ingredients. In some areas sewage has seeped into drinking water supplies, particularly when the ground is very wet. Communities built on sandy soil or on ground that absorbs water poorly are most apt to have trouble. Other sources of pollution are industrial wastes, excess fertilizer that is washed off farmlands, and detergents from home laundering.

Many industries discharge their waste products directly into lakes and streams. This is the largest source of water pollution in the United States In an effort to improve this situation many industries have built waste treatment plants or joined with communities to build such plants. More recently some recycling of waste products has been done. This has been particularly appealing to the chemical industry because their waste products have value in the commercial market. However, the waste products of utilities or steel processors have little or no marketable value.

Modern farming methods require the use of vast amounts of fertilizers for maximum yield. Inevitably, some of this fertilizer, which contains phosphates, is washed down into rivers and streams and gets into water supplies. This is a major source of water pollution.

Home detergents also contaminate water supplies. Since 1945 home laundering has been revolutionized by a combination of the automatic washing machine, synthetic fabrics, and phosphate detergents. Synthetic fabrics and fabric blends with easy care features could be washed in automatic machines with phosphate detergents. As a result the sales of these detergents soared and the use of soap decreased.

After a while people realized that phosphates were polluting waterways. Large green masses of algae began to appear in lakes and waterways, and fish were dying. (As the algae plants increased, they used the oxygen that the fish needed, so the fish died.) Although this process will happen naturally as ponds get older, an increase in phosphates is a stimulant to algae growth. Other factors, such as the size of the body of the water, and the speed at which the water is moving, also affect algae growth.

For a period, some places banned phosphate detergents. But it was found that many alternative detergents were very caustic and harmful to children who accidentally ate them. Also, phosphate detergents were helpful in retaining flameproof finishes on fabrics, such as those used in children's pajamas. A detergent is needed that will not pollute or have other harmful problems.

Fresh water supplies, like other natural resources, are unevenly distributed around the world. There is a great abundance of water in some areas, such as tropical rain forests. Other areas are deserts with little or no rainfall. Population is generally concentrated where there is enough rainfall to maintain some vegetation. However, weather patterns change over a period of time and areas that previously had enough water have experienced long droughts. During the early 1970s the monsoons did not bring enough rain to India, and rice crops withered away. South of the Sahara desert, pasture grass and crops dried up because of a lack of rainfall. The herds of cattle could not survive and many people starved.

Within the United States, the eastern half of the country generally has enough rainfall to provide an adequate supply of water. However, the western half of the country is much drier. Huge dams have been built and water is piped over long distances in many areas.

There is a growing awareness that the United States is using fresh water more rapidly than it is being replaced by the hydrological cycle. Studies suggest that by 1980 we will need more underground water than is available, if the present rate of consumption continues.

Conservation of water is needed on several levels. Industrial processes need to be more efficient in their use of water. Household consumption of water will also need to be cut. One approach is to develop equipment that uses less water. Europe has never had as large a supply of water. As a result, European household equipment generally uses less water. For example, one Swedish washing machine uses only five gallons of water per load. Another approach is to use less mechanical equipment that requires water, such as disposal units. Still another avenue to conserve household water is to use appliances more efficiently. Run the dishwasher or washing machine only when they are full.

There is a growing trend to consider water supplies and waste management on a regional basis. Regional water supply systems and waste disposal plants are now being developed.

Solid Waste Disposal

Waste disposal is a big problem. Have you ever seen the mountains of slag near a mine or the animal refuse from a feedlot where cows are fattened? Big piles of abandoned cars dot the landscape in some places. Cities are running out of places to dump trash.

About 90 per cent of the solid waste is the result of agriculture and mining. Individual homes, stores, hospitals, and so on generate another 6–7 per cent. The rest is produced by industry.

Although individual homes generate only a small proportion of all the solid waste, this amount adds up to a great deal of waste in heavily populated areas. The 1973 report of the National League of Cities and U.S. Conference of Mayors reports that cities spent $6 billion to dispose of trash.

Recycling to salvage useable materials has been proposed as one way to cut costs and conserve scarce resources. This is not a new idea.

Until the end of World War II, significant amounts of materials were salvaged from municipal wastes. Some wastes were set aside in the home for

Figure 6.4. More and better sewage treatment plants are needed in many places. (New York State Department of Environmental Conservation)

separate collection, either by a collection agency, civic group, or social service agency. In some communities, workers on trucks or at dumps and incinerators removed salvageable materials such as newspapers, cardboard, metals, glass, and rags. As labor costs rose and the compactor truck was introduced, picking operations became more expensive and difficult, and so they were slowly abandoned.[1]

Many communities now have recycling programs for newspapers, aluminum cans, and glass. Some cities use poweful magnets to separate metal from other solid wastes. About 55 per cent of U.S. steel production is from scrap metal. It is cheaper to reprocess aluminum than to make it from the raw materials. Cannery waste is being processed into cattle feed. At least one utility company in the United States uses solid waste to generate electricity.

Most of the material presently being recycled comes from manufacturing and businesses. More could be done at several levels to encourage the recycling of materials by communities as well as industry. Federal laws and regulations, such as depletion allowances and schedules, favor the use of natural rather than recycled resources. Shipping rates and policies on federal land use also favor natural resource usage. Also, at present industries and labor are often located near sources of natural resources

[1] U.S. Environmental Protection Agency, "Recycling and the Consumer," 1974, p. 7.

rather than ones that can be recycled. Paper mills are near forests but often far from cities where waste paper is available.

A change in attitude on the part of the individual consumer is also needed if recycling is desired. Recycled paper has gained some acceptance, but reprocessed wool has not. Reprocessed oil for cars has not yet gained wide acceptance.

Much can be done by individuals to reduce the amount of trash. We can buy those products that create the least waste, returnable milk and soda bottles, food and household products in as simple packages as possible.

Reducing the habit of littering is another way to cut waste disposal problems. After a rock concert in Denver the ground was ankle deep in food, candy wrappers, bottles, and cans. Many cities in Europe are noticeably cleaner than those of the United States, partly because people just don't throw as much trash away on the ground.

Industry could be encouraged to package consumer products in ways that would result in less waste materials. This could be done both by legislation and consumer resistance to buying products that are overpackaged.

Figure 6.5. Separation at the source is one approach to recycling. (U.S. Environmental Protection Agency)

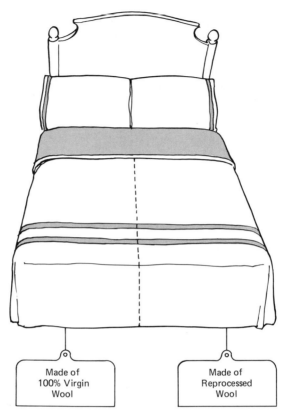

Made of
100% Virgin
Wool

Made of
Reprocessed
Wool

Figure 6.6. Reprocessed wool has not gained the same acceptance as reprocessed steel or paper. (U.S. Environmental Protection Agency)

Also, there needs to be a push for packaging materials that are biodegradable—those that will decompose naturally.

Energy

The people of the United States consume enormous amounts of energy. With only 6 per cent of the earth's population, they consume 30 per cent of the energy used each year. Almost two thirds of this amount is used by industry—the rest by individuals, commercial enterprises, and government facilities.

The American household has a wide variety of appliances and equipment. Ninety-eight per cent of American homes have a television set. Almost half have an air conditioner. Refrigerators, washing machines, dryers, freezers, dishwashers, vacuum cleaners, toasters, electric frying pans, automatic coffeemakers, and electric toothbrushes are commonplace.

Each individual uses about 36 per cent more electricity than he did only ten years ago. And one projection is that by 1985 energy requirements will be double those of 1971.

The energy problem, how to provide enough energy for growing needs without further polluting the environment, is the most difficult environmental problem facing the United States at present.

The United States is faced with a growing shortage of oil, natural gas, and hydroelectric power sources. Sixty-eight per cent of our present energy consumption is from oil and natural gas, 28 per cent from coal, and 4 per cent from hydroelectric and nuclear power.

Tremendous reserves of coal are available. However, soft coal is a big air polluter, and low-sulphur coal is less abundant. Also, there is great opposition to strip mining because it devastates large areas of land. Strip-mined areas can be restored, but this is an added expense. Coal can also be made into gas, but the present process is expensive for use on a large scale.

There is a push to develop new sources of energy—Alaskan oil, off-shore oil and gas reserves, and other sources. Also, there is research being done on alternative fuel sources—breeder reactors, thermonuclear fission, and others.

On a short-term basis, a nationwide computer-controlled power grid would make it possible to transmit high voltages of electricity over longer distances and reduce the possibilities of blackouts. This type of system would also enable local power plants to shut down when air pollution was too great and draw power from farther away.

Industry will have to develop methods and products that utilize energy resources more efficiently at both the producing and consuming levels. Refrigerators and stoves could be even better insulated, and many other products could be more efficient users of energy.

Understanding Your Electric and Gas Bills[2]

You can keep tabs on your use of energy and also doublecheck the utility company's bills.

ELECTRIC. The electricity you use is measured in kilowatt-hours (kwh). A watt is a measure of electricity and a kilowatt is 1,000 watts. You will use 1 kwh of electricity if you leave a 100-watt light bulb burning for 10 hours.

Each dial on your meter shows that you have used a certain number of kwh of electricity. (See Figure 6.8.)

Always start to read your meter with the first dial on the right; it measures a total of 10 kwh. Each time the pointer moves from one number to another on this first dial, you have used 1 kwh.

[2] From "Consumer News," Vol. 4 (October 1, 1974).

Figure 6.7. Open pit mining and strip mining spoil land that is mined. *Above:* This aerial view of a copper company mine in Utah shows the open pit and waste dumps. *Below:* This picture shows an area that has been strip mined for coal and restored. (Soil Conservation Service, USDA)

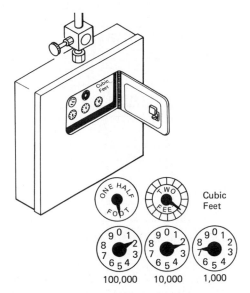

Figure 6.8. An electric meter. (*Consumer News*)

In the meter shown here, 4 kwh are measured on the first dial. The second dial on this meter—measuring a total of 100 kwh—shows that 80 kwh have been used. (Note that some of the dials run clockwise, while others run counterclockwise.)

When you check the third dial—measuring 1,000 kwh—you'll see that the pointer is barely a hair's-breadth away from 5. Do you read this as 5 or 4? First you must check the dial on the right, the 100-kwh dial. Its pointer is now between 8 and 9, showing that it hasn't quite completed its present circling of the dial. Thus, you read the 1,000-kwh dial as 4. You'll read it as 5 after the pointer on the 100-kwh dial reaches 0.

On the fourth dial, of course—the one measuring 10,000-kwh—you read 9. Thus, you have a complete meter reading of 9484.

The sample electric bill (Figure 6.9) may not look exactly like the one you receive in the mail, but it probably includes many of the same items that appear on your own bill. Although utility rates, taxes and other charges vary in different communities, this sample should help to explain your bill. If you still have questions, call your local electric company. Their consumer service department can answer your questions and may also be able to send you a sample bill that will explain the exact items for which you are charged. (Numbers listed below describe items on the sample bill.)

1. This is the number of consumer's account with the electric company. Use it for identification when making inquiry or paying bill.
2. This code indicates the rate schedule that is used in billing the consumer. This rate is usually not shown on the bill; but you do need to know what it is if you want to compute your own bill. You can find the rate at which you are charged by calling your electric company. Usually, electric rates are set on

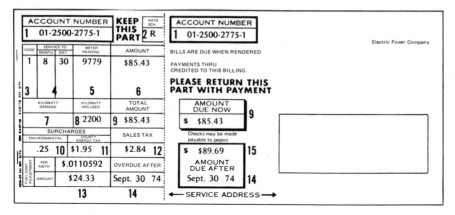

Figure 6.9. A sample electric bill. (*Consumer News*)

a sliding scale, with the rate per kilowatt-hour (kwh) decreasing as you use more kwh of electricity. [However, this is changing in some places.]

3. This code indicates the kind of bill this is—a regular monthly bill or an adjustment bill. Code is explained on reverse side of bill.
4. Cutoff date for billing.
5. Meter reading on which bill is based. You can double-check this figure by reading your meter the same day the electric company reads it. This should be the cutoff date (see item 4); call the company to learn your cut-off date each month.
6. Consumer's monthly charge for electricity.
7. This applies only to commercial installations using more than 6,000 kwh per month.
8. To verify the kwh for which you are charged, subtract last month's meter reading (Item 5 on last month's bill) from Item 5 on this month's bill.
9. This is the total of the following items on the bill: Item 8 multiplied by the rates charged per kwh; Item 10; Item 11; Item 12; Item 13.
10. This state's residents pay an environmental surcharge—collected for the state by the electric company—which helps defray costs of deciding where to locate electric plants.
11. This county levies an energy tax which is collected for the county by the electric company.
12. State sales tax of 4%.
13. The fuel cost adjustment is a "pass-through" charge which represents the electric company's increased costs for the coal and oil used to generate electricity. This state's utility commission allows the electric company to pass along its increased costs to the consumer. The fuel cost increase is figured as a certain amount per kwh (on this bill, it is $.0110592, slightly over 1¢ per kwh). Multiply that figure by kwh used to get fuel cost adjustment ($24.33 on this bill).
14. Date after which bill is overdue.
15. After overdue date, additional 5% is added to bill.

Do you know how to figure your monthly electric costs? You will need the rate schedule used by your local electric company. (See Table 6.1.)

TABLE 6.1
Sample Summer Rate Schedule for Electric Service

Minimum charge (including the first 20 kwh, or fraction thereof)	$2.25 per month
Next 80 kwh	3.55c per kwh
Next 100 kwh	3.21c per kwh
Next 200 kwh	2.96c per kwh
Next 400 kwh	2.65c per kwh
Consumption in excess of 800 kwh	2.20c per kwh

* Electric companies often charge somewhat higher rates in summer when demand for electricity is higher. [This is particularly true in areas where air conditioning is heavily used. In colder areas where electricity is used more for winter heating the rate may be higher in the winter.] Reason: to meet increased demand, company must use additional generators—older ones that are less efficient and produce electricity at a higher cost than newer generators do.

Then you can figure your electric costs by following the step-by-step procedure outlined below. (Numbers in parentheses refer to items on sample electric bill.)

FIRST, take your meter reading, being sure to do it the same day the electric company reads it.

• Today's meter reading: 9779

SECOND, figure out how many kilowatts you have used since the previous month's reading. Remember, your electric meter gives a cumulative reading. To find kwh used for the current month (Item 8), subtract today's meter reading (Item 5) from last month's reading.

• Today's meter reading:	9779
Last month's reading:	−7579
Kwh used this month	2200

THIRD, figure you costs for kwh used, on the basis of the rate schedule now in use by your electric company. (Figures below are based on sample rate schedule.)

• 20 kwh	@	2.25 (flat rate)	=	$2.25
80 kwh	×	3.55¢	=	$2.84
100 kwh	×	3.21¢	=	$3.21
200 kwh	×	2.96¢	=	$5.92
400 kwh	×	2.65¢	=	$10.60
+1400 kwh	×	2.20¢	=	+$30.80
2200 kwh				$55.62

Thus, $55.62 is your basic electricity cost.

FOURTH, figure fuel cost adjustment charge (Item 13) by multiplying the utility company's fuel adjustment rate by the kwh used.

• $.0110592 × 2200 = $24.33.

FIFTH, figure county energy tax (Item 11) by multiplying tax rate (ask electric company) by kwh used.
* $.0008855 × 2200 = 1.95.

SIXTH, add basic electricity cost, fuel cost adjustment & county energy tax.

$$
\begin{array}{rl}
\bullet\ \$55.62 & \text{basic electricity} \\
24.33 & \text{fuel cost adjustment} \\
+\quad 1.95 & \text{county energy tax} \\
\hline
\$81.90 &
\end{array}
$$

SEVENTH, figure state sales tax (Item 12) and add to previous total.

$$
\begin{array}{rr}
\bullet\ \$81.90 & \$\ 3.28 \\
\times\quad .04 & +\ 81.90 \\
\hline
\$\ 3.28 & \$85.18
\end{array}
$$

EIGHTH, figure environmental surcharge (Item 10) by multiplying tax rate (ask electric company) by kwh.
* $.00011235 × 2200 = $.25.

NINTH, add environmental surcharge to previous total to get total amount due on your bill (Item 9).

$$
\begin{array}{rl}
\bullet\ \$85.18 & \\
+\quad .25 & \\
\hline
\$85.43 & \text{total amount due on bill.}
\end{array}
$$

TENTH, to find amount charged if bill is paid after overdue date, subtract environmental charge from total amount and figure 5% of that. Then add the 5% to the total amount of bill.

$$
\begin{array}{rr}
\bullet\ \$85.43 & \\
-\quad .25 & \\
\hline
\$85.18 & \$\ 4.26 \\
\times\quad .05 & +\ 85.43 \\
\hline
\$\ 4.26 & \$89.69\ \text{total late payment.}
\end{array}
$$

GAS.   Your gas meter has two types of dials. (See Figure 6.10.) The recording dials—shown on the bottom line of the meter pictured here—are the ones that measure the cubic feet of gas you use. (A cubic foot is a unit for measuring the volume of natural gas.)

The other dials on your meter—here, the 2 on the top line—are test dials that are used by the gas company to check the accuracy of the meter. You can always spot a test dial because it measures less than 100 cubic feet, and you can always ignore it.

On this meter, the first dial on the right measures 1,000 cubic feet of gas

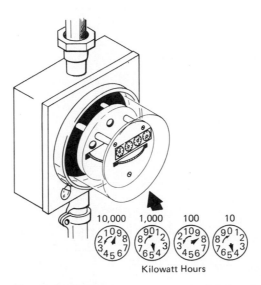

10,000   1,000   100   10

Kilowatt Hours

Figure 6.10. A gas meter. (*Consumer News*)

each time the pointer circles the entire dial. The second dial measures 10,000 cubic feet with each complete circling of the pointer; the third measures 100,000. On a meter having 4 dials, the fourth would measure 1 million cubic feet.

Keeping those figures in mind—and following the rules outlined above for electric meters—you can easily read this meter. The 1,000-foot dial reads 7; the 10,000-foot dial reads 7; and the 100,000-foot dial reads 1. The meter reading is 177.

The sample bill (Figure 6.11) should guide you through your own bill. If you have further questions, call your local gas company. (Numbers listed below describe numbered items on sample bill.)

1. Consumer's account number.
2. Shows how many days' service are covered by bill.
3. Cutoff date for billing.
4. Gas service for consumer's home is connected to plant at this address.
5. Code indicating charges covered by bill—gas usage, fee for repairs or merchandise. Code is explained on reverse side of bill.
6. Meter reading on which bill is based.
7. This is the quantity of gas—expressed in hundreds of cubic feet—that went through the meter during the billing period. This number should equal the difference between this month's meter reading (Item 6) and last month's meter reading.
8. This tells how many therms (therm is a measure of heat energy) were supplied in the average 10 cubic feet of gas during the billing period. A therm is a significant measure for you because consumers of gas are charged by the therm, not by the cubic foot of gas.

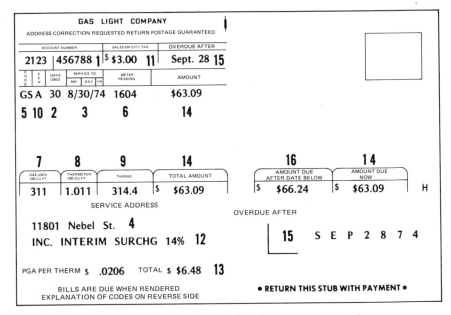

Figure 6.11. Sample gas bill. (*Consumer News*)

9. This shows how many therms the consumer is being charged for. This figure is arrived at by multiplying Item 7 by Item 8.

10. Code for rate schedule that applies to this consumer's type of gas service; rate schedules are built on sliding scales. To learn how much you are being charged per therm of gas, phone your gas company.

11. Sales tax of 5%.

12. This item represents an increase in the consumer's bill—a 14% interim surcharge granted to the company, by the utility commission, until the commission has time to rule on the company's request for an increased rate schedule.

13. This is a "pass-through" charge reflecting increases in the wholesale costs paid for gas by gas company. (See Item 13, "Your electric bill,"). These increases in wholesale costs are passed on to the consumer in the form of an additional charge—a Purchase Gas Adjustment charge (PGA)—for each therm of gas used. Here, the charge per therm is $.0206 (slightly over 2¢)—a total of $6.48 for 314.4 therms.

14. The amount of the bill is the total of the following items: Item 9 multiplied by the rates charged per therm; Item 11; Item 12; Item 13.

15. Date after which bill is overdue.

16. After overdue date, additional 5% is added to bill.

Conserving energy. Each individual can help conserve energy by evaluating his usage and cutting down wherever possible. This will both help cut costs, and reduce the need to use scarce resources.

1. Transportation. Walk or bicycle for short distances. Use public transportation instead of a car, wherever possible. Join a car pool if you can. Work for better public transportation in your area.

To improve gasoline consumption in your own automobile, remember that slower speeds generally save gas. Keep the car in good condition; proper tuning saves gas. Avoid fast starts and stops. Turn off the engine if you stand still for three minutes or longer. Lighten the car by not carrying excess baggage. Keep tires inflated at the pressure recommended by the manufacturer.

If you are buying a car, consider smaller cars that use less gas. Study the government mileage guides to find out about the fuel efficiency of cars.

2. Heating and cooling. New buildings should be designed and constructed so that they will use as little energy as possible. Orientation for maximum sun in winter and shade in summer should be considered.

Good insulation for both new and old homes will cut both heating and cooling costs. Six inches in the ceiling or on attic floors is recommended, and $3\frac{1}{2}$ inches in walls. However, if the winters are severe or electric heat is used, 9 inches in the ceiling is better.

To cut heat loss, install storm windows and doors. Weatherstrip around outside doors and windows. Check and clean the furnace annually. Be sure the fireplace damper is closed when the fireplace is not in use.

To cut cooling costs shade the house with trees and shade windows with awnings, shades, and drapes. Use less light where you can because lights give off heat. Turn on air conditioning only when it is badly needed. Complain about supermarkets, restaurants, movie theatres, and other public places that are too cold, so that they will use less energy, too.

3. Household Appliances. Buy only those appliances that are really useful. When you select new equipment, consider how much energy it uses.

The voluntary labeling program for energy-consuming household appliances can help you select appliances that use energy most efficiently. (See Figure 6.12.)

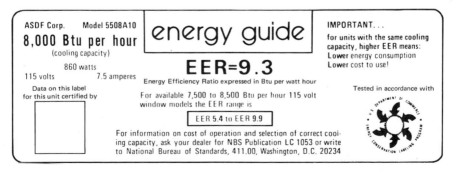

Figure 6.12. Energy guide for appliances. (*Consumer News*)

Want to know how much you will save in operating costs per year by buying a more efficient air conditioner? You need 3 figures: (1) cost of electricity per kilowatt hour in your community; (2) annual hours of air conditioning required for your climate; (3) watts per hour required by each air conditioner. Get the first 2 figures from your local utility company. Get the third from the model or the salesman.

Let's say you need an air conditioner in the 8,000 Btu class. You're considering two models. The more efficient one (with an EER of 8.9) needs 900 watts; the less efficient one (EER—6.2) needs 1,300 watts and costs $40 less. Your utility says you'll need air conditioning for 800 hours a year and electricity costs 4¢ per kilowatt hour.

Use this [National Bureau of Standards] formula: Multiply cost of electricity times hours of cooling needed times watts required by air conditioner. Divide answer by 1,000 to get operating cost in dollars.

- Here's annual cost for running more efficient model: $.04 × 800 × 900 = 28,000 or $28.80.
- Here's annual cost for running less efficient model: $.04 × 800 × 1,300 = 41,600 or $41.60.

[In this example, you will save] . . . $12.80 per year in operating costs on the more efficient model, within about 3 years you will have the $40 difference in purchase price. What's more, the higher-priced model may also offer special features—more fan speed and better insulation, which means less noise. Also consider where you live. In a Florida city like Jacksonville (where you use 1,600 hours of air conditioning per year) you save more with a high-EER model than in a cooler city like Chicago (only about 400 hours of cooling needed).

When you consider operating costs, remember that you're dealing with variables: How good is your insulation? What's the layout of your home? Do you leave doors open and allow cool air to escape? These all affect operating costs. The NBS formula cannot guarantee precisely what you will save in dollars and cents. But it does allow you to figure the difference in operating costs for 2 units under the same conditions.[3]

Operation of the hot-water may account for 15 per cent of a home utility bill. Cut the use of hot water wherever you can. Lower the temperature setting of the water heater. Use cold-water laundering, if possible. Take short showers instead of a bath with a large tub of water. Don't keep the hot water running when you wash dishes.

Refrigerators and freezers are also costly appliances to operate. Over the normal 14-year life of a refrigerator, utility costs are greater than the original purchase price. Contrary to popular belief, a frost-free refrigerator does not necessarily cost more to operate than a standard model, a study

[3] "Consumer News," Vol. 4 (May 15, 1974), p. 4.

by Consumers Unions indicates.[4] Chest-type freezers cost less to operate than those with a vertical door.

Five to 7 per cent of the home utility bill usually is the result of cooking. Use pots that cover the burners to save fuel. Heavy pans usually hold the heat better and thus use less energy. Cover pots when you cook to keep the heat in. Use the oven efficiently. Cook several things at one time if possible. If you only have a small amount to bake, a small appliance may be more efficient, particularly if you have an electric stove.

Extra features on appliances generally use more energy. A color television set consumes more energy than a black and white one of the same size. Large-screen sets use more energy than smaller ones.

It pays to turn off lights when you don't need them. Use lights for specific areas instead of illuminating a whole room. Fluorescent lights use less energy than regular light bulbs and last longer. You can help avoid brownouts and blackouts by using electricity when the demand is lower— early morning, late evening, and weekends.

Air Pollution

Air pollution is generally greatest where people and cars are concentrated. Drive or fly to any big city and you can see how the sky gets grayer as you approach it.

About 215 million tons of air pollutants are discharged into the atmosphere each year. There is some disagreement as to whether automobile emissions or residues from the burning of coal and oil are the biggest pollutants. Both discharge enormous quantities of undesirable material into the air.

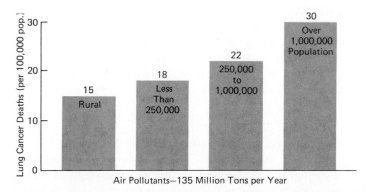

Figure 6.13. Bigger cities result in more air pollution and more deaths from lung cancer. (Department of Health, Education, and Welfare)

[4] "Top-Freezer Refrigerators," *Consumer Reports* (November 1974), pp. 808–814.

Concern with this problem is not new. Physicians in ancient Greece worried about what the winds were blowing over their patients. The burning of soft coal and peat was blamed for atmospheric problems in London during the 1600s.

A small start has been made on improving the situation. The burning of coal has been reduced because coal discharges a lot of soot. Industries and utilities are beginning to install devices for reducing the smoke emitted from chimneys. Emission-control devices are required on new cars. Some states also require older cars to meet emission standards. Changes in automobile engines are also being tried. Airlines are also taking steps to reduce air pollution. New planes have engine modifications and other changes to reduce smoke emission and noise levels.

Noise

Noise is unwanted sound. Most people enjoy hearing the first robin in spring but don't want to hear the washing machine running.

Noise levels in urban areas have increased greatly. Cars, buses, and trains are noisy. Construction crews hammer and bang. Jet airplanes drown out conversations and even debates in Congress as they land and take off.

Rural areas have growing noise problems. More traffic, plus motorcycles and snowmobiles, contribute to the noise level.

Household noise has also increased greatly. Have you ever tried to talk on the telephone in the kitchen while the dishwasher or a fan was running? Many household appliances are noisy.

Apartment dwellers often can hear their neighbors' TV sets and dishwashers. Sometimes they can even hear their neighbor's conversation. An early-rising neighbor whose kitchen is adjacent to your bedroom wall can be just as effective as an alarm clock.

Cars, buses, and airplanes can be muffled further. Have you ever noticed how quietly a big expensive car purrs? Buildings, both residential and industrial, can be constructed to provide sound deadening. Many household appliances could be built to operate more quietly if consumers demand this.

Here are some ways to muffle sound in your home. Use rugs on floors, particularly in busy areas. Install sound-absorbing ceiling tiles, particularly in noisy places like the kitchen. Put noisy appliances on cushioned padding and use insulation and vibration mounts. Buy upholstered furniture rather than hard-surfaced pieces. Hang drapes and curtains to absorb sound.

CHAPTER FOLLOW-UP

1. Make a survey of the important community facilities in your community. If you live in a large city you should limit the survey to a small area.
2. Have a team find out how garbage disposal is handled in your community. Where are waste materials deposited? What are some of the problems? What suggestions for improving the system have been made?
3. Visit your local water treatment plan, if there is one. Find out what is done to the water you drink. Where does it come from? If you live in an area where people depend on individual water supplies, find out what government agencies check on the safety of these supplies. Where can you go to have your water tested?
4. List the household appliances that you consider essential for comfort and convenience in your home.
5. What appliances could you eliminate with little inconvenience?
6. Have a group make a map of nearby outdoor recreational facilities, parks, playgrounds, swimming pools, hiking trails, and so on.
7. Make a bulletin board display of articles from a local newspaper about pollution problems.
8. Discuss in class who should pay for cleaning up the air. Consider the effectiveness of various alternatives and how each possible solution would affect individual families.
9. Invite a representative from a governmental or community agency that deals with environmental problems to talk to the class about environmental concerns in your area.

SELECTED REFERENCES

Aesthetics in Environmental Planning. Washington, D.C.: U.S. Environmental Protection Agency, 1973.

Beale, Calvin L. "Implications of Population Trends for Quality of Life." *Family Economics Review* (March 1973), pp. 3–8.

Bird, Caroline. *The Crowding Syndrome*, New York: David McKay Co., 1972.

Boyer, William H. "Toward an Ecological Perspective in Education: Part II." *Phi Delta Kappan* (February 1974), pp. 397–400.

Call, Dena Lee Child. "Family Conditions and Practices Related to Waste Paper Output." Master's thesis, Utah State University, 1973.

Commoner, Barry. *The Closing Circle*. New York: Alfred A. Knopf, 1971.

Editors of Better Homes and Gardens. *Environment Yes, Hysteria No.* Des Moines, Ia.: Meredith Corporation, 1971.

Field, Anne. "Energy Conversation: A Challenge for Home Economists." *Journal of Home Economics,* Vol. 65 (1973), pp. 23–26.

Fritsch, Albert J., and Barry I. Castleman. *Lifestyle Index.* Washington, D.C.: Center for Science in the Public Interest, 1974.

Goode, William J. "Social Change and Family Renewal." *Families of the Future.* Ames, Ia.: The Iowa State University Press, 1972, pp. 116–133.

Hook, Nancy C., and Beatrice Paolucci. "The Family As an Ecosystem." *Journal of Home Economics.* Vol. 62 (1970), pp. 315–318.

Kneese, Allen V. *Water Resources.* Kansas City: Federal Reserve Bank of Kansas City, 1969.

Latham, Carroll P. "Individual Family Contribution to Paper Pollution in Cache County." Master's thesis, Utah State University, 1972.

The M.I.T. Report. Consumer Appliances: The Real Cost. Massachusetts Institute of Technology for Policy Alternatives with the Charles Stark Draper Laboratory, Inc., n.d.

Pifer, Glenda. "Energy Conservation in and Around the Home." *Family Economics Review* (Spring 1974), pp. 16–17.

"Society and Its Physical Environment." *The Annals of the American Academy of Political and Social Science,* Vol. 389 (May 1970), entire issue.

Steidl, Rose E. "An Ecological Approach to the Study of Family Managerial Behavior." *The Family: Focus on Management,* Washington, D.C.: American Home Economics Association, 1970, pp. 22–34.

Wheeler, James, and Nobuo Shimahara. "Toward an Ecological Perspective in Education: Part I." *Phi Delta Kappan,* (February 1974), pp. 393–396.

part three

---

household operation

chapter 7

food

Eating in this space age reflects the advances of modern technology—from the newborn baby sucking on his sterile, disposable bottle to the harried housewife heating TV dinners or the traveler eating a steak in an airplane high above the Rockies.

Changing Patterns of Eating

Gone are the hearty breakfast and large midday meal (except on Sundays) for most people. Breakfast is light and often eaten on the run. People generally have lunches wherever they are—often at work or at school. Dinner is the main meal of the day and frequently the one time when the family may gather together.

On weekends or holidays, eating may be part of a leisure activity—a hamburger at a roadside restaurant, lunch with a friend, a snack at the bowling alley, or a picnic in the yard, at a park, or while one is traveling.

"More leisure time, with its casual living and irregular home hours, is leading to more frequent eating and nibbling."[1] This pattern of casual eating is made more easily possible by the advances in food processing and vending. Vending machines are growing in use.

Food sales through coin-operated, automatic vending machines are mounting year after year. Vending machines are appearing in new locations, are handling many new food items, and are being adapted to new uses.

The growth in automatic vending of food can be explained by cost and convenience. Automatic vending offers some opportunity to combat rising labor and overhead costs.

The vending operation offers convenience.
1. It places foods in convenient locations close to the consumer.
2. Automatic vending provides convenience in time of purchase. Vending offers round-the-clock services. Few ordinary retailing operations can afford to stay open day and night.
3. Vended foods are usually convenient in use. Little waiting time is involved in their purchase. They can be eaten on-the-spot or readily carried to desk or home for eating.[2]

The older pattern of eating only three widely spaced meals a day grew out of an agrarian economy. Food took a long time to prepare and the family was away from home for most of the day tilling the soil or tending the animals. Today's trend toward more frequent eating, much of it away from home, has evolved in response to the move from an agrarian to an urban culture and to rising incomes as well as to other changes in society.

A growing percentage of meals and snacks are being eaten away from home.

The proportion of some foods eaten away from home appear related to their association with a certain meal and the relative number of times the meal is eaten out. For example, only 7 per cent of the morning meals were eaten out, compared to 23 per cent of noon and 10 per cent of evening meals.

Items consumed away from home in the highest proportion were candy, soft drinks, and alcoholic drinks. Mixtures containing poultry, fish or meat (mainly hamburgers), ice cream and sweet baked goods were nearly as high. These foods are probably related to the high proportion of the snacks (18 per cent) and noon meals (23 per cent) eaten out.[3]

[1] George H. Allen, "What's Happening to Today's Family," *What's New in Home Economics* (Oct. 1966), p. 100.

[2] Excerpt from Roger Murphy, Ruth Hodgson, and Judith Siegel, "Automatic Vending of Food," "Focus on the Food Markets," Feb. 5, 1962, p. 2.

[3] Corinne LeBovit, "Foods Eaten Away from Home," *National Food Situation*, USDA (May 1970), pp. 25–26.

Figure 7.1. Many meals are eaten away from home. *(Top:* Swift and Company; *bottom:* Cooperative Extension Service, Washington State University)

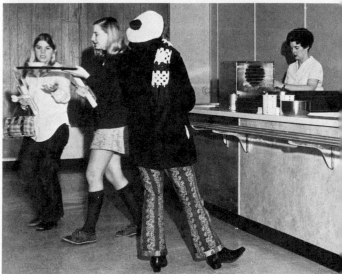

Trends in Food Consumption

Modern supermarkets offer an overwhelming array of products. Many of these are products that did not exist a generation ago.

When Abraham Lincoln clerked in a country store, his customers had around 900 food items to choose from. Until . . . 1940, a . . . shopper had only about a thousand food items from which to make selections. Contrast this with the average supermarket of today with 8,000 or more items—many of which were not available 10 years ago.[4]

There has been a tremendous shift to the use of convenience foods. Today's homemaker is generally a busy woman. She is often involved with activities outside the home as well as within it. Although she may have an attractive, well-equipped kitchen she is still interested in reducing the time she spends on food preparation and cleanup for everyday meals. So the use of convenience foods has boomed. One projection is that "in a few years, our weekly market order may be made up almost entirely of the so-called 'convenience' foods with their built-in maid or chef service."[5]

Canned, frozen, and dehydrated foods are now widely used. Freeze-drying, the newest method of preparing convenience foods is becoming increasingly important. Freeze-dried foods keep without refrigeration.

Foods processed by this method are used as ingredients in other products, [such as] chicken in dry soup mixes and fruit in dry cereals. Campers can purchase a variety of dehydrated meats, dairy foods, eggs, vegetables, fruits, and desserts that take up little space and can be reconstituted rapidly.[6]

Figure 7.2. Freeze-dried foods can be stored without refrigeration. (U.S. Army Natick Laboratories)

[4] Henry H. Harp and William S. Hoofnagle, "Thousands of New Foods Give You a Wide Choice," *Food for Us All,* The Yearbook of Agriculture, 1969, U.S. Department of Agriculture, p. 36.
[5] Ibid.
[6] Ibid., p. 38.

There has been a definite trend for Americans to eat fewer calories than formerly. This is reflected by a decrease in consumption of some foods, such as potatoes.

There has also been a shift in the form in which we consume foods. Our potato might be in the form of potato chips or french fries. A growing part of our milk consumption is as frozen desserts rather than fluid whole milk.

Some of the starches have been replaced by meat and poultry, particularly among higher-income families. Now there is concern as to whether many people are eating more meat than is good for their health. There appears to be a relationship between the high consumption of fats of the type that are found in meat and whole milk and heart disease.

Also, there is growing concern with whether the meat eating pattern of people in the United States uses too much of world's supply of grain, which is badly needed in other countries. Some of the cattle used for the meat supply are fattened on grain, which is used rather inefficiently by cattle.

"Obesity has become a national problem. Because many of our eating patterns developed from the agrarian period, the tendency is for most adults to gain weight. "Adaptation to modern life without development of obesity means either that a person must increase his activity or decrease the amount of food he eats."[7]

Inactivity is the most important factor explaining the frequency of "creeping" overweight. For hundreds of thousands of years . . . men had to be physically active to survive. They required large amounts of food to supply energy for every phase of their work. The present highly mechanized sedentary condition of life has changed this drastically.[8]

The trend away from breakfast as a meal has meant that many young people and adults are low in energy during the morning. One of the reasons for this trend may be the cultural pattern of snacking, another that some people try to lose weight by skipping meals (which is a poor way to do it), and yet another that many people tend to be in a hurry in the morning. However, with careful planning, breakfast can be appealing, easy to prepare, and easily eaten. One of the very important jobs in home management is seeing that the family members are well nourished.

Many adults do not get enough calcium, which younger people

---

[7] Jean Mayer, *Overweight, Causes, Cost, and Control* (Englewood Cliffs, N.J.: Prentice-Hall, Inc., 1968), p. 1.

[8] Ruth M. Leverton, "Nutritional Trends and the Consumer's Food," *Journal of Home Economics*, Vol. 56 (1964), p. 320.

TABLE 7.1
Energy Needs

	(Years)	Weight		Height		Energy
	From up to	(kg)	(lbs)	(cm)	(in)	(kcal)
Infants	0.0–0.5	6	14	60	24	kg × 117
	0.5–1.0	9	20	71	28	kg × 108
Children	1–3	13	28	86	34	1300
	4–6	20	44	110	44	1800
	7–10	30	66	135	54	2400
Males	11–14	44	97	158	63	2800
	15–18	61	134	172	69	3000
	19–22	67	147	172	69	3000
	23–50	70	154	172	69	2700
	51+	70	154	172	69	2400
Females	11–14	44	97	155	62	2400
	15–18	54	119	162	65	2100
	19–22	58	128	162	65	2100
	23–50	58	128	162	65	2000
	51+	58	128	162	65	1800
Pregnant						+300
Lactating						+500

[1] The allowances are intended to provide for individual variations among most normal persons as they live in the United States under usual environmental stresses. Diets should be based on a variety of common foods in order to provide other nutrients for which human requirements have been less well defined.

SOURCE: "Recommended Daily Dietary Allowances," Food and Nutrition Board, National Academy of Sciences–National Research Council, 1973.

generally get from milk. A deficiency of iron resulting in anemia and a lack of energy is also a common problem among college-age girls.

Meal Planning

The goal of most homemakers is to provide food for their family that is wholesome and pleasing "with a reasonable expenditure of available resources."[9]

[9] Paulena Nickell and Jean Muir Dorsey, *Management in Family Living*, 4th ed. (New York: John Wiley & Sons, Inc., 1967), p. 502.

Consider Needs and Tastes

When you are planning food for other people it is important to consider their preferences as well as their nutritional needs if you want them to eat and enjoy the food. Eating is part of our cultural pattern. Even in two closely related countries such as the United States and Great Britain, food preferences differ. Few Americans would elect kippered herring for breakfast or a trifle for dessert.

Within a large country like ours there are many subcultures, each of which may have decided food preferences. The Southerner may like corn bread, the New Englander, clam chowder made with milk, the Puerto Rican American, a baked custard pudding.

In any group of people there are bound to be differing tastes. A husband and wife may have different preferences.

These factors affect food preferences.[10]

1. Religious and cultural background. Special foods and special methods of preparation are sometimes desired. Many people want meatless meals on religious holidays and during Lent. Nationality groups have food which they particularly like: Asians prefer rice; and Italians, spaghetti.
2. Season. People enjoy traditional holiday foods—turkey at Thanksgiving, ham at Easter. They also enjoy cool salads and sandwiches on hot summer days; and even people who seldom go outdoors enjoy hearty soups and stews when the ground is covered with snow.
3. Flavor and appearance of the food. People react first to the way food looks. Attractive color combinations and variety in the shape of foods add to eye appeal. Flavor is important too. Balance your menus with mild and strongly flavored foods, sweet and tart, juicy and dry, spicy and bland. Use familiar foods in unusual flavor combinations for taste interest.
4. Variety. Most people want some variety in their diets, but also want many of the same foods every day. Children do not question milk at every meal, and most adults want no change from their breakfast coffee. Most people want toast and are content with either an egg or a favorite cereal each morning. However, these same people expect variety at other meals. You will learn which foods to serve repeatedly, which only occasionally. There are many ways to obtain variety; in the kind of food, in the day of the week on which a particular food is served, in the method used to prepare the food, in the food combinations, in food garnishes, and in sauces served on the food.

[10] This section and the following one on nutritional needs are excerpts from Roger Murphy, Ruth Hodgson, and Judith Siegel, "Menu Planning," "Highlights of the Food Markets," New York State Cooperative Extension Service, Dec. 31, 1962, pp. 1–2.

Figure 7.3. Low-cost meals can be attractive and interesting. (USDA)

The following factors influence nutritional needs.

1. Age. The food needs of people are different at various stages of life. Preschool children need highly nutritious foods served in small meals and between-meal snacks. Teen-age boys and girls need a well-balanced diet with plenty of protein and calcium and enough calories for rapid growth. Some elderly people need food they can chew without teeth.
2. Sex. Men and women of all ages enjoy many of the same foods. However, beginning in the teen years, the food choices of men and women are different. Teen-age boys may refuse foods as "sissy" foods or "only for girls." Often this attitude remains in the adult man. [Very few men feel that a fruit salad plate is a man's kind of meal.] The weight-conscious teen-age girl is another vexing problem for the menu planner.
3. Activity. The menu should be low in calories but high in other nutrients for people who are inactive. Conversely, for people who are physically active—children and those adults doing strenuous work or participating in athletics—allow extra calories.
4. Health. Many sick people do not need any change in their menus. Others need specially planned or prepared foods to help them regain their health. If the doctor has prescribed a special diet you need to remember this when you plan.

Include Snacks and Food Eaten Away from Home

It is helpful to think of snacks as part of the day's food intake, rather than as an extra. Snacking is so much a part of our cultural pattern. School children come home and head for the refrigerator or kitchen closet. Morning and afternoon coffee breaks are eating times for many people.

Wherever possible, encourage nutritious snacks and serve foods at meals that supplement those that are eaten outside or as snacks.

Many people, including youngsters, know the rules of good eating (see Figure 7.4), such as how to use the Basic Four Plan for three meals a day. But they may find it difficult to adapt these rules to situations such as travel, business lunches, a party, or snacking.

Menus at Various Cost Levels

It is possible to be well nourished at several levels of expenditure. Table 7.2, "A Day's Menu at Different Costs," gives an example of meals planned at three levels of expenditure.

Table 7.3 shows a week's meals for a family at the low-cost level. Table 7.4 gives the quantity of food needed for these meals for a family of four or six.

Figure 7.4. (National Dairy Council)

Build Good Eating Habits

Food habits start early. They begin with nursing or bottle feeding. The very young child is quite adaptable and will learn to like whatever he is given, within reason, as the varied food patterns of people around the

TABLE 7.2
A Day's Menu at Different Costs

Low	Moderate	Liberal
BREAKFAST		
Orange juice (canned)	Orange juice (frozen)	Sliced oranges
Oatmeal with reconstituted nonfat milk	Wheat flakes with whole milk	Sugarfrosted rice cereal with fruit and half-and-half
Enriched white toast	Whole wheat toast	Rolls
Margarine	Margarine	
Jelly	Jelly	
Reconstituted nonfat milk for children	Whole milk for children	Whole milk for children
Instant coffee	Coffee	Coffee
LUNCH		
Cream of tomato soup (made with dry nonfat milk)	Dehydrated onion soup	Frozen tomato bisque
Peanut butter and raisin sandwich (enriched bread)	Bologna sandwich (enriched bread)	Boiled ham on dark rye bread
Celery and carrot sticks	Head lettuce salad, thousand island dressing	Deviled egg, pickles, olives, potato chips
Reconstituted nonfat milk	Whole milk	Whole milk
SNACK		
Lemonade	Cider	Fruit juice punch
Oatmeal cookies	Brownies	Assorted butter cookies
DINNER		
Spaghetti with meat sauce	Beef stew with potatoes, carrots, onions	Standing rib roast
Winter squash	Tomato and lettuce salad with mayonnaise	Baked potato
		Zucchini and onion casserole
		Romaine salad with blue cheese dressing
Biscuits		
Margarine		
Bread pudding	Custard	Toffee ice cream
Reconstituted nonfat milk	Whole milk	Whole milk
Instant coffee	Coffee for adults, if desired	Coffee for adults if desired

SOURCE: Adapted from Helen Denning Ullrich, "Food Planning for Families at 3 Different Cost Levels," *Food for Us All*, Yearbook of Agriculture 1969, U.S. Department of Agriculture, p. 285.

TABLE 7.3
Ideas for One Week's Low-Cost Meals

	Morning	Noon	Evening
Sunday	Oranges, quartered (in season) Pancakes Sirup Milk for children	Stewed chicken Mashed potatoes Green beans Bread Margarine Milk for children	Baked beans Apple Spice cake Cocoa
Monday	Oranges, quartered Oatmeal or grits Milk Toast or bread Margarine	Peanut butter and Apple butter sandwiches Raw carrots Spice cake Milk	Creamed chicken Rice Cabbage salad Bread Margarine Peaches Milk for children
Tuesday	Peaches Ready-to-eat cereal Milk Cinnamon toast or bread	Frankfurter-bean soup Banana or apple Graham crackers Milk	Chili con carne Potato salad Biscuits Applesauce Milk for children
Wednesday	Applesauce Oatmeal or grits Milk Biscuits Margarine Jelly Milk for children	Hard-cooked egg sandwiches Crackers Potato salad Lemonade	Frankfurters Spinach or other greens Hash-browned potatoes Bread Margarine Peanut butter cookies Milk
Thursday	Juice Ready-to-eat cereal Milk Cinnamon toast or bread	Potato and onion soup Crackers Hard-cooked egg Banana Milk	Fried liver and onions Creamed potatoes Vegetable salad Bread Margarine Peanut butter cookies Milk
Friday	Juice Oatmeal or grits Milk Toast or bread Jelly	Cheese sandwiches Raw carrot Graham crackers Milk	Oven fried fish fillet Mashed potatoes Cole slaw Cornbread Margarine Apple pie Milk for children

	Morning	Noon	Evening

Saturday	Juice
	Eggs, fried or
	    scrambled
	Potato cakes
	Toast or bread
	Jelly
		Bologna sandwiches
		Apple pie
		Milk
			Macaroni and
			    cheese
			Kale or other greens
			Carrot strips
			Bread Apple butter
			Graham crackers
			Milk for children

NOTE: Adults may want coffee or tea at two meals. If milk is served as a drink, adults and children under nine years get ¾ cup and boys and girls nine to twenty years get 1 cup. At least one half of the milk is made from nonfat dry milk.

SOURCE: "Money Saving Main Dishes," Home and Garden Bulletin No. 43, U.S. Department of Agriculture, Washington, D.C.

world attest. Through food management in the family, young people can learn to build good eating habits.

While we all tend to get set in our tastes as we get older, new foods can be introduced to many people. Dickins, in discussing the data from a study of the acceptance of new recipes, identifies three types of consumers:

1. Those who will try the new, who like to experiment.
2. Those who hesitate, who do not really trust their own judgment, who must have the "go" sign from a friend or relative, and, in case of a recipe with food not used before, must have tasted it themselves or know people who have tasted it and can vouch for it.
3. Those who won't try a new recipe at all, who like to go along in the same old way, or do not have imagination to see something good in the new.[11]

Wightman adds that a homemaker was more likely to try a new recipe if the ingredients were familiar.[12] For example, someone who was unfamiliar with cornmeal would be less likely to try a recipe using cornmeal than a person who had used cornmeal in other dishes. This hesitancy about using new foods has been noted among families who receive donated foods. Unfamiliar foods are often discarded, even when the family needs food badly. When the United States gave wheat to rice-eating nations in an effort to avert famine, many people would not eat the wheat.

[11] Dorothy Dickins, "Factors Related to Food Preferences," *Journal of Home Economics*, Vol. 57 (1965), p. 429.
[12] Mildred R. Wightman, *Kentucky Urban Homemakers' Attitudes, Preferences and Practices Concerning Dairy Products.* Progress Report 123, University of Kentucky, Agricultural Extension Station, n.d., p. 25.

TABLE 7.4
Food Used in the Week's Low-Cost Meals

	Amount for family of—	
	Four Persons	Six Persons
Milk Group		
Nonfat dry milk	1½ lbs.	3 lbs.
Whole fluid milk	3 half-gals.	6 half-gals.
Cheese, processed	1 lb.	2 lbs.
Meat Group		
Ground beef	½ lb.	¾ lb.
Frankfurters	1 lb.	1½ lbs.
Bologna	½ lb.	¾ lb.
Beef liver	1 lb.	1½ lbs.
Chicken, ready-to-cook	3 lbs.	4½ lbs.
Fish fillet	1 lb.	1½ lbs.
Eggs	2 doz.	3 doz.
Kidney beans, dry	½ lb.	¾ lb.
Navy beans, dry	½ lb.	¾ lb.
Peanut butter	½ lb.	1 lb.
Pork and Beans	28-oz. can	52-oz. can
Bread–Cereal Group		
Flour, all purpose	2 lbs.	3 lbs.
Cake mix, spice	18 oz.	18 oz.*
Cereal, ready-to-eat	12-oz. pkg.	18-oz. pkg.
Rolled oats or grits	1 lb.	1½ lbs.
	4 oz.	6 oz.
Rice	½ lb.	¾ lb.
Macaroni	4 oz.	6 oz.
Bread, white (1½ lb. loaves)	6	9
Crackers	1½ lbs.	2 lbs.
Graham crackers	1 lb.	2 lbs.
Vegetable–Fruit Group		
Fresh		
Apples	4 lbs.	6 lbs.
Bananas	2 lbs.	3 lbs.
Oranges	6	9
Cabbage	2 lbs.	3 lbs.
Carrots	1½ lbs.	2¼ lbs.
Green pepper	1	2
Kale or other greens	1 lb.	1½ lbs.
Lettuce	1 lb.	1½ lbs.

* Families of six would use the whole cake on Sunday and use graham crackers for lunch on Monday.

	Amounts for family of—	
	Four Persons	Six Persons
Onions	1 lb.	1½ lbs.
Potatoes	12 lbs.	18 lbs.
Canned:		
Juice (tomato, orange, or grapefruit)	1 can (46 oz.)	1 can (46 oz.)
Applesauce	1 can (29 oz.)	1 can† (29 oz.)
Peaches, cling	1 can (29 oz).	1 can† (29 oz.)
Green beans	1 can (16 oz.)	1 can (29 oz.)
Tomatoes	1 can (16 oz.)	1 can (29 oz.)
Spinach	1 can (16 oz.)	1 can (29 oz.)
Other Foods		
Margarine	1 lb.	1½ lbs.
Lard shortening	1⅔ lbs.	2½ lbs.
Salad dressing	⅛ pt.	¼ pt.
Sugar, granulated	1½ lbs.	2 lbs.
Sugar, brown	¼ lb.	⅓ lb.
Jelly	½ pt.	⅔ pt.
Apple butter	1 pt.	1⅓ pts.
Sirup	6 fl. oz.	8 fl. oz.
Lemonade, frozen	6-oz. can	26-oz. cans
Coffee	⅔ lb.	⅔ lb.
Tea	—	—
Baking powder, spices seasoning	—	—

SOURCE: Home and Garden Bulletin No. 43, U.S. Department of Agriculture, Washington, D.C.

† Families of six would use the whole can of peaches and applesauce for evening meals on Monday and Tuesday, and use juice for Tuesday and Wednesday breakfast.

Prestige may be a stimulant to change in food habits. In Mysore [India], ragi, once ridiculed as poor man's food is now accepted as rich man's food because His Highness, the Maharaja Krishnaraja Wuadiar, eats ragi at every meal.[13]

[13] Excerpt from Rajimmal P. Devadas, "Social and Cultural Factors Influencing Malnutrition," *Journal of Home Economics,* Vol. 62, No. 3 (1970), p. 169.

Food Costs

Food costs vary with a number of factors in addition to the current level of prices. The following are some of the most important of these factors.

Income Level

As family income increases there is a tendency to spend more for food, but this often represents a decreasing portion of the family's income.

Costs for food budgets at three levels of spending—low, moderate, and liberal—are published quarterly in *Family Economics Review*.[14] These costs are based on a hypothetical market basket for a family of four, consisting of a father of thirty-eight, a mother, and two elementary school children. Tables are given so that you can develop costs for families with a different composition. These figures are useful as guidelines in planning menus at various cost levels.

Family Size

Two cannot live as cheaply as one, a close look at the weekly food bills reveals. A survey of expenditure patterns of United States families made jointly by the U.S. Departments of Labor and Agriculture gathered data on how the nation's families spend their money.

Large families spend a great proportion of their money for food. As the size of the family grows, a greater proportion of the family's money goes for food. Of the families studied, smaller family units used a larger proportion of their money to buy things other than food. The proportion going for food ranged from 24 per cent of all money spent in the one-member family to 29 per cent in the family of six or more.

The rate of increase goes down as the family grows larger. Although the weekly food bill increases with family size, the rate at which it increases becomes smaller.

1. Large families may be able to effect savings through quantity purchases and use of large-size packages.
2. Diets differ among families. Large families may use more of the less expensive foods, such as cereals, whereas small families may have a more expensive food consumption pattern.
3. Large families waste less food than small family units. Small families generally report loss of food due to inability to buy and prepare small quantities of food.

[14] *Family Economics Review* is published by the U.S. Department of Agriculture for home economics extension specialists. However, subscriptions are available free to home economics teachers.

4. Large families may have more young children who do not consume as much food as adults or teenagers. The addition of a baby to a two-person family increases the food bill about one fourth the cost of food for an adult eating alone, according to U.S. Department of Agriculture studies. As the child reaches adolescence, this volume of food increases and surpasses that needed for the adult.
5. Small one- or two-person families of adults may have incomes sufficiently large that the need for food economy is less than in large families.
6. Small families spend more money per person on food away from home than large families.

Families differ in money spent on food groups. Large families spent a few cents less of each food dollar for meats, fruits, and vegetables and a few cents more for cereals and bakery products than did small families. Large families also allocate more of each food dollar for milk, probably because they had more children.

Small families with one or two persons, all adult families, and older families gave greater emphasis to meats, fruits and vegetables, and beverages than large families with young children. Small families spent relatively more for beverages such as tea and coffee than did large families.[15]

Comparative Shopping

If one is willing to spend time and energy to save money, comparative shopping for food usually can result in considerable savings. There are several ways to do comparative shopping. Some people study the advertisements in newspapers and circulars before leaving home. They plan their shopping around the sale items.

They may buy the specials at several different stores. Or perhaps they decide to do all their shopping at the store that has the greatest number of sale items that they want. Going from store to store is practical in a monetary sense only if the savings on food outweigh the transportation and time costs, and if necessary transportation is available.

In one sense, the homemaker may earn more per hour through comparative shopping than can the family breadwinner. If by spending 15 extra minutes the shopper can save 5 per cent of a $20 food purchase, or $1.00, this equals a rate of $4.00 per hour—more than many workingmen earn.[16]

---

[15] Excerpted from Roger Murphy and Ruth Hodgson, "Focus on the Food Markets," N.Y. State Cooperative Extension Service, May 2, 1966, pp. 1–3.

[16] Excerpt from Roger Murphy and Ruth Hodgson, "Comparative Shopping Counts," "Focus on the Food Markets," New York State Cooperative Extension Service, Feb. 8, 1965. Data from a study by Heinz Biesdorf, New York State College of Home Economics, Cornell University.

Figure 7.5. Comparative shopping can result in savings. (USDA)

Stretching Food Dollars

DO PENNIES COUNT? . . .

Do pennies count? When you're shopping for food, there's no doubt about it. Three to four cents off on a 25-cent can of beans, for example, is a 10 to 15 per cent savings. Not bad for just a few pennies. Applying this kind of shopping sense—plus the other shopping tips offered [here]—could save you as much as $5 on a $30 weekly bag of groceries. At the end of a month, that's an extra $20 in your pocket.

MAKE OUT A SHOPPING LIST . . .

- Plan your menus with an eye on the ads.
- Make a list of the foods you'll need.
- Then stick to the list, but be open minded should you spot an unadvertised bargain.
- Shop alone if you can. You'll be able to concentrate better. And besides, Dad and the kids tend to run up the food bill.

TRY NEW RECIPES, NEW MEAL IDEAS . . .

Get out the cookbooks, watch newspapers, magazines, and television for new recipe ideas, unusual casseroles, or recipes using old favorites in new ways. You can cut your food bill 20 per cent by using lower-priced items in your menus.

SHOP THE SPECIALS . . .

- Shop the ads. Shop the specials. Shop the stores.
- Check ads particularly for meat, poultry, and fish on special. Plan your

meals accordingly. These items can amount to a third of your family's food bill.

COMPARE THE BRANDS . . .

- Try the lower priced grades and brands. You may like them as well as more expensive items.
- Some stores carry as many as six different brands of canned green beans with prices sometimes varying considerably. While quality and cut may differ, nutritional values vary little.
- By looking for lowest priced brands in one store, you can save—for example —5 to 7 cents on a 6-ounce can of frozen orange juice, a nickel on a can of peas, as much as 20 cents a pound on bacon.

BE WILLING TO SWITCH WHEN THE PRICE IS RIGHT . . .

- Beef or pork liver for calves' liver.
- Poultry and fish for red meats.
- Dry milk for fresh milk.
- Bean, cheese, and egg dishes for meat dishes.
- Cabbage for lettuce.

BUY IN QUANTITY . . .

- Buy in quantity when there's a sale and if you've checked to see that it's a good buy.
- But be careful! Buy only what you need and can use. It's not a bargain if the food is wasted or spoils before you can use it.
- Buy the large can or package only if it fits your family's needs—and you have a proper place to store it.
- Figure the cost per ounce, per pound, per serving. Cornflakes—for example —range from 2 cents an ounce in the large box to 4 cents an ounce in the individual packs.

CHECK THE COST OF CONVENIENCE . . .

Chances are the partially prepared items will cost you more than the fresh. But not always. Some convenience foods, like frozen concentrated orange juice, frozen green peas, canned orange juice and fruit cocktail, and some cake mixes, are often cheaper than their fresh counterparts.
- Other convenience foods, like frozen corn on the cob, stuffed baked potatoes, cheese in a spray can, and frozen dinners, usually cost you more.
- BUT—if time is short, you may be willing to pay the cost of convenience. Just remember the choice you are making.

FRUITS AND VEGETABLES

- Be willing to switch one vegetable for another, one fruit for another—if the price is right and your family likes it.
- Play one form of fruits and vegetables against another. Is it cheaper to serve it fresh, canned, or frozen?

- Buy fresh in season—but not at first. Prices usually go down as supply increases.
- Look for lower priced fruits and vegetables. For instance, apples that are smaller and not so red. You could save 8 to 12 cents on a 5-pound bag.
- Watch for canned or frozen specials as new supplies come to market.
- Save money by selecting fruits packed in light rather than heavy syrups.
- Whole fruits and vegetables in a can are usually higher priced than slices, chunks, or halves. Small or "mixed" pieces cost even less.
- Special frozen vegetable combinations and butter-added, boil-in-the-bag vegetables add to your food bill. If you have the time, prepare them yourself.
- Big bags of frozen fruits and vegetables are money savers. You can pour out only as much as you need, save the rest.

CEREALS AND BAKED GOODS . . .

- Some stores offer specials on day-old bakery products. Watch for these.
- Buy the big package of cereal and save.
- Hot cereals cost less than ready-to-eat varieties.
- Sugared cereals cost more than unsweetened. Sugar them yourself and save [or skip the sugar].

DAIRY PRODUCTS . . .

- For cooking, try nonfat dry milk and canned evaporated milk.
- Use nonfat dry milk to make skim milk for family drinking. It costs half the price.
- Buy milk in quantity. . . .

MEAT, POULTRY, AND EGGS . . .

- Know USDA grades. They help you compare price and quality.
- When buying meat, it's the price per serving not the price per pound that counts. Figure four servings per pound of lean boneless meat, two servings per pound of bone—in meat. . . .
- Buy a big chuck roast and cut it three ways for three meals—a steak, a stew, a roast.
- When chicken is "on special," you can save as much as 25 per cent.
- Buy whole chickens and save 2 to 10 cents a pound.
- Compare the various sizes of eggs. If medium eggs are at least 7 cents a dozen cheaper than large eggs in the same grade, buy mediums. You get more for your money.[17]

Table 7.5 gives a comparison of the edible servings for various cuts of meat. Figure 7.6 shows how various meat and meat alternatives compare in cost.

[17] Adapted from "Shopping Sense: Ideas for Stretching Food Dollars," President's Committee on Consumer Interests, Washington, D.C., n.d.

TABLE 7.5
Servings Per Pound of Red Meat and Poultry

Retail Cut	Per Pound	Retail Cut	Per Pound
BEEF:		**PORK—FRESH:**	
Sirloin steak	2½	Center cut or rib	
Porterhouse, T-bone,		chops	4
Rib steak	2	Loin or rib roast	2½
Round steak	3½	Boston butt—bone-in	3
Chuck roast, bone-in	2	Blade steak	3
Rib roast—boneless	2½	Spare ribs	1⅓
Rib roast—bone-in	2		
Rump, sirloin roast	3	**PORK—CURED:**	
Ground beef	4	Picnic—bone-in	2
Short ribs	2	Ham—fully cooked:	
Heart, liver, kidney	5	bone-in	3½
Frankfurters	4	boneless and canned	5
Stew meat, boneless	5	shankless	4¼
		center slice	5
		POULTRY:	
LAMB:		Broiler, ready-to-cook	1⅓
Loin, rib, shoulder		legs, thighs	3
chops	3	breasts	4
Breast, shank	2	Turkey, ready-to-cook:	
Shoulder roast	2½	under 12 lbs.	1
Leg of lamb	3	12 lbs. and over	1⅓

SOURCE: Ellen H. Semrow, "Money Stretching Ideas for Making Your Food Dollar Go F-u-r-t-h-e-r," *Food for Us All*, Yearbook of Agriculture 1969, p. 293, U.S. Department of Agriculture.

Federal Food Stamps

The federal government has tried various methods of increasing and improving the food consumption of low-income families. Donated foods (commodities that are generally in surplus supply) were available for some years to families receiving public assistance and nonprofit organizations that serve food.

More recently, federal food stamps have been introduced in counties where the county government elects to participate. In these counties eligible families can purchase food stamps from designated agencies. For each dollar the purchaser gets more than a dollar's worth of food stamps. Thus it increases purchasing power and gives the family the option to choose its own food. Most large chain stores, many small stores, as well as some specialty food stores, honor food stamps in areas where they are available.

There is a formula to determine who is eligible to buy these stamps,

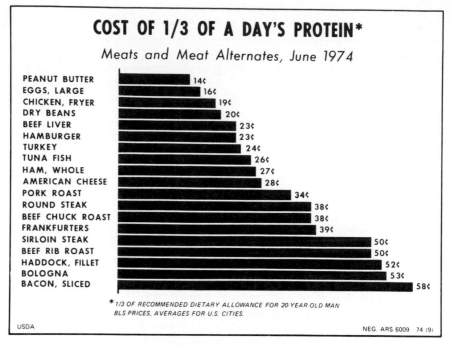

Figure 7.6. (USDA)

but one need not be receiving public assistance to qualify. Depending on the family income, a graduate student and spouse or an older person on a pension might be eligible.

In counties that are participating in the food stamp plan, nonprofit institutions are still eligible for donated foods although individual families are not.

Becoming a Wise Buyer

Shopping in the well-stocked stores of today is a complicated business, particularly if one wants to get good value for his money.

Where Do You Shop?

Consumers don't always shop where food prices are lowest for comparable quality products. According to a study of food prices in four major Ohio cities, the food stores with the most services did the largest volume of business.[18]

---

[18] Lois Simonds, "Variations in Food Costs in Major Ohio Cities," *The Journal of Consumer Affairs*, Vol. 3 (Summer 1969), pp. 52–58.

Table 7.6 lists some of the reasons consumers use in deciding where to shop.

TABLE 7.6
Items Important or Essential to Shoppers
in Their Choice of Food Stores

Store Attribute	Per Cent of Shoppers Interviewed	
	Absolutely Essential	Essential or Important
Is easy to shop	45	75
Has wide selection of items	43	71
Has best quality of meats in area	54	67
Is easy to get to	39	63
Has top vegetable and fruit department	43	62
Has favorite brand	33	62
Is nearby	34	53
Gives best value on canned products	32	52
Has low prices in area	31	52

SOURCE: D. B. DeLoach, "A 'Showcase' for Food, at Your Local Supermarket," *Food for Us All*, Yearbook of Agriculture 1969, U.S. Department of Agriculture, p. 46.

Generally, the largest supermarket chain stores have lower prices than small private food stores. In some areas "discount" stores may charge lower prices for food than supermarket chain stores.

However, some people choose to shop in small stores for a variety of reasons. They may like the personalized nature of the small store. In parts of New York City the small *bodega* serves as a social center for Puerto Rican families. Also, the small specialized store may carry specialty foods that are hard to get elsewhere, such as real Italian olive oil, or special seasonings. Most important, many small food stores provide credit. Some families count on being able to buy food on credit when funds are low.

Food Store Promotions

With the great similarity of merchandise and prices in large markets, some stores have tried to compete and build shopper loyalty by offering various extras, such as discount coupons, games, free or low-priced dishes, and trading stamps.

Most stamp plans operate on a basis where the shopper gets $2\frac{1}{2}$ cents in stamp purchasing power for every dollar spent. The stores who give out these stamps purchase them and must absorb the cost for them either in higher prices, or through a much greater volume of sales.

It is very difficult to measure realistically how far food stamps raise

Figure 7.7. The trend of the future may be for computerized checkout counters in supermarkets. There is considerable controversy about this because stores would not need to stamp the price on each item for the checkers to read. However, it would also be harder for shoppers to see what price is being charged for each item.

prices. "Sperry and Hutchinson, the leading stamp company, . . . concedes that for stamps to pay their way, they must produce at least a 12 per cent increase in sales."[19] (There are a number of studies on stamps and prices. Some of these are listed in the Selected References at the and of this chapter.) Generally, the first store in an area to introduce trading stamps can increase its volume significantly. But those that follow often fail to make any real gain in sales volume. When this is the case, the cost of the trading stamps must be reflected in higher prices.

Many people have hypothesized why trading stamps are popular with consumers. One of the most reasonable explanations is that when so few differences exist between markets trading stamps represent a visible extra. Furthermore, the saving of trading stamps gives some people a feeling of thrift, much like the popular Christmas Club plan for savings. (The latter is popular even though it pays little or no interest.) Some states have adopted laws banning trading stamps, others stipulate that only cash redemptions are allowed, and some require that money be offered as an alternative to merchandise at stamp redemption centers.

[19] Frederick E. Waddell, "The Case Against Trading Stamps," *The Journal of Consumer Affairs*, Vol. 2 (Summer 1968), p. 21.

Figure 7.8. Under the grade labeling program those plants that qualify are permitted to use the USDA grade mark on their consumer packages of cheddar cheese. Such factors as flavor, texture, finish, appearance, and color are considered.

Food Grades

Grade labeling is a great help in intelligent selection of food. However, except for meat and eggs, most foods are not graded at the retail level although they are frequently graded at the wholesale level as an aid to purchasing agents.

Of the few food processors who do grade food for retail customers, many use their own system of grading. Others, however, use U.S. Department of Agriculture grades.

> The use of U.S. Department of Agriculture grades for food products sold in retail stores is strictly voluntary. However, if USDA grades are used, the product must meet their standards. The food processor, handler, or producer who wishes to use U.S. grades must request the service from the Agricultural Marketing Service of the United States Department of Agriculture and pay for it.
>
> The grades apply to the quality at the time the food is graded. All USDA grades are preceded by the letters, "U.S." and enclosed in a shield-shaped mark. Foods labeled by a processor according to his own standards may not be labeled with "U.S." preceding the grade.[20]

Except for meat, consumer grades are generally designated by the letters A, B, or C. The federal grades for beef are as follows:

USDA Prime. Beef with this label comes from young, well-fed beef-type cattle. The generous amounts of fat that run in streaks through the lean make this meat tender, juicy, and flavorsome. About 30 per cent of all beef from

[20] Irene Oppenheim, *The Family As Consumers* (New York: Macmillan, 1965), p. 80.

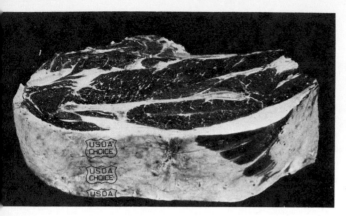

Figure 7.9. Grade labeling on a chuck roast. (USDA)

steers and heifers makes this grade. Steaks and roasts are tender and adapted to cooking with dry heat. (Most prime beef goes to restaurants.)

USDA Choice. This grade of beef has less fat than Prime beef, and is more economical. More beef of this grade is produced than of any other grade —usually around 50 per cent of all beef comes from steers.

USDA Good. As the name implies, this grade of beef pleases many families. "Good" beef is less juicy than "Choice" or "Prime" but it may be preferred by beef-eaters who like their meat lean.

USDA Commercial. Older animals and some young ones fall into this grade. Cuts of meat of this grade have a very thin covering of fat and practically no fat through the lean. Slow cooking with moisture helps make the meat tender.

USDA Utility. Beef from animals that are well along in years is usually this grade. There is very little fat on any cuts of Utility beef. Meat of this and lower grades seldom goes to retail stores; usually they are made up into processed meat products.[21]

There are also five grades for lamb and veal. For lamb and veal the lowest two grades are USDA Utility and USDA Cull instead of Commercial and Utility. Poultry is graded as A, B, or C. Some of the other commonly used grades are shown in Table 7.7.

Meat Inspection

All meat and poultry that are shipped in interstate commerce must be inspected for wholesomeness. Because most beef, veal, and lamb are shipped across state lines, the bulk of these meats is federally inspected. Since 1970, federal law requires each state to inspect meat and poultry according to federal standards. If the states do not do this satisfactorily, the federal government can step in and inspect the meat at a charge to the state.

Meat inspection stamps are placed directly on the carcass of the animal,

[21] Extension Service, State Colleges of Agriculture and Home Economics, New York, New Jersey, and Connecticut, *Food Marketing Handbook* (Ithaca, N.Y.: Cornell University, n.d.), pp. 2–4, 5.

TABLE 7.7
Some Commonly Used Grades

Butter	U.S. Grade AA (U.S. 93 Score)	U.S. Grade A (U.S. 92 Score)	U.S. Grade B (U.S. 90 Score)	
Cheddar cheese	U.S. Grade AA	U.S. Grade A	U.S. Grade B	
Swiss cheese	U.S. Grade A	U.S. Grade B	U.S. Grade C	U.S. Grade D
Nonfat dry milk	U.S. Extra Grade	U.S. Standard Grade		
Cottage cheese	No Grades—May be marked USDA "Quality Approved"			
Eggs	U.S. Grade AA	U.S. Grade A	U.S. Grade B	U.S. Grade C

SOURCE: "U.S. Grades at a Glance," U.S. Department of Agriculture, n.d.

except for poultry. With poultry the stamp is generally placed on the box in which poultry is shipped and is not visible to the store customer. If the meat is packaged or canned an inspection stamp must appear on the label.

Food Labels

Food products sold in interstate commerce must be labeled in a way that is not misleading according to federal law. If there is more than one ingredient in a product, the ingredients must be listed in order of amount, except where there is a standard of identity. A standard of identity is a recipe filed with the Food and Drug Administration. For instance, there are standards of identity for catsup, mayonnaise, and a number of other foods.

Food Dating

Open dating of food products, especially perishable and semiperishable items, is currently receiving a great deal of attention. Although food manufacturers have dated products for many years, the date (and certain other manufacturing information) has usually appeared in some form of code. Today, there is a growing demand that the date appear uncoded. Advocates of uncoded, or open, dating argue that such information will help reduce the sale of spoiled or stale food. They say it will help consumers to find fresher food as well as help foodstores rotate the products on their shelves.[22]

[22] *Food Dating: Shoppers' Reactions and the Impact on Retail Foodstores* (Washington, D.C.: U.S. Department of Agriculture, 1973), p. 2.

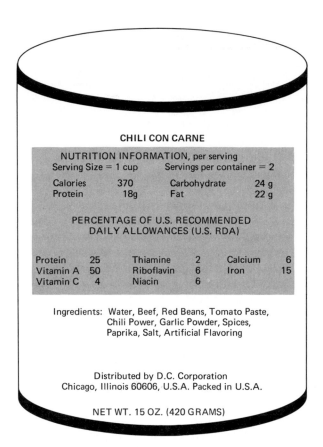

CHILI CON CARNE

NUTRITION INFORMATION, per serving
Serving Size = 1 cup   Servings per container = 2

Calories	370	Carbohydrate	24 g
Protein	18g	Fat	22 g

PERCENTAGE OF U.S. RECOMMENDED
DAILY ALLOWANCES (U.S. RDA)

Protein	25	Thiamine	2	Calcium	6
Vitamin A	50	Riboflavin	6	Iron	15
Vitamin C	4	Niacin	6		

Ingredients: Water, Beef, Red Beans, Tomato Paste,
Chili Power, Garlic Powder, Spices,
Paprika, Salt, Artificial Flavoring

Distributed by D.C. Corporation
Chicago, Illinois 60606, U.S.A. Packed in U.S.A.

NET WT. 15 OZ. (420 GRAMS)

Figure 7.10. A nutrition label. Information about the cholesterol and sodium content of the food may also be included to help people on restricted diets. (U.S. Department of Health, Education, and Welfare)

Food Additives

Food additives date back to the time when man first tried to store food for periods of scarcity. Salt was used to preserve food in biblical times, and so, too, were spices. But the varied uses of modern food additives are new. Additives are substances other than those that occur naturally in food. They are usually chemicals used in crop production or added during food processing to preserve quality in getting food to market.

Perhaps it is easier to understand why additives are used if we examine the purposes of some common food additives.

Nutrient Supplements. These are vitamins and minerals added to food to improve its nutritive value. For example, Vitamin A is added to margarine and Vitamin D to milk. Thiamin, riboflavin, niacin (another B vitamin), and iron are added to "enriched" bread. Iodine added to salt makes it "iodized."

Figure 7.11. Food dating. (USDA)

Nonnutritive Sweeteners. These are sugar substitutes for people who must restrict their intake of ordinary sugar because of diabetes or prefer to do so as a reducing aid. Saccharin is the most frequently used substitute.

Preservatives. Preservatives are used to prevent spoilage and other undesirable chemical changes. The preservatives in fat are called antioxidants; those in bread are called mold or rope inhibitors or antimycotic agents. Additives to dairy products help to prevent changes that spoil the color, flavor, texture, or appearance of dairy foods. Some of the other common preservatives are benzoic acid, sugar, salt, and vinegar.

Emulsifiers. These help to improve the uniformity of volume, the fineness of grain, smoothness, homogeneity, and keeping quality of foods. Many baked products, ice creams, cake mixes, and frozen desserts contain emulsifiers.

Stabilizers and Thickeners. These help to add smoothness and evenness as well as to thicken such foods as ice cream, candy, frozen desserts, chocolate milk, sweet beverages, and some fruit juices.

Acid, Alkalis, Buffers, and Neutralizing Agents. These are important in many processed foods. Soft drinks are often flavored by the addition of an organic acid. The acidity of cream to be used for butter is controlled with organic acids.

Other Types of Additives. Flavoring agents are added to bakery goods and ice cream. Bread is improved in color by the addition of oxidizing agents that whiten the flour and prevent caking, hardening, and drying.

Regulations covering food additives were part of the original federal Food, Drug, and Cosmetic Act of 1906 and of the later one of 1938. Both Acts prohibited the sale of any food containing harmful ingredients. Under these laws the Food and Drug Administration had to prove an additive harmful before it could be removed from the market. Since 1960 . . . the burden of proving food additives harmful has shifted from the FDA to the food processors and chemical manufacturers. Now food processors and chemical manufacturers must run extensive tests on new additives and have them approved by the Food and Drug Administration before the additive may be used.

Another problem arose when pesticidal residues remained on fresh fruits and vegetables. Procedures for the setting of safe limits or tolerances for pesticidal residues remaining on fruits and vegetables have been established, and are reviewed regularly. Processed food can contain amounts that never exceed the tolerance allowed on raw products. Some foods, such as milk, are not permitted to have any pesticidal residue.

A new concern has been added by our atomic age. Radioactive fallout can contaminate our food supply. Extensive study is now going on to watch its effects and control it.[23]

Using Food Wisely

The aim of good food management is to provide the family with wholesome and attractive food at reasonable costs in time, money, and energy. Therefore, it is necessary

1. To store food so that it will keep in good condition until it is to be used.
2. To cook it in ways that will conserve the nutritive value and enhance its appeal.
3. To avoid unnecessary waste of both food and nutrients.

We use food in a variety of forms—fresh, frozen, dried, canned, and frozen. Food in these different forms requires care in the home to keep it in good condition.

Dried Foods

Dried foods generally require very little care in the home. Some, such as dried milk, must be protected from excess moisture once the package is opened, so that it will not become lumpy. Some cereals tend to attract insects, and should be stored in tightly covered containers. However, most dried foods, particularly before they are opened, keep well for long periods of time in the average home in the packages in which they are bought.

Canned Foods

Canned foods are really our oldest type of convenience food. They have the great advantage of being able to store well for long periods

---

[23] Oppenheim, op. cit., pp. 97–99.

of time at room temperature. The following are some questions that are frequently asked about canned foods.

1. *Is anything added to make canned foods keep?* No. Heat is the only thing used to make canned foods keep.
2. *Why are gold-colored enamel-lined cans used for some foods?* Enamel-lined cans are highly desirable for some kinds of foods to retain an attractive appearance; for example, to preserve the color of red fruits or to prevent sulphur staining of the can interior.
3. *What are dietetic canned foods?* A number of different canned foods are being canned without the addition of salt or sugar. This provides foods that are palatable, economical, and easily prepared for persons who are on low-sodium diets, or are restricted to a low sugar or low calorie allowance by their physicians.
4. *Is it safe to leave unused portions of canned foods in the can after it is opened?* It is perfectly safe to leave opened food in the can. The U.S. Department of Agriculture states in Home and Garden Bulletin No. 105 (1965): "Food may be left in tin cans after opening. Put a cover on the can and store in refrigerator." The important thing to remember in storing any unused portion of canned food is to put it in the refrigerator, just as any other cooked food is kept.
5. *Where should a supply of canned foods be stored?* Canned foods preferably should be stored in a cool, dry place. In a humid climate where even a cool basement may be damp it helps to avoid the danger of sweating and rusting if the cans are stored in tight cupboards or closets. (Rust, however, does not damage canned foods unless it is severe enough to perforate the can.) High storage temperatures should be avoided since they tend to impair the color and flavor of many products, though not their wholesomeness.
6. *How long will canned foods keep?* Indefinitely, if nothing happens to the container to cause a leak. They are thoroughly heat processed. Extremely long periods of storage at high temperatures may result in some loss in color, flavor, and nutritive value. We recommend that canned foods be stored in a fairly cool area . . . away from steam pipes or radiators. (See 5.) Place on shelves, or put cases on racks rather than directly on the floor.
7. *What effect has freezing on canned foods?* Except for a slight breakdown of texture of a few products, a single thawing and freezing does not usually affect canned foods adversely.

   Some foods of creamy consistency may curdle or separate upon freezing. Heating the product in preparing it usually restores the original consistency. Repeated freezing and thawing will injure the texture of some of the delicate fruits and vegetables.
8. *Do canneries use the so-called surplus crops for canning?* No. Fruits and vegetables used by the majority of canners are grown by farmers under contract. This permits the canner to supply special seed to insure getting the variety most suitable. It also permits the supervision of growing and harvesting by the canner's trained fieldmen.

TABLE 7.8
Common Can and Jar Size*

Industry Term	Container		Approx. Cups	Principal Products
	Consumer Description			
	Approx. Net Weight or Fluid Measure (Check Label)			
8 oz.	8 oz.		1	Fruits, vegetables, specialties‡ for small families. 2 servings.
Picnic	10½ to 12 oz.		1¼	Mainly condensed soups. Some fruits, vegetables, meat, fish, specialties.‡ 2 to 3 servings.
12 oz. (vac.)	12 oz.		1½	Principally for vacuum pack corn. 3 to 4 servings.
No. 300	14 to 16 oz. (14 oz. to 1 lb.)		1¾	Pork and beans, baked beans, meat products, cranberry sauce, blueberries, specialties. ‡ 3 to 4 servings.
No. 303	16 to 17 oz. (1 lb. to 1 lb. 1 oz.)		2	Principal size for fruits and vegetables. Some meat products, ready-to-serve soups, specialties. ‡ 4 servings.
No. 2	20 oz. (1 lb. 4 oz.)	18 fl. oz. (1 pt. 2 fl. oz.)	2½	Juices§, ready-to-serve soups, some specialties‡, pineapple, apple slices. No longer in popular use for most fruits and vegetables. 5 servings.
No. 2½	27 to 29 oz. (1 lb. 11 oz. to 1 lb. 13 oz.)		3½	Fruits, some vegetables (pumpkin, sauerkraut, spinach and other greens, tomatoes). 5 to 7 servings.
No. 3 cyl. or 46 fl. oz.	51 oz. (3 lb. 3 oz.)	46 fl. oz. (1 qt. 14 fl. oz)	5¾	Fruit, vegetable juices§, pork and beans. Institutional size for condensed soups, some vegetables. 10 to 12 servings.
No. 10	6½ lb. to 7lb. 5 oz.		12-13	Institutional size for fruits, vegetables and some other foods. 25 servings.

Meats, fish, and seafood are almost entirely advertised and sold under weight terminology.

Infant and Junior foods come in small cans and jars suitable for the smaller servings used. Content is given on label.

SOURCE: "Focus on Canned Foods," 5th ed., National Canners Association, p. 8.
* The labels of cans or jars of identical size may show a net weight for one product that differs slightly from the net weight on the label of another product, due to the difference in the density of the food. An example would be pork and beans (1 lb.), blueberries (14 oz.), in the same size can.

‡ Specialties—Food combinations by special manufacturer's recipe.
§ Juices are now being packed in a number of other can sizes including the one quart size.

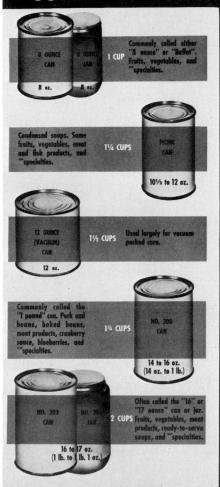
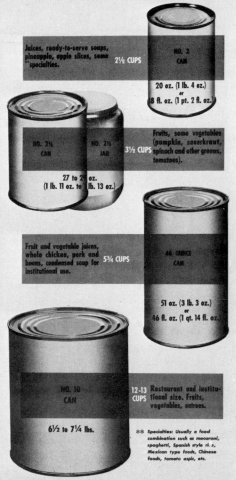

Figure 7.12. (National Canners Association)

9. *Is very much canned food eaten in the United Stated today?* The following examples illustrate the proportion of the total food supply of each that is consumed in canned form.

	Per Cent Canned (Approx.)
Asparagus	50
Beets	90
Corn, sweet	65
Peas, green	65
Tomatoes and tomato products	80
Apples	20
Apricots	65
Cherries, red tart; cranberries; grapefruit, juice and sections; peaches; pears	50 of each
Pineapples	Most of it

10. *Who discovered how to can food?* It began in the kitchen of an obscure Parisian confectioner, Nicholas Appert. Through his experiments he won in 1809 the coveted prize offered by Napoleon to the person who could find a new way to preserve foods to feed his large army the year around. Appert's "rule of thumb" canning method worked, but he didn't know why. Half a century later Louis Pasteur discovered the cause of food spoilage, and thus was launched the scientific application of heat to preserve foods.

Commercial canning of foods began in America in 1819 and developed rapidly with the historic events taking place in a new country. Canned foods were depended upon by pioneers in their westward trips seeking gold and new homes. . . . They have formed a basic part of the diet of armed forces in each major war. And here at home canned foods supply nutritious meals for infants and adults and assist in furnishing special diets for the sick and ailing.[24]

Frozen Foods

Many people believe that a home freezer, or large freezing compartment, is a great convenience (which it can be) and that it saves the family a lot of money (which it may not do). In general, the people who really save money by having a freezer are those families who grow much of the food they freeze. The cost of operating a freezer is not insignificant, and unless the food is obtained at very little cost it is hard to effect any major savings in money.

U.S. Department of Agriculture studies show the following yearly

[24] This section is from "Know Your Canned Foods," 3rd ed., National Canners Association, n.d.

expenses for a freezer: net depreciation (15 years expected life), interest foregone, repairs (2% of purchase price), electricity for maintaining 0°F., packaging (packaging and electricity costs vary with the amount of food that is frozen). Families who want to insure their frozen food should add ½ to 1 cent per pound to the above storage costs.

From a money-saving point of view it makes sense to freeze foods that

TABLE 7.9
How Long Can Frozen Foods Be Kept?

	Months
Fruits and fruit juice concentrates	12
Vegetables	8–10
White bread and plain rolls	3
Cakes	
Angel and chiffon	2
Chocolate layer	4
Fruit	12
Pound and yellow	6
Danish pastry and doughnuts	3
Fruit pies	8
Meat	
Chopped beef and thin steaks	3
Beef roasts and steaks	12
Lamb patties	4
Lamb roasts	12
Pork cured and sausages	2
Pork fresh roast	8
Veal cutlets and chops	6
Veal roasts	8
Cooked meat, meat dinners, pies, pot roast	3
Poultry	
Chicken whole and chicken and turkey pies	12
Chicken cut up, goose whole, turkey cut up and whole, cooked chicken and turkey	6
Fish	
Cod, flounder, haddock, halibut, pollack fillets	4
Mullet, ocean perch, sea trout, striped bass fillets	3
Pacific Ocean perch and salmon steaks	2
Sea trout, striped bass (whole and cleaned)	3
Cooked fish, shellfish	3
Ice cream and sherbet	1

SOURCE: "Home Care of Purchased Frozen Foods," Home and Garden Bulletin No. 69, U.S. Department of Agriculture.

provide the most savings. Because the average family spends about one fourth of its food dollar for meat, a larger share that for any other food group, many families devote a large portion of the freezer space to meat. Some people buy weekly specials in quantity. Others purchase half or a quarter of an animal from a meat market or freezer meat firm.

Approximately one third of all freezers are purchased through freezer food plans. Many of these plans are reliable and furnish good products at reasonable cost. But a great many charge enormous prices for freezers and are misleading about the quantity and quality of food that the purchaser of the plan will receive.

Good management practices enable the family to use frozen foods at their best. To maintain frozen foods at peak condition the homemaker must see that they are wrapped in a way to keep out air and maintained at 0°F. or colder. (See Table 7.9, "How Long Can Frozen Foods Be Kept?")

Meat that has been frozen can be cooked from a frozen state, partially thawed before cooking, or thawed completely before cooking. (See Table 7.10.)

TABLE 7.10
Approximate Time for Cooking Frozen Meats

Kind	How Cooked	How much	Thawed Before Cooking (min. per lb.)	Cooked from Frozen State (min. per lb.)
Standing rib	Roast at 300°F.	Rare	18	43
roast of beef		Medium	22	47
		Well done	30	55
Rolled rib	Roast at 300°F.	Rare	28	53
roast of beef		Medium	32	56
		Well done	40	65
Pork loin roast				
center cut	Roast at 350°F.	Well done	30 to 35	50 to 55
shoulder or loin	Roast at 350°F.	Well done	50 to 55	70 to 75
Leg of lamb	Roast at 350°F.	Well done	30 to 35	40 to 45
Beef rump	Braise	Well done	30 to 35	50
Porterhouse				
steak			*Total*	*Total*
1 inch chick	Broil	Rare to medium	8 to 10	21 to 35
1½ inches thick	Broil	Rare to medium	10 to 15	23 to 38
2 inches thick	Broil	Rare to medium	20 to 30	33 to 43
Beef patties	Broil or			
1 inch thick	Panbroil	Medium	10 to 12	16 to 18

SOURCE: *Meat and Meat Cookery* prepared by a Committee of the National Livestock and Meat Board, n.d.

The Metric System

The United States is moving toward converting our present system of weights and measures to the metric system. Great impetus for this change has come from manufacturers who sell products both in this country and abroad, where the metric system is already being used.

You may already know many metric measurements. Our currency is based on the metric system, units of ten. Many athletic events, swimming

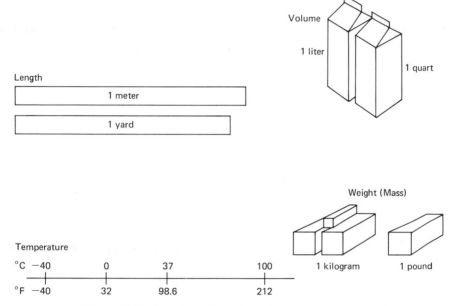

Figure 7.13. Metric units and customary measurements.

Figure 7.14. Many food products will probably be sold in metric units. (National Bureau of Standards, U.S. Department of Commerce)

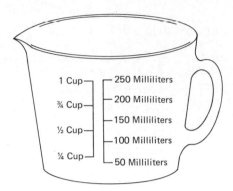

Figure 7.15. Initially, measuring utensils with two sets of measurements will probably be used. (National Bureau of Standards, U.S. Department of Commerce)

meets and races, are measured in meters. Film for cameras, camera lenses, and ski lengths are now sized in metric units. Medical prescriptions are written in metric units, grams, and milligrams.

Food labeling is one of the first areas where conversion will take place. Many canned foods and boxed cereals presently state the weight of the contents in both pounds and grams. Eventually, we probably will have foods sold in metric units, rather than pounds and ounces. Initially, the change-over may be eased by the use of recipes and measuring utensils that give both our present system of measurements and metric units. However, there is a big push for everyone to learn to think in metric units.

Summary

Today's eating patterns reflect the advances of modern technology. There has been a tremendous shift to the use of convenience foods. Americans are eating fewer calories, less starchy foods, and more meat and poultry.

Gone are the hearty breakfast and large midday meal, except on Sundays. Dinner is the main meal of the day and frequently the one time of the day during the week when the family may gather together.

When planning food for other people it is important to consider their preferences as well as their nutritional needs, if they are to eat and enjoy their food. Good food management enables people to have wholesome and attractive food with a reasonable expenditure of time, money, and energy.

Shopping in the well-stocked stores of today is a complicated business, particularly if one wants to get good value for his money. Good food management requires planning and organization to maximize family resources in shopping as well as in care and use of food. As the changeover to the metric system takes place everyone will need to learn to work with metric measurements instead of our present ones.

CHAPTER FOLLOW-UP

1. Compare the taste, appearance, and cost per serving of each of the following items.[25]

   - Orange juice: frozen vs. concentrate vs. canned vs. fresh squeezed from juice oranges (per serving).
   - Fresh milk, evaporated, non-fat dried solids.
   - Waffles: homemade, made from a mix, frozen.
   - Baking powder biscuits: homemade, made from a mix, ready-to-bake, bakery-made.
   - Broccoli: fresh vs. frozen (per serving).
   - Spinach: fresh vs. frozen (per serving).
   - Green beans: fresh, canned, frozen (per serving).
   - Apples (for pie): canned vs. fresh.
   - Applesauce: homemade vs. canned.
   - Pie, any kind: homemade, homemade with a pie-crust mix, frozen ready-to-eat, bakery.
   - Cheddar cheese: unwrapped bulk, wrapped and unsliced, wrapped and sliced.
   - Lemon juice: fresh, bottled.
   - Whipping cream: heavy cream, various ready-whipped products in pressurized cans, topping made from evaporated milk, topping made from non-fat dry-milk solids.
   - Tea: bulk, bags, instant.
   - Shrimp: shelled and deveined frozen, breaded and frozen, unshelled frozen, fresh.
   - Sweet potatoes: fresh, canned, frozen candied.
   - Potatoes: bulk, washed and bagged, frozen mashed, instant.
   - Bologna and liverwurst: whole vs. sliced.
   - Ham: uncooked with bone and skin vs. cooked canned, boneless and skinless.
   - Coffee: ground vs. instant (use the same brand).
   - Grapefruit: fresh vs. canned.
   - Butter: bricks vs. quarter pound sticks. Sweet vs. whipped.
   - Eggs: Which size is the best buy now?
   - Tuna: Study the various types. Compare prices, recommend best buys for various uses.
   - TV dinner.

2. Plan a week's meals for two people in their early twenties. Decide whether you want to plan for a man and woman, two girls, or two men.

[25] List from: Doris Ruslink, "Projects in Food Purchasing," *Forecast for Home Econo mists* (November 1961), pp. 28–29. Copyright by the McCall Corporation.

3. Plan a week's meals for a family of four (father of twenty-eight, mother, and two preschool children) at three levels of expenditure.
4. Revise the plans made in questions 4 and 5 in order to use a minimum of time and energy. Assume that the home manager has heavy responsibilities.
5. Using the shopping guide[26] that follows compare the cost of the same items in several stores. This guide is designed to help a homemaker who rates cost as the single most important determining factor in where, when, and how she buys. The best store in terms of cost may not be the best in terms of closeness to one's home or extra services. Each homemaker has to decide which factors are important in his or her situation.

Thirty-seven items have been selected that are commonly found on most families' shopping list. Where brands are necessary, we have left that space open so that you may fill in your favorite brand. Always remember to price the same brand in each store. Where brands do not make a difference, we have indicated certain standards that will make your comparisons more accurate. Size and weight have been indicated for each item. Always remember to price the same size for each item in each store. If the correct size or brand is unavailable in any store, omit it from your list.

Supermarkets should be compared with supermarkets and grocery stores should be compared with grocery stores. Do not attempt to compare the prices in a grocery store with those in a supermarket. Grocery store prices are usually higher than a supermarket's and they usually offer additional services such as charge accounts, check cashing and deliveries. These additional services cost more money but their added convenience is more important to many people than increased food costs.

Most meats and fresh produce have been omitted from this list because their prices fluctuate daily in the wholesale market. Moreover, there are seven grades of meat and one must be an expert in these varying grades before price comparisons can be attempted. The same variety in grades and standards applies to fresh fruits and vegetables.

Sue and Frank Foster[27]

Sue and Frank Foster sent invitations for a buffet supper to six close friends soon after returning from their wedding trip. Just one week before the buffet, Frank's aunt and uncle called to say they would be in town on Friday. Frank felt he should invite them home for dinner, and Sue agreed. Thus she is faced with giving a dinner for four on Friday night, and a buffet supper for eight the following night.

[26] Developed by the Office of Consumer Protection, Department of Law and Public Safety, State of New Jersey.
[27] Extract from *Echo*, a publication of the Department of Home Economics of the National Education Association, 1967. The material was developed in a project of the Washington Gas Light Company with home economics teachers in the Washington, D.C., area.

Shopping Guide

Name and Address of Establishment	Type of Establishment
_____	individual ____ chain ____
_____	supermarket ____ grocery ____

Item	Brand	Weight or Size	Price
Peeled tomatoes		1 lb. can	
Potatoes	any U.S. #1 select	10 lb. bag	
Yellow onions	any U.S. #1 small	3 lb. bag	
Chickens	whole broilers	per pound	
White pea beans	any U.S. #1	1 lb. bag	
Milk	any homo., Vit. D.	½ gallon container	
Corn flakes		12 oz. package	
Peas		1 lb. can	
Solid white tuna		7 oz. can	
Strained baby food		4½ oz. jar	
Gelatin		3 oz. package	
All-purpose flour		2 lb. bag	
Laundry bleach		½ gallon	
Laundry detergent		1 lb., 4 oz. box	
Hand soap		Personal size	
Frozen orange juice		6 oz. can	
Frozen french fries		12 oz. package	
Toilet tissue		1 roll, 2 ply tissue	
Sugar		5 lb. bag	
Salt		1 lb., 10 oz. box	
Thin spaghetti		1 lb. box	
Pork and beans		1 lb. can	
White rice		1 lb. box	
Regular grind coffee		1 lb. can	
Evaporated milk		13 oz. can	
Enriched white bread	lowest price available	1 lb. loaf	
Skinless franks	any all beef	1 lb. package	
White fresh eggs	any large, grade A	1 dozen	
Cream cheese		3 oz. package	
Margarine, stick		1 lb. package	

(Continued overleaf)

Shopping Guide (Cont.)

Item	Brand	Weight or Size	Price
Frozen lima beans		12 oz. package	
Bacon		1 lb. package	
Whole cured ham	#1 grade	per pound	
Toothpaste		family size	
Shaving cream		11 oz. aerosol	
Shampoo		7 oz. bottle	
Peanut butter		12 oz. jar.	

Sue has a full-time job, which limits the amount of time available for food preparation. And though there are two regular paychecks, Sue and Frank have set up a strict budget to cover the initial cost of setting up housekeeping. They had decided that [forty] dollars was the maximum they would spend for the buffet supper, and Sue must now revise that menu so that the same amount of money will cover expenses for both occasions.

Prepare menus and serving plans Sue could use and work schedules for both meals. You must account for purchases of food and decorations for both occasions, and must not exceed . . . [forty dollars]. You may plan for Sue to begin her shopping and advance preparations as early as the Saturday before the dinner, remembering that she works each weekday from nine until five. There is a combination refrigerator-freezer in the apartment, and a good collection of cooking and serving equipment. The dining area in the apartment is large enough for Sue's table (which seats six people) and a serving cart. This is where she will serve at least the main course of her dinner, but she will use it only to arrange the food for her buffet supper, and have guests take their food to individual folding trays in the living room, or, if the weather is nice, on the patio. Since there is no duplication of guests, the two menus do not have to be completely different. The most important factors are adherence to time and money limitations, and appropriateness of menus for serving style.

CRITERIA FOR EVALUATION

Menu should
   be nutritionally well balanced,
   have a pleasing appearance,
   provide good and varied textures,
   allow for advance preparation of some foods,
   be appropriate for the occasion.
Plan of work should
   include major steps in preparation,
   determine time needed for each operation,
   include a planned sequence of preparation: shopping, storing, planning
      and setting table, serving, and cleaning up.

Cost must
   be within specified amount,
   be itemized for food and decorations (if purchased).
Preparation of food involves
   choice of recipe,
   taste,
   orderliness in preparation,
   appearance.
Serving entails
   correctly and attractively set table,
   correctly and attractively served food,
   ease of management.

7. Measure several baking pans in metric units. Label them in metric units.
8. Prepare a recipe that is given in metric units. Use measuring utensils in metric sizes for this.

SELECTED REFERENCES.

Alexander, Milton. "An Analysis of a Rhode Island University Study of Trading Stamps and Prices." The Sperry and Hutchinson Co., 1965.

Baldwin, Ruth E., Dorothy Borchelt, and Marion Cloninger. "Palatability of Ground Beef Home Frozen and Stored in Selected Wraps." *Home Economics Research Journal* (December 1972), Vol. 1., pp. 119–125.

Batcher, Olive M., and Louise A. Young. "Metrication and the Home Economist." *Journal of Home Economics,* Vol. 66 (1974), pp. 28–31.

Biesdorf, Heinz B., and Mary Ellen Burris. *Be a Better Shopper: Buying in Supermarkets.* Miscellaneous Bulletin 86, Cornell University, 1970.

Bivens, Gordon E. "An Exploration of Food Price Competition in a Local Market." *Journal of Consumer Affairs,* Vol. 2 (Summer 1968), pp. 62–73.

Boyd, Jacque. "Food Labeling and the Marketing of Nutrition." *Journal of Home Economics,* Vol. 65 (1973), pp. 20–24. '

"Buying Beef: Bulk Buying vs. the Supermarket." *Consumer Reports* (September 1974), pp. 659–663.

"Buying Beef: How Much Is Enough?" *Consumer Reports* (September 1974), pp. 666–668.

"Buying Beef: What a Good Label Can Tell You." *Consumer Reports* (September 1974), pp. 664–665.

Cromwell, Cynthia, and Dianne Odland. "Convenience and the Cost of Plate Dinners and Skillet Main Dishes." *Family Economics Review* (Summer 1974), pp. 10–13.

Cross, Jennifer. *The Supermarket Trap.* Bloomington, Ind.: Indiana University Press, 1970.

Dickins, Dorothy. "Factors Related to Food Preferences." *Journal of Home Economics,* Vol. 57 (June 1965), pp. 427–430.

Family Economics Review, published quarterly. Washington, D.C.: Federal

Extension Service, U.S. Department of Agriculture. (Free to home economics teachers and extension specialists.)

Fleck, Henrietta. *Introduction to Nutrition*, 3rd ed. New York: Macmillan, 1976.

"Food and Your Weight." Washington, D.C.: U.S. Department of Agriculture, 1973.

Food Dating: Shoppers' Reactions and the Impact on Retail Foodstores. Marketing Research Report 984, U.S. Department of Agriculture, 1973.

"Food for the Family with Young Children." Washington, D.C.: U.S. Department of Agriculture, n.d.

"Food for the Young Couple." Washington, D.C.: U.S. Department of Agriculture, latest ed.

Food for Us All. The Yearbook of Agriculture 1969. Washington, D.C.: U.S. Department of Agriculture.

"Food Guide for Older Folks." Washington, D.C.: U.S. Department of Agriculture, latest ed.

Fox, Hazel M., Beth A. Fryer, Glenna H. Lamkin, Virginia M. Vivian, and Ercel S. Eppright. "Family Environment." *Journal of Home Economics*, Vol. 62 (1970), pp. 241–245.

Gussow, Joan Dye. "Improving the American Diet." *Journal of Home Economics*, Vol. 65 (1973), pp. 6–10.

"Keeping Food Safe to Eat." Washington, D.C.: U.S. Department of Agriculture, 1971.

Klicka, Mary V. "Convenience: Keynote of the Future." *Journal of Home Economics,* Vol. 61 (1969), pp. 707–716.

Lamkin, Glenna, Mary Louise Hielscher, and Helena B. Janes. "Food Purchasing Practices of Young Families." *Journal of Home Economics*, Vol. 62 (1970), pp. 598–604.

Lawyer, Josephine H. "Freezer Food Concerns." *Family Economics Review* (Spring 1974), pp. 11–13.

LeBovit, Corinne. "The Changing Pattern of Eating Out." *National Food Situation*. U.S. Department of Agriculture (May 1973), pp. 30–34.

Mayer, Jean. *Overweight, Causes, Costs, and Control*. Englewood Cliffs, N.J.: Prentice-Hall, Inc., 1968.

Moody, Marilyn S. "Supermarket Specials in Manhattan, Kansas." Master's thesis, Kansas State University, 1971.

Peterkin, Betty. "The Cost of Meats and Meat Alternatives," *Family Economics Review* (Fall 1974), pp. 11–13.

Raper, Nancy R. "Vegetarian Diets." *Family Economics Review* (Summer 1974), pp. 14–16.

Peterkin, Betty. "Nutrition Labeling for the Consumer." *Family Economics Review* (Summer 1973), pp. 7–14.

Simonds, Lois A. "Variations in Food Costs in Major Ohio Cities." *Journal of Consumer Affairs*. Vol. 3 (Fall 1969), pp. 52–58.

Tinklin, Gwendolyn L., Nancy E. Fogg, and Lucille M. Wakefield. "Convenience Foods: Factors Affecting Their Use Where Household Diets Are Poor." *Journal of Home Economics*, Vol. 64 (1972), pp. 26–28.

Waddell, Frederick E. "The Case Against Trading Stamps." *The Journal of Consumer Affairs*, Vol. 2 (Summer 1968), pp. 21–38.

Wilkinson, J. B., and J. Barry Mason. "The Grocery Shopper and Food Specials: A Case of Subjective Deception?" *Journal of Consumer Affairs*, Vol. 8 (Summer 1974), pp. 30–36.

chapter 8

---

ergonomics:
the management
of work

This chapter is concerned with the management of household work. Family members generally are the ones who supply the energy and skill for household work. Often they want to save time, avoid messy jobs, and be able to carry on some activities near other family members. It is possible for family members to have more time for leisure, recreation, and other interests through the use of improved work arrangements and techniques. This is more than just doing things efficiently. It involves knowing when to spend a lot of time doing something, when to "cut corners," and when the job should be omitted entirely. Work management involves the changing of homemaking standards, the use of tools, the rearrangement of storage and work centers, the development of better work methods, and the use of new products that save work.

Homemaking Standards

Many of us enjoy a certain amount of graciousness and luxury in living. If we didn't it wouldn't be possible to sell the wide variety of products designed to make life pleasanter, and hotels wouldn't provide some of the services that they do. But the feeling that some things are just not worth the bother if we have to do them ourselves is a very personal one, and it may influence what we do at home.

Gradually, most families build up a set of standards with which they are willing to live. Perhaps they have a tablecloth for guests, and place mats when they are alone. Good dishes might be used only for festive occasions because they require extra care. Some things that require lots of upkeep, such as silver and crystal, are put away for occasional use.

When one needs to reduce the time and effort spent on household work, because either the demands on the homemaker's time are too heavy or the homemaker wishes to take on some new activity such as a job, or any of a number of community activities, then one of the first steps in reducing household work is to re-examine standards. In many cases it is possible to change these standards in a way that will cut down household work. Paper plates can be used for children's lunches, picnics might be substituted for more formal parties, children's play clothes might be more casual, meals might have fewer courses, or marketing might be reduced by shopping at less frequent intervals, which would make for a little less variety in fresh fruits and vegetables.

Standards for how a home should be operated are part of our value system. Many a marriage has had rough going because the husband and wife did not have the same idea of how the home should function. The husband may expect the wife to be a meticulous housekeeper, and she is not. Or the wife may feel that she should keep an immaculate home and the husband does not feel that it is worth the bother and is very careless about picking things up. Or perhaps the wife has very high standards of how her house should look but is unable to keep to them. There may be several young children who need her attention and just more work than she can manage.

In order to minimize family disagreement, standards for the operation of the home need to be a compromise between the values of the members and what is possible to maintain at the time. At periods when the demands on family time and energy are greatest, when children are small or someone is ill, standards may need to be relaxed even more than usual. Standards that are unrealistic for the situation just make everyone miserable.

Another approach is to share family responsibilities differently. This often involves changing a standard or perhaps accepting the standard of the individual to whom a job is delegated. For example, if children make the beds they may not look quite as neat as if the homemaker made them. The same might be true of setting the table or folding the laundry.

Or one might decide to organize the household differently. Perhaps when you empty the dishwasher after breakfast you set the table for lunch or dinner instead of putting the dishes away and then taking them out to set the table later. The house wouldn't look quite as tidy as if the dishes were put away, but it might save a few minutes at a busy time.

Another homemaker might decide to wash the sheets and then put them back on the beds. This would enable her to air the beds and avoid folding the sheets, but it might also mean that the beds wouldn't be made as early that particular day and that the sheets might not last as long as if they were rotated and not used continuously.

There are many ways to reduce household work by changing standards. Each family has to make decisions as to what compromises are happy for them.

The Use of Tools

One of the most significant developments in the home during recent years has been its mechanization. Early in the century few homes were wired for electricity and equipped with gas or running water. Household equipment often consisted of a coffee grinder, a food chopper, and a wind-up clock. Today the middle-income home boasts a wide variety of small and large mechanical equipment, which has greatly reduced the backbreaking work involved in homemaking.

These tools have created new types of problems in homemaking. Which tools should the family own? Where can they be stored for efficient use? And how can they be kept in good working condition?

Many homemakers, both experienced ones and those just starting out, need to step back and look at household equipment from a new perspective. Equipment in the home is really a tool. If it reduces work or makes work easier or pleasanter and one has room for it and can afford it, then it is worth buying. But many people collect more tools than they can reasonably use or store. Small kitchen equipment particularly has been promoted like women's fashions; there is always a new thing to toast, bake, or mix. Many of these are useful, but few homes need two or three types of mixers, and most kitchens have too little cabinet space for many things in addition to dishes and food.

Assistance in selecting the right tools can be given by such magazines as *Consumer Reports* and *Consumers Research Magazine*. They try to test new products as they come on the market from the point of view of the family who might buy them.

Household equipment needs the same care and attention that are given to tools in industry in order to keep them working effectively. Household appliances must be handled carefully and given regular maintenance. A very high percentage of service calls are made because appliances are incorrectly or carelessly used.

The maintenance of equipment has become a big annoyance for many families. We have come to depend on our appliances. When the washing machine is out of order in a household with small children, life becomes more difficult. Facilities for servicing appliances have not kept pace with the profuse production of them.

Trends in the Use of Equipment

There have been growing sales of small washers, dryers, refrigerators, and, most recently, freezers. Small appliances fit into apartments, trailers, and boats. They fit the needs of small households who do not need to do things in a big way but still want the ease and convenience of these tools.

Many people are using portable electric appliances instead of bigger equipment, an electric broiler or roaster instead of an oven, a hand mixer instead of a large one. Probably the ease of cleaning the equipment and its counter-top availability have stimulated this trend.

There is a growing market for unusual kitchen equipment.

> Exotic utensils are becoming standard kitchen equipment. Wire whisks and gleaming copperware, fat chopping blocks, . . . fondue pots, omelet pans, souffle dishes—all are moving into homes as a result of the conversion of the "meat and potatoes" American of two decades ago into a diner with somewhat exotic tastes.[1]

The Arrangement of Storage and Work Centers

One of the most obvious differences between contemporary houses and those of a century ago is in the arrangement of storage and equipment. Much of the planning of space is done around homemaking aids that did not exist one hundred years ago.

The Kitchen

Most homemakers regard the kitchen as their chief work center in the house. In many families it is also the center of family activity. As a result

[1] *Business Week*, April 4, 1970, p. 98.

there has been an increasing trend to have the kitchen and family room opening on to each other in new houses.

One study of what homemakers wanted in their kitchens brought out that the kitchen should be

> Planned and arranged to permit the homemaker to do her work easily and quickly,
> Part of the family room so the family can spend more time together,
> One that friends and neighbors admire.[2]

Although this study did not list appearance first, many real estate agents believe that the appearance of the kitchen is often the chief selling point in a house.

Arrangement.   Many homemaking activities take place in the kitchen. "A well arranged kitchen with organized work centers providing convenient working space and storage facilities to suit your particular needs helps you work efficiently and comfortably."[3] (See Figure 8.1.)

There are four basic kitchen shapes, the L-shaped, the U-shaped, parallel walls, and straight line. The straight line is the least efficient, and generally used only where kitchen space is very limited.

A kitchen should be planned around work centers so that one can work efficiently. Kitchen planners often suggest three work centers:

1. A mixing and preparation center with the refrigerator next to it and preferably opening toward the work area.
2. A preparation and clean-up center that includes the sink.
3. A cooking and serving center with the range and oven as part of it.

These three work centers should be located so that there is a "flow of work," that is, the homemaker moves with a minimum of motion from one to another in the sequence in which food is prepared. One measure of the efficiency of the kitchen is the "work triangle."

> Paths between the three work centers form the "work triangle." (See Figure 8.2.) Traffic through this triangle interferes with meal preparation. The

[2] Frances Elizabeth Fortenberry and Tessie Agan, "Shall We Continue Teaching Work Simplification in Kitchen Planning?" *Journal of Home Economics*, Vol. 56, No. 6 (1964), p. 407.

[3] Alice M. Burton and Virginia Y. Trotter, "Easy-to-Use Kitchens," Bulletin No. EC 66–2200, sponsored by Nebraska Heart Association and Extension Service, University of Nebraska College of Agriculture and Home Economics and U.S. Department of Agriculture, n.d., p. 2.

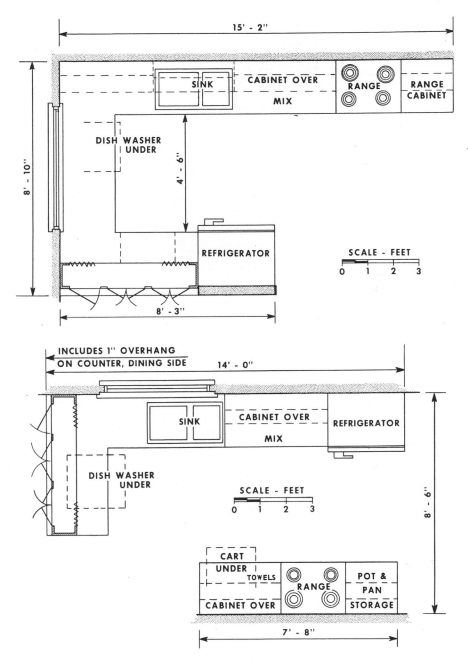

Figure 8.1. Two different kitchen arrangements designed for ease of work. (USDA)

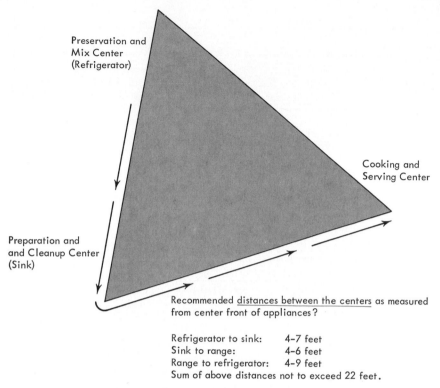

Preservation and
Mix Center
(Refrigerator)

Cooking and
Serving Center

Preparation and
and Cleanup Center
(Sink)

Recommended <u>distances between the centers</u> as measured
from center front of appliances?

Refrigerator to sink: 4–7 feet
Sink to range: 4–6 feet
Range to refrigerator: 4–9 feet
Sum of above distances not to exceed 22 feet.

Figure 8.2. A work triangle. *(Easy-to-Use Kitchens*, Bulletin No. EC 66-2200, Nebraska Heart Association and Extension Service, University of Nebraska College of Agriculture and Home Economics in cooperation with the U.S. Department of Agriculture)

distances between the centers should be comfortable for working, allowing for enough counter and storage space appliances but not so much as to waste space and require extra steps and effort.[4]

"The sink area is the most used center in the kitchen."[5] It should have the choice location. Most model homes put the sink under a window so that the homemaker will have a view of outdoors. The cooking and serving center is second in importance, and should be located conveniently to the sink and for serving.

The height of work areas, kitchen equipment, and storage units should be convenient for the homemaker. A common complaint of many women

[4] Ibid., p. 4.
[5] Rose E. Steidl, "Arrangement of Kitchen Centers," Cornell Extension Bulletin No. 1028, New York State College of Home Economics, 1961, p. 7.

Within each work center <u>organize</u> articles <u>within</u> the <u>area</u> <u>you</u> <u>can</u> <u>reach</u> while <u>working</u>. When your shoulders arms or hands are limited you probably have a limited reach.

To find the area you can reach while working, stand or sit — whichever position you normally use — and face a large piece of brown paper thumbtacked to a wall. With a crayon in each hand, draw arcs to form the circles of your "Easy Reach" and "Maximum Reach" areas.

"Easy Reach Area"

Swing an arc with each arm, keeping elbows comfortably close to your body.

In this area store most-used articles.

"Maximum Reach Area"

Swing an arc with each arm extended to full length. Bend forward slightly if measuring from a seated position.

In this area store articles used a little less frequently.

"Outside of Maximum Reach Area"

In this area store articles used occasionally.

Figure 8.3. Determining work and reach areas. *(Easy-to-Use Kitchens*, Bulletin No. EC 66-2200, Nebraska Heart Association and Extension Service, University of Nebraska College of Agriculture and Home Economics in cooperation with the U.S. Department of Agriculture)

is that men design the kitchens and tend to place cabinets too high for the average woman.

Storage. Items to be stored in cabinets in the kitchen include food, utensils, dinnerware, kitchen linens, empty food containers, and cleaning supplies used at the sink. In addition, many families keep packaging supplies for use in freezer, wrapping sandwiches, and refrigerator storage.

The quantity of items is tremendous, as anyone who has moved knows. A limited supply of packaged goods would be about one hundred items, of utensils, eighty-four items, and of cleaning supplies nine items.

Finding a convenient place for everything in the kitchen is not easy. Many homes have inadequate or poorly planned kitchen storage space. When adequate storage space is available and articles can be placed within reach while working, kitchen jobs are much easier and pleasanter.

How much *total storage space* do you need? This depends on the kinds and amounts of food, equipment, utensils, and appliances you use in your kitchen. No need to move or reach around that bulky never-used kettle to get your saucepans. *Discard articles you don't use.*

A *definite place to store each article* you use in your kitchen saves you much time and energy—less reaching and hunting.

Figure 8.4. Well-planned kitchen storage. (USDA)

Why cross the kitchen to get first one thing, and then another? With sufficient storage space, or even a rearrangement of present storage at each work center, you can *store articles where you use them first.*

Groups items together that are used together. Sugar, shortening, mixes, mixing bowls, measuring cups and spoons, and baking dishes should be stored together at the mix center. Canned foods that need water added for cooking and saucepans should be stored at the sink center. Pot holders, pancake turners, stirring spoons and skillets belong together at the range.

You will want to store articles so they are accessible—*easy to see, easy to reach,* and *easy to grasp.* Store them in the type of storage unit that provides this accessibility and is within your reach while you work....

Arrange storage units to fit the articles to be stored. Recommended inside heights of storage units for various types of supplies are:

3″ to 3½″—silver, small tools, spices
3½″ to 4″—linens for sink and table
6″ to 7″—saucepans, canned foods
10½″ to 11½″—canisters, large packaged foods
11½″ to 12¼″—shallow utensils stored vertically

The time, effort, and energy you need are reduced when good storage arrangements save you trips across the kitchen.[6]

Evaluating a kitchen. Most homemakers are not able to plan a dream kitchen from scratch. Generally, a family chooses a house or apartment with a kitchen already installed.

There are a number of ways in which one can evaluate a kitchen from the point of view of ease of work. The "Evaluation Guide for Existing Kitchens" by Bard, which is shown in Table 8.1, is one useful method.

Other Areas of the Home

Group working materials into activity centers in order to make it easier to do household jobs. Try to put all the tools and supplies for each activity in one area. Have an area for reading, another for mending and ironing, and one for bathing the baby if there is an infant in the family. Duplicate some small equipment if necessary to save steps. Group working materials so that you can do as many activities as possible with the least amount of time and effort to get ready for them.

Arrange storage space so that things are easy to find and use.

One of the first rules for good home management is "a place for everything and everything in its place." But, as every homemaker knows, it's one thing

---

[6] Excerpts from Alice M. Burton and Virginia Y. Trotter, "No-Stoop, No-Stretch Kitchen Storage," Bulletin No. EC 66-2201, sponsored by Nebraska Heart Association and Extension Service, University of Nebraska College of Agriculture and Home Economics and U.S. Department of Agriculture, n.d., pp. 2, 7, 8.

TABLE 8.1
Evaluation Guide for Existing Kitchens

	Home Size		
Item	Under 1,000 sq. ft.	1,000–1,400 sq. ft.	Over 1,400 sq. ft.
Storage and Counter Space			
1. Total base-cabinet frontage	72"+	96"+	120"+
2. Total wall-cabinet frontage	120"+	144"+	168"+
3. Counter adjacent to latch side of the refrigerator	15"+	15"+	18"+
4. Counter to either side of the range or surface units	15"+	18"+	24"+
5. Counter to either side of the oven	15"+	15"+	18"+
6. Counter length for mixing	42"+	42"+	54"+
7. Total amount of counter frontage	72"+	96"+	108"+
Arrangement			
8. Clearances between opposite appliances, cabinets, wall or table	48"+	54"+	60"+
9. Adjustable shelves in wall cabinets *or* cabinets with the third shelf not more than 72" above the floor	yes	yes	yes
10. Traffic through the work triangle (unless there is an alternate route)	none	none	none
11. Door openings that interfere with work areas	none	none	none

SOURCE: Ella Mae Bard, "An Evaluation Guide for Existing Kitchens," M.S. thesis, Ohio State University, 1967, p. 52. Based on recommendations from "Kitchen Planning Standards" by William H. Kapple, Small Homes Council—Building Research Council, *University of Illinois Bulletin*, Vol. 62, No. 65, Circular Series 0532 (March 1965).

to know the rule and another to live up to it. This is especially true if you live in one of the new "compact" homes, or in a city apartment, where places to put things are at a minimum.

The shortage of storage space in homes of all sizes, both new and old, is a universal complaint of today's homemakers. There are a number of reasons why:

You have more possessions than your parents had. These include everything from household appliances and equipment for family leisure activities to the personal belongings of each member of your family.

Or, maybe your family has "outgrown" your present home but you're not yet ready to move to a larger one.

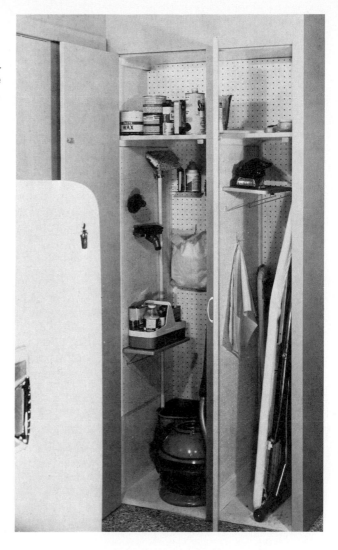

Figure 8.5. Group working materials where they are easy to find. (USDA)

Then there's the matter of economy in modern home-building. In the effort to give a maximum amount of "living" space at the lowest possible cost, home designers have eliminated many storage areas taken for granted in homes built a generation or so ago.[7]

Stretching storage space. The best way to stretch storage space is to take a deep breath and toss out absolutely everything that hasn't been used in a year. Most of us find it hard to be quite so ruthless. We're sentimental about some things. We think we might be able to use others in the future. Or we paid so much for something that we hate to part with.

Obviously, it will take a little effort to consider what to throw out and

---

[7] "Put Your Storage Problems on the Shelf," S. A. Hirsh Manufacturing Company, 1962.

what to keep. One way to handle this is to sort over personal and household possessions at regular intervals. Look over clothing at the start of each season. Check household items once or twice a year. If you do a seasonal cleaning this might be combined with it. Or just sort things out at convenient times. Some people like to get rid of excess clothes and toys before Christmas because they are planning to buy some new things for the holidays. A college student going away to school might sort clothes and personal articles out before packing. You could recycle some things by giving them to a person or organization that can use them.

Frequently, we have our most convenient storage spaces cluttered with things we don't use often. Items that are frequently used should be stored where they are visible and easy to reach. The others can be put in less accessible spots.

Adjustable shelves and shallow shelving make it easier to arrange small and odd-sized things conveniently. Dividers in drawers and trays with compartments for jewelry, gloves, or underwear make it easier to keep everything in place.

Look at closets and storage areas. Are the closets a mix-up jumble of shoes, clothes, sports equipment, and other things? Do you have to move your suitcase every time you want to get something else out? Then it's time to reorganize your storage space.

Streamlining Methods of Work

The first step in making work easier is a desire to simplify the job. Then, new methods must be developed and used long enough to lose their awkwardness and become habits.

There are six key questions to ask in simplifying work methods.

1. *What* is being done?
2. *Who* is doing it?
3. *Where* is it being done?
4. *When* is it being done?
5. *Why* is it being done?
6. *How* is it being done?

The why and how are of particular importance.

Why raises the question of whether the job should be done at all. If it should be done, could it be done differently to accomplish the same purpose? *How* naturally leads to considering the skills needed for the task, the ways in which it might be done better, and the satisfactions that might result from an improved method.

Figure *8.6.* Storage space can be attractively arranged. (USDA)

Questioning the *how* of a task may be approached by way of the concept of classes of change. Mundel (1960) proposed that simplification could be classified into five groups according to the origin of change. Gross and Crandall (1963) condensed these into three: Class I, change originating in the activity of the worker; Class II, change originating in work space and tools; Class III, Change originating in the product. These classes of change can serve as the basis for study and simplification of a task of narrow definition, having hot rolls for a meal, or of a task of broad definition, cleaning a room.[8]

The Use of Body Mechanics

An important approach to the improvement of work methods is through the proper handling of one's body. Good posture in working, lifting, stretching, and other activities can do much to reduce the physical effort involved in household activities.

Figures 8.7a and b are representations of the body divided into the three main weights—the head, the chest, and the pelvic or hip section. Proper alignment (a) locates in a vertical arrangement the first two weights over the base of support, the third weight. In this balanced position, the muscles can maintain good posture with a minimum of strain and effort whether you are working, playing, sitting, standing, walking, or climbing. Obviously, however, you

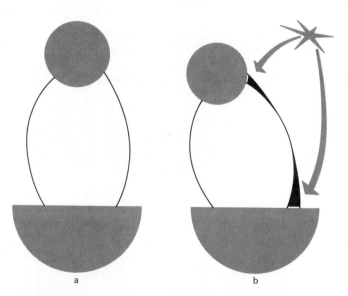

a   b

Figure 8.7. Good and poor body alignment. (Katherine H. Sippola, "Your Work and Your Posture," Cornell Extension Bulletin 1139)

[8] Rose E. Steidl and Esther Crew Bratton, *Work in the Home* (New York: John Wiley & Sons, Inc., 1968), p. 345.

cannot accomplish all your work with your body in this straight, erect position. You must do countless jobs of lifting and carrying each day.

Whenever these weight are out of alignment (b) the force of gravity tends to increase their misalignment. This force, combined with the weight of the misaligned body, causes the muscles to contract constantly to keep the body from toppling over. Constant contraction of the muscles results in local fatigue, particularly at the base of the neck and in the lower back where most of this weight must be supported.

Changing your position will prove restful when it is necessary for you to stand or sit in one place for a long period of time. Misaligned body positions for a short period of time are not harmful and will allow some muscles to relax. These positions must be used *for change only*, however, since the well-aligned body should be the basic position, not only when standing and sitting but also during activity. Selecting a good height for work surfaces, either when standing or sitting, is an additional help in maintaining proper body alignment.

Knowledge of the principles of good body alignment and good work heights is, however, only the first step in acquiring a habitually efficient posture. Persistent practice, along with a desire to make this a part of one's life, is essential if a well-aligned body is to become a habit.

Keep the Body Sections in Alignment

Lifting heavy objects from the floor is one of the tasks homemakers most often perform incorrectly. Body alignment has particular significance in lifting weights since you obviously have to bend the body. Figure 8.8 indicates how you can bend and still maintain body alignment. Notice that the head is directly over the chest and the trunk bends forward from the pelvic region. The heavier the object to be lifted, the more important it is for you to maintain correct body position since you have that weight to lift in addition to your own body weight.

Spread the Base of Support

Widening the base of support in a forward-backward stride position as well as spreading the feet apart gives greater stability to the body segments in the direction the body will be moving.

Hold Any Object You Lift As Close to Your Body As Possible

Any weight must be held close to your body if it is to be lifted most easily and if body balance is to be maintained. To test this principle, hold your pocketbook at arm's length for a few seconds, then hold it in close to your body. Notice the difference in pull on the muscles. This effect is multiplied when the object to be lifted is heavy. Think of lifting a roast out of the oven. Think, too, of passing a heavy serving dish at the table.

Use the Strong Leg Muscles

Following these guides when lifting heavy objects not only helps to keep those three body weights in line but also makes use of the good leverage of the

Figure 8.8. Effective use of the body in lifting.

long bones of the legs; moreover, the long, strong muscles of the legs and thighs can do the lifting job more easily than the small muscles of the back.

Think of Ways to Avoid Heavy Lifting

A load of clothes weighs almost twice as much when it comes out of the washing machine as when it goes in. A basket of damp clothes on the floor has to be lifted. If you place the basket on a bench or cart before adding the damp clothes, you have eliminated a bad lifting job. Another great muscle saver is the use of wheels—on your ironing board, your vacuum cleaner, your serving cart, or any other piece of portable equipment. Grocers have been capitalizing on this idea for years.[9]

Techniques for Analyzing Work Methods

A sizable body of literature has developed about the ways in which work methods can be analyzed. Time exposures have been made of a worker with a light (or lights) attached to him that show the various movements involved in an operation. Charts can be made of the routes used in

[9] Katherine H. Sippola, "Your Work and Your Posture," *Cornell Extension Bulletin 1139*, 1966, pp. 3–5.

performing a task by using a floor plan and having an observer diagram each route used with paper and pencil or string charts. The actual number of steps involved in an activity, such as preparing a particular meal, can be counted. Time charts can be kept to compare various methods. Or notes can be taken to count each type of operation, such as getting ready, cutting, and so on. (A form of note taking on work methods that is widely used was developed by the Gilbreths; it is called *therbligs*.[10])

The method of charting a person's route was used in a study of food shopping.

The U.S. Department of Agriculture researchers watched more than 3,000 shoppers wind their way through 13 Boston supermarkets. As shoppers moved through the store, their individual paths and shopping activities were recorded on an outline of the store's selling area. Whenever a shopper picked up and examined an item, it was recorded. If she bought anything, that, too, was noted.

[The study showed that] the number of purchases were related to store coverage. Those who shopped the entire store spent more than twice as much money per visit as those who shopped selected areas only. . . . Shoppers spent more money in stores with continuous gondolas because the lack of cross-aisle traffic encourages staying longer in the store and covering a greater area of the store. Because of this, you will sometimes see advertised specials mid-gondola rather than at the end.

Shoppers seldom bypass a department to return to it later.

Some foods are power items, that is, they are the most regularly purchased. Bread, milk, butter, and eggs are such. The location of items within this group influences what shoppers will buy. For example, bread on display at the end of the bakery counter so that the shopper passes cakes, pies, and rolls en route encourages the purchase of these items as well as bread. In Boston, cake sales rose and bread sales remained the same when this arrangement was tried.

Thirty per cent of the shoppers used shopping lists. Shoppers with pre-pared lists shopped longer and spent more money per minute. This observa-tion does not necessarily mean use of a list increases food purchases. It may mean that those with lists were thorough shoppers.[11]

Most analysis techniques were developed for use in industry, where a small saving of time or effort in a repetitive operation might result in a large saving of money by reducing the work required for a specific job. Some of these techniques are useful in analyzing homemaking activities,

[10] Lillian M. Gilbreth, Orpha Mae Thomas, and Eleanor Clymer, *Management in the Home* (New York: Dodd, Mead & Company, 1960), Chap. 4, "Charts."

[11] Roger Murphy, Ruth Hodgson, and Judith Siegel, "Shopping Patterns," *Focus on the Food Markets*, March 6, 1961, pp. 1–2. Based on Nick Havas and Hugh M. Smith, "Customers' Shopping Patterns in Retail Food Stores," Market Research Division, Agri-culture Marketing Service, U.S. Department of Agriculture, 1960.

TYPICAL PATH OF SHOPPER COVERING ENTIRE STORE

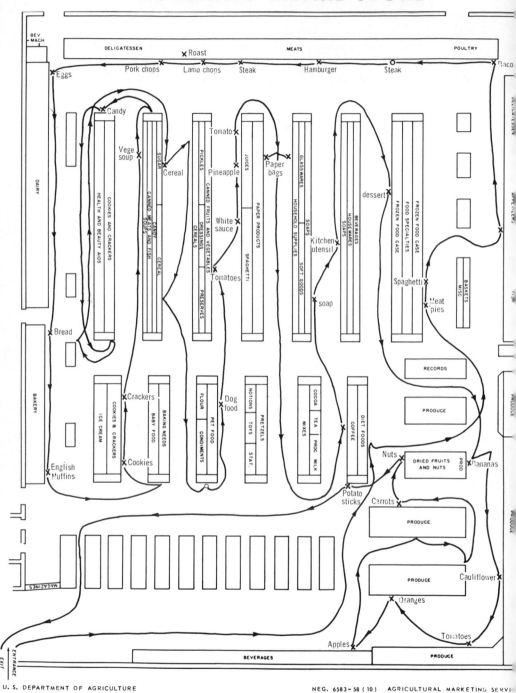

U. S. DEPARTMENT OF AGRICULTURE   NEG. 6583-58 (10)   AGRICULTURAL MARKETING SERVI

Figure 8.9. (USDA)

such as deciding which type of kitchen layout would be most efficient and how to save effort for a homemaker with limited time or energy. But in many cases the homemaker decides about the timing of activities and what she is willing to do in the way of work based on factors other than economy of effort. For example, it would be efficient to leave bedspreads off so that the beds would be ready to use in the evening, but many families use bedspreads because they like their appearance.

The Use of New Products

The use of new products that save time for homemakers has boomed.

Convenience Foods[12]

Today's homemakers are often willing to spend more money on food to save time and energy in the kitchen. The most obvious advantages of convenience foods are that they usually save time in food preparation and that they are generally less bulky to carry home. On the other hand, most convenience foods cost more than home-prepared ones.

The bulk of the convenience foods being used at present are canned or frozen. Freeze-dried foods that can be stored in the package without refrigeration are growing in use but are still only a small proportion of convenience foods.

It is possible to prepare meals quickly without using commercial convenience foods if you are willing to do advance preparation. Many casseroles can be prepared ahead and frozen or refrigerated until needed. A pot roast can be cooked in advance and then heated through and sliced at the last minute. Chicken can be prepared for baking and then frozen in the baking pan. Then it can be thawed and baked in the same pan. Or it can be put directly in the oven to thaw and cook.

Hamburger patties can be made when the meat is purchased, then separated with foil or freezer wrap and frozen. In this way they will separate easily for thawing or cooking directly.

Baked products such as cakes, pies, and cookies freeze very well. Pies and cookies may be frozen either cooked or uncooked. Many people like to freeze the dough for cookies or pies ahead of time. This is often helpful at

[12] A technical definition of convenience foods is given by Mary V. Klicka, "Convenience: Keynote of the Future," *Journal of Home Economics*, Vol. 61, No. 9 (1969), p. 707. "A convenience food is a menu item in a preserved state that, with objective finishing instructions, allows the serving of that menu item without need for a skilled cook or baker to assure customer acceptance of that item. A convenience recipe component is an ingredient or recipe subassembly in a preserved state that allows the user to proceed directly with the formulation of a menu item without the need for further preparation labor for that component."

a busy holiday period like Christmas. Dough can be made weeks in advance, at a time when one is not as busy.

In considering when to use various types of foods and what to prepare ahead, the homemaker has a wide variety of choices. The decision should include consideration of whether it is important only to save time and energy at mealtimes, whether it is possible to use less busy times to save work at peak periods, and how tight the budget is.

Other Products

Another way some homemakers save work is with dishes that can be used to freeze or refrigerate foods, cook them, and then serve them at the table. This saves lots of extra dishwashing. Some of these are made with easy to clean surfaces.

Many people use aluminum foil and aluminum foil pans to save dishwashing and oven cleaning. They put foil under baking dishes in the oven, use it to line baking pans, use it as a pan to heat small items in the oven, and line burners and drip trays on the stove.

Figure 8.10. Non-stick bakeware eases the job of cleaning the pan. (E. I. DuPont de Nemours & Company)

Personal Space

In recent years the idea of "personal space" has received more attention.

Human affairs have been arranged on the assumption that human beings "have" to have a certain amount or kind of space. Building codes require that buildings be set back from the street and that ceilings be of a certain height so that individuals will have "enough room." There are safety rules limiting the number of persons in a restaurant, a theatre, an elevator, even a subway car, and whatever the reasons for the limit, the number must be less than the physical capacity of the space or it would not be necessary to have a rule.

The space a person needs seems so self-evident that it comes as something of a shock to discover that behavioral scientists can't really give architects and institutional managers a universal square or cubic-foot per-person figure as a guideline. We can be explicit about how much we need in one particular situation, but the amount varies as soon as the circumstances change.[13]

Consider for a moment how closely packed teen-age girls like to be at a slumber party, but how much space they need in a college dormitory. You may enjoy crowding around the table with a big family group for Thanksgiving or Christmas dinner, but you would hardly accept such closeness at a public restaurant. Astronauts function well for long periods in small capsules, but their homes are more spacious. We enjoy some people closer to ourselves than others.

Safety in the Home

Safety is an important consideration in the planning and carrying on of household activities. The placement of equipment is important. Many people have to reach over the stove to get things out of a cabinet. Can you think of other situations where the placement of equipment might present safety problems?

The design of equipment is also an important consideration.

The National Bureau of Standards and kitchen range manufacturers, for example, have recently begun a comprehensive program that will result in re- commended design changes for gas and electricity ranges particularly from the standpoint of danger of accidental clothing fires. Among the changes being considered are control knobs that cannot be turned on accidentally, burner arrangements that do not necessitate reaching over one burner to use another, and elimination of the dangers of invisibly hot burners. A hazard that I had not

[13] Caroline Bird, *The Crowding Syndrome* (New York: David McKay Company, Inc., 1972), pp. 83–84.

Figure 8.11. Consider how differently chairs are arranged in an airport waiting room (A) and the lounge of an apartment for senior citizens (B). (*Top:* Pan American World Airways; *bottom:* Courtesy Medical Tribune and Crestview, Sylvania, Ohio)

Figure 8.12. These are some sources of frequent home accidents. (Textile Industry Product Safety Committee)

previously considered in relation to door opening and body position in use of the oven was brought to my attention by a friend recently. She told me that she had "frizzled" her wig when she opened the door to her hot oven. Her solution was to buy a new wig made of less vulnerable material, but perhaps some attention should be given by manufacturers to design of the oven-opening arrangement on ranges.[14]

Also, the manner in which an activity is carried on influences whether it is hazardous or not. One can cut carrots safely against a breadboard. However, many people hold the carrots in their hand and cut against their thumbs, which is much more dangerous. Electric light cords can cause accidents if they are placed where the insulation gets worn or are on the floor where people can trip over them.

Summary

It is possible for homemakers to have more time for leisure, recreation, and other interests through better work management. This can be accomplished through a variety of methods.

1. *The changing of homemaking standards.* When one needs or wants to reduce the time and effort spent on household work one of the first steps is to re-examine standards for housekeeping. In many cases it is possible to change these standards in a way that will cut household work.

2. *The use of tools.* Today a wide variety of tools is available to ease the work involved in maintaining a home. These tools have created new types of problems for the family. Which tools should the family own? Where can they be stored? How can they be kept in good working condition?

3. *The arrangement of storage and work centers.* Finding a convenient place to keep everything in the home is not easy. Many homes have inadequate or poorly planned storage space. Or the family may have a great many things that require storage. When adequate storage space is available and frequently used articles can be placed within reach, homemaking jobs are much easier and pleasanter. Often, with careful planning, many things can be placed in more convenient locations.

4. *Streamlining methods of work.* There are six key questions to ask in simplifying work methods. What is being done? Who is doing it? Where is it being done? When is it being done? Why is it being done? How is it being done? By considering the answers to these questions, one can often

---

[14] Fern E. Hunt. "Innovations in Teaching: Ergonomics," *Actualizing Concepts in Home Management* (Washington, D.C.: American Home Economics Association, 1974), p. 6.

plan new work methods that are more efficient. Proper use of the body can make some jobs easier.

5. *The use of new products.* The use of convenience foods and disposable products that save time for homemakers has boomed. Frozen foods are widely used, as are paper products, aluminum foil, and dishes that can be used to store, cook, and serve.

In recent years the idea of personal space has received more attention. There are no clear guidelines as to how much space is needed for all activities, although there are some for certain specific situations.

Safety in the home is an important consideration in the planning and carrying out of household activities. The location of equipment, the design of equipment, and the manner in which activities are carried on all affect safety.

CHAPTER FOLLOW-UP

1. What are some of the standards of homemaking that you feel are important to maintain? If you had to cut corners, what things would you eliminate? What things would you be most reluctant to change?
2. Look at your present clothing closet. It probably doesn't meet all your qualifications for good storage. Replan it to provide better storage for the things you now have.
3. Most college students have some housekeeping chores such as laundry or cleaning even if they are living in a dormitory. Take the housekeeping job you like the least and consider how you might do it more efficiently.
4. Assume that you will give a party for some of your friends at home or where you have access to a kitchen. How might you plan the evening to reduce work for yourself?
5. Look at your home, or a friend's, carefully to find safety hazards. List these and indicate how they might be corrected.
6. Draw a plan of your family's kitchen. Then replan it to improve its efficiency.
7. Draw a chart indicating your easy-to-reach area when you are standing.
8. Keep a list for a day of all the places you sit with people. Where was the amount of space for you too small? Were there any cases where you had too much space?
9. How could you improve your study area so that it would be easier to work. Make a plan to reorganize this area.

SELECTED REFERENCES

Bard, Ella Mae. "An Evaluation Guide for Existing Kitchens." M.S. thesis, Ohio State University, 1967.

Bird, Caroline. *The Crowding Syndrome.* New York: David McKay Company, Inc.. 1972.

Burton, Alice M., and Virginia Y. Trotter. "Easy-to-Use Kitchens." Bulletin No. EC 66-2200, sponsored by Nebraska Heart Association and Extension Service, University of Nebraska College of Agriculture and Home Economics and U.S. Department of Agriculture, n.d.

———. "No-Stoop, No-Stretch Kitchen Storage." Bulletin No. EC 66-2201, sponsored by Nebraska Heart Association and Extension Service, University of Nebraska College of Agriculture and Home Economics and U.S. Department of Agriculture, n.d.

Cavner, Linda Susan. "Organization of Activities Performed in Cleaning the Living Room As Reported by 265 Homemakers in Lincoln, Nebraska, 1967." Master's thesis, University of Nebraska, 1973.

Dickerson, F. Reed. *Product Safety in Household Goods*. Indianapolis, Ind.: Bobbs-Merrill Co., 1968.

Gilbreth, Lillian M., Orpha Mae Thomas, and Eleanor Clymer. *Management in the Home*. New York: Dodd, Mead & Company, 1960.

Gross, Irma H., Elizabeth Walbert Crandall, and Marjorie M. Knoll. *Management for Modern Families*. New York: Appleton-Century-Crofts, 1973, pp. 128–147.

Havas, Nick, and Hugh M. Smith. "Customers' Shopping Patterns in Retail Food Stores." AMS Bull. 400, Market Development Research Division, Agricultural Marketing Service, U.S. Department of Agriculture, 1960.

Hunt, Fern E. "Innovations in Teaching: Ergonomics." *Actualizing Concepts in Home Management*. Washington, D.C.: American Home Economics Association, 1974, pp. 4–6.

Kapple, William H. "Kitchen Planning Standards." Small Homes Council-Building Research Council, *University of Illinois Bulletin*, Vol. 62, (March 1965).

McCullough, Helen E. "Household Storage Units." Small Homes Council, *University of Illinois Bulletin*, Vol. 50 (Jan. 1953).

Magrabi, Frances M., Beatrice Paolucci, and Marjorie E. Heifner. "Framework for Studying Family Activity Patterns." *Journal of Home Economics*, Vol. 59 (Nov. 1967), pp. 714–719.

———, Avis Woolrich, Kathryn Philson, Ruth H. Smith, and Anna L. Wood. "Space Standards for Household Activities." Bulletin 686, University of Illinois Agriculture Experiment Station in cooperation with Alabama Agriculture Experiment Station; College of Home Economics, Pennsylvania State University; Washington Agriculture Experiment Station; Agriculture Research Service, U.S. Department of Agriculture.

Peet, Louise Jenison, Mary S. Pickett, and Mildred G. Arnold. *Household Equipment*. New York: John Wiley & Sons, Inc., 1970, Chap. 16 "Maximizing Satisfaction in Work in the Home."

Sippola, Katherine H. "Your Work and Your Posture." Cornell Extension Bulletin 1139, New York State College of Home Economics, 1966.

Steidl, Rose E. "Organization and Activity Management." *Proceedings: Southeastern Regional Conference-Family Economics-Home Managements*. University, Ala.: The University of Alabama, 1972, pp. 94–114.

———, and Esther Crew Bratton. *Work in the Home*. New York: John Wiley & Sons, Inc., 1968.

Walker, Florence S. "Standards in a Managerial Context." *Actualizing Concepts in Home Management.* Washington, D.C.: American Home Economics Association, 1974, pp. 12–19.

Wanslow, Robert. *Kitchen Planning Guide.* Small Homes Council-Building Research Council, University of Illinois, 1965.

White, Linda Souther, and Betty Jane Johnston. "Use of Electric Housewares and Convenience Foods." *Journal of Home Economics,* Vol. 58 (1966), pp. 675–677.

part four

special management situations

chapter 9

the low-income family

The poor inhabit a world scarcely recognizable and rarely recognized by the majority of their fellow Americans. It is a world apart, whose inhabitants are isolated from the mainstream of American life and alienated from its values. It is a world where Americans are literally concerned with day-to-day survival, where a minor illness is a major tragedy, where pride and privacy must be sacrificed to get help, where honesty can become a luxury and ambition a myth. Worst of all, the poverty of the fathers is visited upon the children.[1]

Poverty is not as visible as it once was. With mass production of clothing poor people dress much like everyone else. Their homes tend to be out of sight or in central cities.

Poverty is the absence of money, or the means to secure the basic essentials of life. . . . The general level of production

[1] "Poverty in America," *Monthly Labor Review*, Vol. 87, No. 3 (March 1964).

249

of goods and services, together with the fairness of their distribution, determines the degree and extent of poverty among various groups.[2]

Who Is Poor?

The following are brief descriptions of some people who are poor.[3]

A permanently and totally disabled man with a family. Mr. Doe, a permanently bedfast man of fifty, applies for Aid to the Permanently and Totally Disabled. He has a wife and four sons aged thirteen, eleven, nine, and six. Three years before he was disabled, Mr. Doe bought a house, on which he is still making monthly payments. While employed, he was covered by Social Security. He has no other income, owns no other property, has no cash on hand. He cashed in his insurance to live on and, after exhausting this, he applied for assistance.

A divorced mother with three children. Mrs. White, aged thirty-five and divorced, applies for assistance from the Aid to Families with Dependent Children program for her three daughters, aged ten, eight, and six. Mrs. White has diabetes. She has no income, owns no property, and has no cash on hand, and no insurance.

A blind man with earned income. Mr. Gray, a blind man, applies for Aid to the Blind. He lives alone in an apartment and has a small income from the operation of a vending stand. He has no other income, owns no property, has no cash on hand, and no insurance.

An elderly widow living alone. Mrs. Jones, a widow of seventy-three who lives alone in her own home, applies for public assistance. She rents one room in her home and receives a very small income. At the time of application, she has $175 in the bank. She has an insurance policy with a small cash value. She has no other income or resources. She has never been employed. Her husband . . . [was not covered by Social Security]. She has no children.

An aged man living with a married daughter. Mr. Smith lives with his married daughter and her family. The daughter provides shelter, utilities, and household supplies for him. She is unable to make any other

---

[2] Statement by Elizabeth Wickenden, Technical Consultant on Public Social Policy, National Social Welfare Assembly, Inc. (mimeo.) January 23, 1964.

[3] Adapted from Gladys O. White, "Yardstick for Need." Bureau of Family Services, Welfare Administration, U.S. Department of Health, Education, and Welfare, 1964, pp. 16–25.

contributions. Mr. Smith receives a [small] . . . monthly benefit from Federal Old-Age, Survivors, and Disability Insurance, commonly called Social Security. He owns no property, has no cash on hand, and has no private insurance.

A child with earned income. Mrs. Green, a widow of forty, applies for assistance through the Aid to Families with Dependent Children program for herself, a son of sixteen, and a daughter of thirteen. The mother has no income, owns no property, has no cash on hand, and no insurance. The son has a paper route and works at a grocery store after school.

The causes of poverty are not the same for everyone, as the preceding examples suggest. Consideration of how poor people can be helped should be based on this fact. The following six categories describe the major groups of poor people.

1. *Those who are not able to work* because they are too old, disabled, too young (and deprived of normal parental support) or tied down by social responsibility. For these people the only answer is higher social insurance, assistance, and pension payments together with direct benefits such as housing, health services, and . . . [help in getting more food].
2. *Those who are able and qualified for work but can't find it.* For these people the answer lies in more jobs produced through a growing adaptive economy, publicly provided . . . employment, and liberalized unemployment insurance.
3. *Those who are under-employed, under-paid, or disadvantaged in market exchange* (as with some farmers). Again a growing economy is basic but so also are a higher minimum wage and better adapted farm policies.
4. *Those who are not equipped to fill available jobs,* either because they are

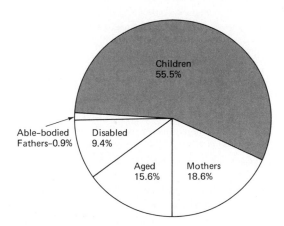

Figure 9.1. Who gets U.S. welfare? (U.S. Department of Health, Education, and Welfare)

under-educated or their old skills have become obsolete. For these people education, new work experience, occupational counseling, and placement services are the answer.

5. *Those who are living in a locality or area* where the former means of livelihood has ceased to exist or [where they are unable] to afford tolerable living standards. For the employable persons in such an area new means of livelihood must be brought in or they must be assisted to move out. The unemployable persons in such depressed areas fall within the same situation as in (1) above.

6. *Those whose social and personal problems have brought* them to a point of self-defeating discouragement. These are the people who have sought escape in delinquency, mental illness, alcoholism, chronic dependency, and other forms of social isolation. These people may need individual supportive help in addition to the other remedies listed if they are to break the bonds of poverty.[4]

Members of minority groups are much more likely to be living in poverty, as the following study indicates.

A survey of the major poverty areas of New York City—Central Harlem, East Harlem, the South Bronx, and the Bedford-Stuyvesant area of Brooklyn —in 1968–69 brought out the following facts. *The poverty areas had a higher rate of unemployment for all men and women, sixteen years of age and over, in the labor force, than New York City as a whole or the nation.* Unemployment was greatest for Puerto Rican* residents, then Blacks, and least for whites.

The data on annual work experience show that one out of every seven adult men was unemployed at some time during the year. About one third of those who experienced unemployment were jobless for 15 weeks or more.

As might be expected, teenagers sixteen–nineteen years old, living in the poverty areas studied, experienced particular difficulty in the labor market. Among those seeking work, the unemployment rate averaged 25.3 per cent for the survey year.

In this area, more than four out of every ten households were headed by women—nearly half the Black and one third of the white and Puerto Rican households had female heads. Among the area's 77,000 women household heads aged twenty to sixty-four, nearly half were out of the labor force, neither working nor looking for work. Labor force participation of Puerto Rican women was lower than of Black women, with 30 per cent of them actively in the labor force as against a 57 per cent rate for Black women.

Marked differences in age distribution among the racial-ethnic groups residing in the poverty-slum areas were found. Among Blacks, close to half of the working age population was found to be forty-five years of age or more. In contrast, the average age of the Puerto Rican population was considerably

4 Wickenden, op. cit.
* This category usually covers all Spanish-speaking people.

younger with nearly three fourths under forty-five years of age. The small proportion of whites living in the poverty-slum areas was largely concentrated in the older age groups, with roughly three fifths forty-five years and over.

Occupationally, the men and women workers living in the areas surveyed were concentrated in low-paid and low-skill, low-status jobs. Three fifths of the employed adults worked as semiskilled operatives, laborers, domestics, or were in other service jobs. While better than a fourth of the men and over a third of the women were in white-collar jobs, only about 10 per cent were in professional, technical, or managerial jobs.

Occupational patterns among employed teenagers in the survey areas differed strikingly from those of adult workers. Sixty per cent of the employed sixteen–nineteen year olds held white-collar jobs (mostly clerical—nearly double the national percentage). On the other hand, only one tenth of the teenagers held service jobs, half the national average.

The educational attainment of the labor force in these areas, as measured by median years of school completed, suggests that a large proportion was at a critical disadvantage in the competition for good jobs. Years of school completed by employed workers eighteen years of age and over averaged 10.8 years compared with the national median of 12.3 years in March 1968. About three fifths of the employed Blacks eighteen years of age and over had not completed high school, as was the case for about three fourths of Puerto Ricans. In fact, among Puerto Ricans nearly half of all the employed workers had eight years or less of school. Unemployed workers in these areas had even lower levels of educational attainment.

Black male household heads earned more than Black women heading households who were working full time. Puerto Rican women employed full time earned less than Puerto Rican men who were working full time. A substantial proportion of families and single individuals—better than one in four—reported incomes below the poverty line as defined by the Social Security Administration.[5]

Another study in New York City, of families who received welfare assistance points out some other aspects of the family situation of poor families. Husbands were present in only about one fourth of the households. The mothers tended to be young, nearly 40 per cent were under thirty, 40 per cent were in their thirties, and the remainder were forty and over. About two thirds of the families had three or more children at home who were under nineteen. Eleven per cent of the families lived in public housing. One out of two mothers grew up in a small town or rural area. About half of the mothers grew up in homes with two parents, the rest had only one parent. About half of the mothers had attended high school, but only one out of six of these had graduated.[6]

[5] Condensed from *News*, Bureau of Labor Statistics, Middle Atlantic Regional Office, New York, U.S. Department of Labor, Oct. 30, 1969.
[6] I. Cox, "Families on Welfare in New York City," *Welfare in Review*, Vol. 6 (March–April 1968), pp. 22–26.

Children and Poverty

Older people and children under the age of eighteen were the two groups most heavily represented among the poor. Often two fifths of the population in poverty areas are children under age eighteen.

Poverty is a problem particularly for the children of the poor. Through no fault of their own they are very likely to enter adulthood poorly prepared to cope with the world.

Wickenden has made a plea for children's right to a better chance in life:

> I am against people being forced out of school by the discouragements of poverty and then being denied the right to earn a livelihood because they have no diplomas. I am against children growing up with bad teeth, poisoned tonsils, and uncorrected defects. . . . I am against the small heart-breaks that seem inconsequential only to those who do not experience them; the child to

Figure 9.2. Poverty is found in many places. This girl lives in a large city. (USDA)

Figure 9.3. Many programs have been tried to help youngsters from low-income families. *Left:* Children of migrant farm workers at a child-care center in New York State. *Right:* Youngsters at a camp for underprivileged boys and girls. (USDA)

whom Santa Claus cannot bring the tricycle . . . the adolescent girl who cannot dazzle with a new dress at the high school dance.[7]

Children learn early that they are poor, and because they are poor they may be treated differently from children who are more fortunate. A mother who received welfare payments to supplement her earnings testified at a Congressional hearing: "Where I live children feel the stigma of being welfare recipients. . . . They'd rather go hungry than let the neighbors know they're on welfare."[8] Another woman described what happened when her children had a free lunch at school. "They push the welfare children aside until the paying children are served."[9]

Proposals for improving the situation of the poor child abound. As a nation we seem to have accepted the premise that the school, from pre-kindergarten up, should be used to help disadvantaged youngsters.

[7] Elizabeth Wickenden. "The Legal Right to a Minimum But Adequate Level of Living," *Journal of Home Economics*, Vol. 59 (1967), p. 14.

[8] *The New York Times*, June 6, 1969, p. 45.

[9] Ibid.

Effective implementation has bogged down because of differences in how this could best be accomplished and an unwillingness to commit the funds that are needed.

Also, we do not yet seem committed to the idea that it is necessary to improve the home setting at the same time that we help the youngsters directly. And yet one of the most widely heralded studies of why poor children don't succeed in school suggests that this may be the most important factor in influencing their school performance.[10]

Life Styles of Low-Income Families

Money is the yardstick by which some people measure another's worth or status. It may not be a good yardstick, but it is widely used. When a person has very little money he tends to be classified at the bottom of the social structure. In addition, one's financial status determines the specific environment in which he lives as well as his relationship to it.

In our society, a continuously low income is directly associated with certain life situations. Poorer, more crowded living quarters, reduced access to education and recreation, occupational restriction to simpler, manual types of work—these similar characteristics of the very poor are sufficiently obvious to need no underlining. The result of these circumstances is a set of life conditions that is not so obvious. These conditions consist of four general limitations:

1. *Limited alternatives.* The poor, of all the strata in society, have the slightest opportunity to experience varieties of social and cultural settings. Their own setting is one of the least intricacy and flexibility. Throughout life, they experience a very narrow range of situations and demands. Their repertoire of social roles is limited. They seldom participate in any activity which takes them out of the daily routine. They rarely play roles of leadership or fill any position calling for specialized functioning. On their jobs they confront less complex situations and have fewer, less diverse standards to meet. Socially, they seldom go beyond the borders of kinship and neighborhood groups—people very like themselves.

2. *Helplessness.* The position of the poor vis-à-vis society and its institutions is one of impotence. They have practically no bargaining power in the working world. Unskilled and uneducated, they are the most easily replaced workers. The skills they do have are minimal, of little importance in productive processes. On the job itself, the very poor man can exercise little autonomy and has small opportunity to influence conditions of work. He is close to helpless even to acquire information and training which would change this situation. He has neither the knowledge nor the means to get it.

3. *Deprivation.* It is reasonable to suspect that this general condition, almost universally associated with poverty, is felt with particular intensity in

[10] James S. Coleman, et al., *Equality of Educational Opportunity* (Washington, D.C.: U.S. Government Printing Office, 1966).

American society. Deprivation is, after all, relative. When it is defined as lack of resources relative to felt wants and needs, it is evident that America has one of the greatest gaps between generally accepted goals and the extent to which the lower class can realistically expect to attain them. As a nation, we stress, perhaps inordinately, the value and virtue of high attainment. We expect and applaud efforts at self-improvement and upward social mobility. Commercial advertising attempts to stimulate and increase desire for status achievement. The richness of life in the rest of society is well displayed—on television, in newspapers, on billboards, in store windows, on the very streets themselves. All this, plus awareness that some people have actually succeeded in the strenuous upward move, make the condition of the unachieving poor one of unremitting deprivation. Their relative deprivation is, perhaps, the condition which more than anything else affects the life-view of the poor. Constant awareness of their own abject status and the "failure" which it rightly or wrongly implies understandably leads to embarrassed withdrawal and isolation.

4. *Insecurity*. People of low income are more at the mercy of life's unpredictability than are the more affluent. Sickness, injury, loss of work, legal problems—a range of hazardous possibilities—may overwhelm anyone. But to the poor man they are especially fearful. His resources are more sparse. His savings, if any, are quickly expended in any sizable emergency. Certain conditions of his life make emergencies more likely. His work skills are more expendable, sometimes more dependent on seasonal demands. He is more likely to lose his job on short notice. An emergency expenditure of funds may mean the postponing of rent payments and the fear of eviction. He is unable to secure for himself and his family the regular, preventive health measures which would fend off medical emergencies. He often finds that he cannot successfully navigate the channels involved in using public sources of emergency help, such as clinics and legal aid agencies.[11]

Isolation, as well as a great deal of friction, may arise from the general expectations low-income husbands and wives have of each other. The husband regards the home as a retreat for the satisfaction of physical needs. Accordingly, the husband places primary value on the nonemotional aspects of the wife's role. A "good wife" is one who prepares the meals for the family, keeps his clothing in order, raises the children, and frees him from everyday worries. In short, the husband conceptualizes the wife's role as housekeeper-mother. This is antithetical to the wife's wish for emphasis on the interpersonal aspects of marriage. It is not that she resists the performance of household and motherly duties but rather, that she resents the husband's limitations of the marital relationship to these tasks. It has been suggested that much of the tension observed in the families of the poor arises from this basic conflict in role expectation.

Hence, the low-income wife must endure emotional deprivation as well

[11] Lola M. Irelan and Arthur Besner, "Low-Income Outlook on Life," in Lola M. Irelan, ed., *Low Income Life Styles*, Division of Research, Welfare Administration, U.S. Department of Health, Education, and Welfare, 1966, pp. 1–3.

as the fear of physical-economic deprivation. She is handicapped, however, by her subservient position vis-à-vis her husband and by her view of men from managing the marital relationship to serve her needs better. What might also be thought of as a handicap is the special significance of marriage to the low-income woman. Women in the lower socioeconomic strata are likely to find it difficult to think of themselves in a role other than the familial one. They tend to feel somewhat lost after outgrowing the daughter role and look to the wife-mother role to regain a clear-cut familial status. Some family sociologists have suggested this as a reason for the fact that women in the lower socioeconomic classes marry at a younger age than women in higher social classes. Furthermore, from the low-income woman's viewpoint, a husband offers the most tangible opportunity for love and security and represents a defense against the workings of the unpredictable world. The wife is wary about asserting herself against the husband lest he leave her, though the gap between the ideal and the real husband may be great.

The special significance of motherhood may arise from economic deprivation as well as the emotional deprivation in the husband-wife relationship. Being denied most of the tangible and intangible satisfactions of marriage, the low-income woman defines herself mainly as a mother and seeks gratification in life through this function. The limited outside interests also increase the significance of motherhood.

The female-based household is a widely prevalent and persisting form among the poor. It has been estimated that between 25 and 40 per cent of the child-rearing units in urban "slum" areas are of this type. Usually such a household will consist of one or more women of child-bearing age, often related by blood or through marriage and spanning two or more generations—for example, the "single parent" and her mother and/or aunt. Associated with this household type is a marriage pattern in which the woman has a succession of temporary partners during her procreative years.

Some research suggests that this type of family is not entirely disadvantageous. We have noted the minimal economic contribution of the husband and father and his insistence on being recognized as the family head without making substantial commitments to the family. Frequently it is the husband who is the economic burden—low-income women often have more success in obtaining and holding a job than men. It may be a gamble to marry and risk losing control over a small income. In short, middle-class ideals of marriage for economic support, love, and companionship simply are not realistic.

The permissive psychological techniques of child rearing are often impossible in a low-income setting. A middle-class child with a temper tantrum can be sent to his own room until the storm is over. When an entire family lives in two rooms, however, a screaming child cannot be isolated and must be silenced. When a husbandless woman works all day to support

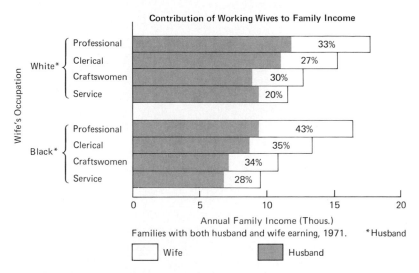

Figure 9.4. Black women workers earned a greater proportion of family income than did white women, reflecting, in part, the lower incomes of black male workers. (USDA)

her family, it is next to impossible for her to avoid making more than ordinary demands on her older children.

In almost every phase of health care and behavior, the poor behave differently from the middle-class and more affluent sectors of American society. They have higher prevalence rates for many diseases, including schizophrenia. They have less accurate health information. Illness is defined differently. They are less inclined to take preventive measures, delay longer in seeking health care, and participate less in community health programs.

When income is uncertain and not always enough to cover rent and food, "health" is understandably likely to be defined as the ability to keep working. Treatment is postponed until disability is threatened. In reasonable sequence with this economic definition of health, a family's wage earner often gets medical care that other members do without. Going to the clinic for a child may mean that the mother has to take a day off without pay.

The hardships of poverty seem to nudge health downward in the hierarchy of values. When a household is operating with a minimum of material necessities, first aspirations are for concrete, physical improvement— for a better place to live, for more and better household equipment, even for some luxuries. Health comes further down the list.[12]

[12] This discussion of health is based on Lola M. Irelan, "Health Practices of the Poor," in Lola M. Irelan, ed., *Low-Income Life Styles*. Division of Research, Welfare Administration, U.S. Department of Health, Education, and Welfare, 1966, pp. 51, 57.

Figure 9.5. This family has just moved into a low-rent house built with a government subsidy. (Bureau of Indian Affairs, U.S. Department of the Interior)

The Spending of Low-Income Families

Low-income families spend a high proportion of their income on food, clothing, and shelter. Consequently, they have a tiny proportion of their small income available for other things.

From a practical point of view a low income severely limits one's choices in the market place. First of all, a person with a low income is limited to buying things when he desperately needs them, from a place that he can get to, or uses because he can get credit there. Secondly, the low-income buyer is less likely to know all the alternatives available or where to go for information and help. Third, he cannot take advantage of sales by buying extra amounts. "If a mother has to feed a family, she cannot forego buying milk in order to purchase five extra cans of beans which happen to be on sale at six for a dollar."[13] Nor can they delay purchasing until a time when prices might be lower. "Can you imagine the effectiveness of telling a poor family that buying clothes a half-year ahead of time will save them money?"[14] They haven't enough money for their immediate needs and, therefore, cannot afford to commit money for future needs.

There have been a number of studies to determine whether or not prices in low-income areas are higher.[15] In general, the prices of food in certain stores, such as supermarkets, seem to be close to those in similar stores in middle-income neighborhoods nearby. The big difference is that in many low-income neighborhoods there are very few big supermarkets. Most of the stores are small food stores, which tend to have higher prices than the chain-store supermarkets. Where there are supermarkets the quality of food sold is often poorer than in middle-income neighborhoods. Also, some stores in low-income areas raise prices on days when people in the neighborhood get money, as, for instance, the day welfare checks are received.

Prices for nonfood items such as television sets, furniture, and pots and pans generally are higher in low-income neighborhoods. Among the reasons that have been given for this are that the cost of doing business is higher in low-income areas, and also that merchants take advantage of the people.

Rents for apartments in low-income areas of cities generally are high for poor facilities, in comparison with the rents in many middle-income areas.

Home Management Problems

Who is the homemaker with a low income? She is likely to be the mother of a large family with a husband who is absent, ill, unemployed, or earning very little. Perhaps she is a widow past the age of sixty-five, living on a modest pension of Social Security. In some cases the homemaker is a man.

---

[13] Treinah Meyers, "The Extra Cost of Being Poor," *Journal of Home Economics,* Vol. 62 (1970), p. 381.

[14] Ibid., p. 380.

[15] These studies are listed in the Selected References at the end of this chapter.

The home management job of the low-income homemaker is much more difficult than that of a more fortunate person.

> One of the first things we saw was hunger. . . . Lack of money means no food and no food means hunger. . . . I can still hear the angry retort of one of my neighbors in the housing project when the welfare department said it could not make a needed adjustment in her check until the following month, June. "And what am I supposed to do," she asked, "starve in May?"[16]

Usually the family with a low income lives in a place that is run-down and dirty. Perhaps it is a decrepit slum apartment or a crumbling farmhouse. Often the family is cramped together in a very few rooms. The combination of an old run-down structure and cramped quarters makes it hard to organize the living space into an easy working arrangement.

Then, too, it is much more difficult to take care of a place that is in poor condition. Many families live in places that haven't been painted in a long time. Often the plumbing is poor. There may be inadequate heat and hot water. The home may be badly in need of other repairs.

There are few, if any, convenience tools. Some lucky families own a washing machine. Most do not. The refrigerator may be small and not work well. It probably doesn't hold frozen foods, or, if it does, can't keep them frozen. Time-saving cleaning products are too expensive to buy.

The homemaker with a low income is often a woman trying to do two jobs. In the city she may work outside the home as well as care for her family. If she lives in a rural area she may be trying to farm poor, neglected land and care for her family.

Moreover, her family is frequently larger than average. This means that she has more housework than the oft-quoted middle-income family with two or three children.

The homemaker and her family may not have much energy or may have chronic health problems. A wholesome diet may have been lacking for a long time. Medical care was probably a hit-or-miss affair at best.

In actual fact, the low-income homemaker must be more efficient than the average woman just to keep things going at home. She probably cannot afford to buy everything new and must reuse hand-me-down clothing and castoffs to some extent, particularly for children. Cleaning has to be done the slow, hard way in a home that is not easy to care for. Outside services are a luxury that the homemaker cannot afford. If the stove or bathroom needs repair, she and her family will probably have to do what they can without skilled help. Food shopping for a larger than average family must be done frequently because of inadequate or poor storage facilities.

[16] Camille Jeffers, "Hunger, Hustlin' and Homemaking," *Journal of Home Economics*, Vol. 61 (1969), pp. 756–757.

	Police Charges	2.5 times more
	Ambulance Runs	almost twice as many
	Fire Calls	almost twice as many
	Visiting Nurse Calls	4 times more
	Health Services	2.2 times more
	Welfare Services	14 times more

Figure 9.6. Poverty is expensive for the community. (U.S. Department of Health, Education, and Welfare)

Unfortunately, the homemaker with a low income is often more poorly prepared for her job than the woman with a better income.

> Poverty means much more than lack of cash, it means lack of education, lack of capacity to plan and direct your life . . . lack of capacity to change the conditions under which you live.[17]

Except for special groups who are living for a portion of their lives at a low-income level, such as graduate students or retired couples or families

[17] Address by Ronald V. Perrin, director of the New Jersey Antipoverty Migrant Opportunity Program at the annual meeting of the Consumers League of New Jersey, Montclair, New Jersey, May 1966.

who have had a major reverse of one sort or another, most homemakers with low incomes are poorly educated and unaware of how to change their own situation. They may not only lack job skills but also the ability to deal effectively with their environment, the landlord, the school, the health department, and the many problems that arise.

On top of all this, the family with a low income often lacks money even for their family's basic needs. Certainly, it is very far from being able to afford the package of goods and services that most people have come to believe is the right of every American.

Case Studies of Minority Groups

One of the major problems in working with people from minority backgrounds is that it is hard for outsiders to recognize how deeply their values and behavior are rooted in their culture and needs. The following case studies suggest some of the difficulties that subgroups must face when they are trying to enter the mainstream of American life.

The Black Family

That the Negro American has survived at all is extraordinary—a lesser people might simply have died out, as indeed others have. But the Negro American community has . . . paid a fearful price for the incredible mistreatment to which it has been subjected over the past three centuries.

In essence, the Negro community has been forced into a matriarchal structure which, because it is so out of line with the rest of the American society, seriously retards the progress of the group as a whole, and imposes a crushing burden on the Negro male and, in consequence, on a great many Negro women as well.

There is, presumably, no special reason why a society in which males are dominant in family relationships is to be preferred to a matriarchal arrangement. However, it is clearly a disadvantage for a minority group to be operating on one principle, while the great majority of the population, and the one with the most advantages to begin with, is operating on another. This is the present situation of the Negro. Ours is a society which presumes male leadership in private and public affairs. The arrangements of society facilitate such leadership and reward it. A subculture, such as that of the Negro American, in which this is not the pattern is placed at a distinct disadvantage.

There is much evidence that a considerable number of Negro families have managed to . . . establish themselves as stable, effective units, living according to patterns of American society in general. While this phenomenon is not easily measured, one index is that middle-class Negroes have even fewer children than middle-class whites, indicating a desire to conserve the advances they have made and to insure that their children do as well or better.

It might be estimated that as much as half of the Negro community falls into the middle class. However, the remaining half is in desperate and deteriorating circumstances. Moreover, because of housing segregation it is immensely difficult for the stable half to escape from the cultural influences of the unstable one. The children of middle-class Negroes often as not must grow up in, or next to the slums, an experience almost unknown to white middle-class children. . . .

Most Negro youth are in danger of being caught up in the tangle of pathology that affects their world, and probably a majority are so entrapped. Many of those who escape do so for one generation only: as things now are, their children may have to run the gauntlet all over again. That is not the least vicious aspect of the world that white America has made for the Negro.

Obviously, not every instance of social pathology afflicting the Negro community can be traced to the weakness of family structure. If, for example, organized crime in the Negro community were not largely controlled by whites, there would be more capital accumulation among Negroes, and therefore probably more Negro business enterprises. If it were not for the hostility and fear many whites exhibit towards Negroes, they in turn would be less afflicted by hostility and fear and so on. There is no one Negro community. There is no one Negro problem. There is no one solution. Nonetheless, at the center of the tangle of pathology is the weakness of the family structure. Once or twice removed, it will be found to be the principal source of most of the aberrant, inadequate, or antisocial behavior that did not establish, but now serves to perpetuate the cycle of poverty and deprivation.

A fundamental fact of Negro American family life is the often reversed roles of husband and wife. The matriarchal pattern of so many Negro families reinforces itself over the generations. This process begins with education. Although the gap appears to be closing at the moment, for a long while, Negro females were better educated than Negro males, and this remains true today for the Negro population as a whole.[18]

The Puerto Rican Family

Not long ago, I met a Sister who had been in Puerto Rico for many years teaching school. Now she is teaching here in a parochial school that has many Puerto Rican students. She was complaining of how different the children here are from those she had taught on the Island. She said to me: "With such a beautiful Island, why do they come up here where they lose all their gracious manners?"

It seemed to me that the Sister had missed a point. While she taught in the Island, she did not acquire a knowledge of the personality and culture of the Puerto Ricans and she could not understand the struggle that these poor children were having in trying to grow up in an environment so alien to their warm personality. The terrible confusion that the family goes through in the uprooting from one country to another is keenly felt by the children and adolescents and they reflect it in their behavior.

Many studies have been made of Puerto Rican society and culture to determine what distinguishes them from others. These studies have not been

[18] Excerpt from *The Negro Family: The Case for National Action*, Office and Policy Planning and Research, U.S. Department of Labor, 1965, Chap. IV.

able to pinpoint any particular trait that distinguishes Puerto Ricans in terms of national character, from other peoples of the western world. However, these studies pointed out what we Puerto Ricans knew long before, that class differences in cultural patterns were in many particulars more significant than the common factor. In-other words, Puerto Ricans from the mountain sections are different from those of the city slum areas, and an upper class family's way of acting differs greatly from that of a working man's family at a coffee plantation. Although there are differences in behavior and although the studies came to the conclusion that there is nothing distinctive about the Puerto Rican people's culture, I feel that the Puerto Rican is identified by common sentiments and traditions which we term "dignidad," "respeto," and "cariño": dignity, self-worth, respect and love. These characteristics are hard to analyze. They are not learned from books but are transmitted from family to family through the years.

"Dignidad" is a quality which gives depth to a person in the feeling of being someone. It is an inner value of himself expressed in many of the circumstances of life. Because of this "dignidad," a man will choose the intangible rather than the materialistic desires of life. This quality is complemented by "respeto" which makes a Puerto Rican understand his place and act accordingly. It does not matter whether he is rich or poor, white or black, a Puerto Rican knows what is expected of him in his relations with his friends, relatives, and other people. Because of this, he acts with "dignidad" and expects "respeto" just as he will give "respeto" to others as his obligation in the extensive network of his loyalties.

Let me tell you little stories that illustrate some of our traditions of "dignidad," "respeto," and "cariño."

R—— is a young teenager in Brooklyn. His family is poor but hard working, and both parents have tried to raise their children in the traditional Puerto Rican way and the family has tried to live with "dignidad." R needed shoes, but Sister knew he would never accept money from us. So we asked him to wash our car and then Sister gave him an envelope with money as a "little gift." That afternoon he came back to us with a beautiful African violet plant. He had spent the money in a grateful gift to the Sisters. Wasteful, some practical minds may say but, to me, watching R going down the stairs, he expressed his "dignidad," "respeto," and "cariño" as a Puerto Rican would ever do. This was part of his great Spanish heritage, the depth of which he could not put into words, except to feel that it was a major justification of his behavior.

Another story: Last year when I was in Puerto Rico in the summer, I went to visit the little town of Cabo Rojo where I had worked as a missionary for nine years. As I visited some old friends, I saw this old lady waiting for me on the road. She said: "Sister, while you were with us, I never was able to give you anything. But today when I saw you down the street, I rejoiced because I could give you a little present." Putting her hands in her apron pocket, she brought out five beautiful fresh eggs as her gift.

To a Puerto Rican, it does not matter whether he is poor or rich, or how much or little education, he has a place with *dignidad* as a person in his society. He has self-respect and he is aware that other people in his society respect him. So, you can imagine what happens when he comes to this country and finds that honor and prestige here are measured by achievement and success and that to uphold his "dignidad," he must compete and grow rich in material possessions.

Juan is an example of this clash of values. When Juan came to New York, he had a happy family. His wife, Lola, and his four children respected him as the head of the family, the provider, and the authority for all. Juan worked hard and kept them reasonably happy. But as time went on and the children became older, he could not keep up with the society around him. His teen-age girls wanted special clothes; his boys wanted to be better dressed; the wife wanted better furniture. Juan's job was not enough. The wife went to work to help and Juan lost part of his authority because he was not the sole provider. To cover up, he began to gamble, hoping to make the money to provide what he could not do by work. When the man loses his "dignidad," his sense of self-worth, he loses his sense of his obligations to others. Conflict began and poor Juan's family is fast becoming a "problem family."

As one becomes acquainted with the Puerto Rican people and their life "back home," one realizes the staggering list of things they must accept and become accustomed to in adapting to city life. So let us look at some aspects of the Puerto Rican way of life at home which will help you to understand them better in their assimilation into this new way of life.

The family is extensive. The family is the integral unit of Puerto Rican society and differs in many ways from the typical American family, because the culture stresses different values. To a Puerto Rican, family life is a key-stone. His innate joy of living, born of his hospitality and generosity, pre-vails over interests in material things. The Puerto Rican family is extensive. Someone has called this extensive family the Puerto Rican social security plan. Everyone knows his neighbors and depends upon family and friends for sup-port in situations of crisis. The extensive family does not only comprise the members of the nuclear family. It also includes the many relatives, such as aunts, uncles, cousins, grandparents, and especially the *padrinos* and *com-padres*, godparents and co-parents of the baptismal ceremony. With these latter, there is a special network of relationship which is very sacred. A child is brought up to feel that he is never alone, but that around him there is a network of relationships that will ever sustain him and help him. Therefore, if a child is deprived of his parents because of sickness, death or some other cause, the relatives usually take over and, without any legal procedure, adopt the child. There is great security for the child in the environment of Puerto Rican culture.

When I was working in Puerto Rico, the mother of 10 children died when her 11th baby was born. I felt sorry for the father and worried about the children and who would take care of them. The day after the funeral I visited them. All was in perfect order. The oldest girl, 14 years old, had taken over the care of her father and two children. The baby and the rest were already happily adjusting, each one to a new family that had adopted them im-mediately after the mother died.

The Puerto Rican child accepts the responsibility of belonging to this extended family as an integral part of himself and in his role he knows he cannot fail them if he wants to win "dignidad-respeto-cariño" as he grows older.

To the Puerto Rican, emphasis on his family is the training he gets from the very beginning of his life. He learns that whether in business or in feasting, you always defer to your own relatives first. You can see one of the great stresses the Puerto Rican child has in the United States where his extended family is not around him to give him support and security and when he sees his own family losing face in the many problems that confront the stranger in a big city.

Last summer, a young teacher at the University of Ponce told me he was driving in a "público" (a taxi) and asked the chauffeur if he had a big family. "Muy grande, maestro" (very big, teacher), so the teacher thought 10 or 12 children. He asked, "How old is the oldest child?" The chauffeur answered, "Oh, I have no children, but a big family, four uncles, five aunts, ten cousins."

A public health nurse in New York City was quite perturbed because of the conduct of Mrs. Ramos, a young Puerto Rican mother. Mrs. Ramos brought her child to the clinic and the nurse told her that the child had to be vaccinated for diphtheria. Mrs. Ramos refused because she said she had to ask her husband. The nurse was very upset and thought Mrs. Ramos was avoiding or neglecting her duty to her child. Great was her surprise when Mrs. Ramos returned to the clinic the next day all smiles; her husband had said "yes."

The family structure in Puerto Rico is a patriarchal unit and is under the complete domination of the husband or father. Man is head of the house. His authority is unquestioned. He is expected to be the provider, to do the family shopping, to make the important decisions, to discipline the children. This is so much a part of our life that it seems strange to expect any other attitude in family relations. In the incident which was related, the woman could not make a decision unless her husband consented.

The woman's role is one of submission and dependency. She is expected to obey her husband and to ask his permission to go visiting or to do anything outside her established duties. She is not allowed to dance or talk to any man unless her husband gives her permission. In all things, she defers to her husband. The man is very jealous. She serves and cares for her husband and children. She does not sit or leave until all is well. That is why some come late for meetings.

. . . In return, the man protects the woman in a way which reminds us of the old-time Spanish chivalry. . . . There are variations, and we begin to see these even in . . . Puerto Rico.

Children are expected to obey implicitly the head of the house. They are given responsibility early in their lives, sometimes beyond their capacity. Older children are assigned the task of caring for younger brothers and sisters. It is taken for granted that the oldest son is next in authority, with almost the same rights as his parents to enforce the family discipline.

The contrasting social education of the children gives the male in Puerto Rican society a different outlook about sex conduct. Boys are given more freedom; girls are well protected. Girls have little freedom to associate with boys.

Although the boy is given a great amount of freedom, the girl is often overprotected. Once she becomes a teenager, she is not allowed out of her parents' sight. Here we see a source of conflict for the adolescent . . . where other children are given much more freedom than Puerto Rican parents can accept as possible to give their children.[19]

Older Americans

Many older people lack enough money to maintain themselves comfortably in spite of benefit programs such as Social Security. Retirement benefits have not kept pace with the rising cost of living, so older people

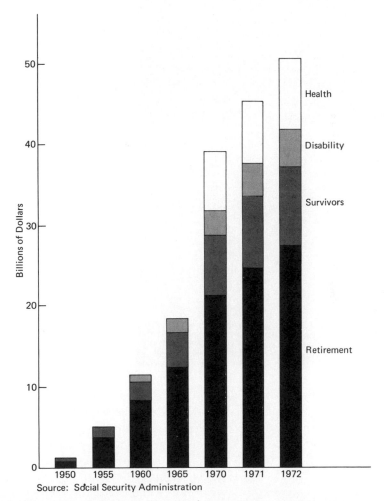

Figure 9.7. Total benefits paid under the Social Security Program have increased greatly from 1950 to 1972. (Social Security Administration)

[19] Excerpt from Sister Thomas Marie, "Puerto Rican Culture," *Public Health News,* New Jersey State Department of Health, Vol. 43 (Aug. 1962), pp. 235–240.

Figure 9.8. Some people develop hobbies and interests as young people that they can continue all their lives. (U.S. Department of Health, Education, and Welfare)

are particularly hard hit by inflation, which means greater costs for the things they buy. Medical expenses, which have been rising in cost faster than some segments of the economy, are a big expense item for many older people. A great deal of help has been provided by the government programs of Medicare and Medicaid, but a major illness is still a problem financially as well as functionally for many.

Older people may need to spend more time doing the regular household chores and caring for their own personal needs. They may have less energy, in addition to physical limitations that make it harder and slower to do some things.

Older people often have time on their hands. They need to make new friends and develop new interests. Old friends move away, become ill, or die. Their children may be far away and busy with their own jobs and families. Some interests and activities are no longer possible to carry on because of limitations of energy or income.

> At present most people dread old age. A much more sensible approach would be to prepare for old age, to provide the conditions in which the aging population would have a place and a function, and to educate people so that their later leisure years are happy ones.
>
> Facilities and good care are needed, but these are not enough. What is also needed is for people to approach the later leisure years with the attitudes and skills for a successful retirement. This is a job of education. Just as people now prepare for working years, they might also prepare for retirement ones.
>
> Schools and community agencies could expand their function by helping people develop a constructive attitude toward older people and their own old age. They might also do more to help young people develop interests in activities they could carry on through their later years.
>
> Community service projects also offer an opportunity to use the abilities of older people. Many could contribute more if the channels of communication were expanded so that older people would feel wanted and also learn where in the community they could contribute.
>
> Modern science and medicine promise still longer life and healthier later years. Will this be a gift or a burden? [20]

Summary

Old people and children under the age of eighteen are the two groups most heavily represented among the poor. Poverty is particularly a problem for the children of the poor. Through no fault of their own they are very likely to enter adulthood poorly prepared to cope with the world.

In our society, a continuously low income is directly associated with certain life situations—poor and crowded living quarters, reduced access to education and recreation, and occupational restrictions. As a result of these conditions the poor have four types of limitations. The first is limited alternatives, in work, living situations, and experience in the world. The second is helplessness in relation to many of the institutions and organizations of society. The third is deprivation. Sometimes even the most basic needs may not be met. Psychological needs are rarely met. The fourth limitation is insecurity. People with low incomes are more at the mercy of life's unpredictability than are the more affluent.

From a practical point of view a low income severely limits choices in the market place. The person with a low income is limited to buying

---

[20] Irene Oppenheim, *The Family As Consumers*, New York: Macmillan, 1965, p. 271.

things when he desperately needs them, from a place that he can get to, or must use solely because he can get credit there.

In fact, the low-income homemaker needs to be more efficient than the average woman just to keep things going at home. She probably has a larger than average family, is more likely to have an outside job, has a home with poor equipment. which is in poor condition, may live far from shopping, have little transportation, and has very little money to spend.

One of the major problems in working with people from low-income backgrounds is that it is hard for outsiders to recognize the extent to which their values and behavior are rooted in their culture and needs.

Older people often lack enough money to maintain themselves comfortably. Also, they often do not have a feeling of functioning or belonging in our youth-oriented culture. Much could be done to improve their economic, physical, and social situation.

CHAPTER FOLLOW-UP

1. If you were planning to work with mothers or students from a low-income group, what would be some of the things that you ought to know before you meet with them?
2. How would you go about finding these things out?
3. One of the most frequently voiced criticisms of programs for the low-income group is that the people for whom the program is designed have had no part in planning it. How could you involve the participants in planning a program?
4. Try and picture yourself as the mother in a poor family new to the city. What are some of the things that you might find helpful in a community program? In a school program?
5. Do you think that a single type of program can be effective, such as a nutrition education program, or a child care program? If so, why? If not, why not?
6. Many people are fearful of "outsiders" from groups they have not known before. How might you try to handle this fearfulness if you were planning to work in a low-income housing project or a school in a poverty-stricken area?
7. What are some of the things that you think might be done to eradicate or reduce poverty in this country?
8. Have a committee investigate what programs and facilities for older people are available in your community.

SELECTED REFERENCES

Brooks, Mildred J. "Home Management Field Experiences in a Welfare Department." *Actualizing Concepts in Home Management*, Washington, D.C.: American Home Economics Association, 1974, pp. 49–50.

Caplowitz, David. *The Poor Pay More*. New York: The Free Press, 1963.

Chilman, Catherine S. "Child-Rearing and Family Relationship Patterns of the Very Poor," *Welfare in Review* (Jan. 1965). Reprinted by the Welfare Administration, U.S. Department of Health, Education, and Welfare.

Coleman, James S., et al. *Equality of Educational Opportunity.* Washington, D.C.: U.S. Government Printing Office, 1966.

"Consumer Problems of the Poor: Supermarket Operations in Low Income Areas and the Federal Response." Thirty-eighth Report by the Committee on Government Operations, House Report No. 1851. Washington, D.C.: U.S. Government Printing Office, 1968.

Family Budget Standard. New York: Community Council of Greater New York. (Revised annually.)

"Federal Trade Commission Report on District of Columbia Consumer Protection Program." Washington, D.C.: U.S. Government Printing Office, 1968.

Goodman, Charles S. "Do the Poor Pay More?" *Journal of Marketing.* Vol. 32 (Jan. 1968), pp. 18–24.

Gould, Nathan. "Cultural Perspectives on the Education of the Poor," in Milly Cowles, ed., *Perspectives in the Education of Disadvantaged Children.* Cleveland: The World Publishing Co., 1967, pp. 33–53.

Groom, Phyllis, "Prices in Poor Neighborhoods." *Monthly Labor Review* (Oct. 1966), pp. 1085–1090.

Herzog, Elizabeth. "Facts and Fictions About the Poor," in "Perspectives on Poverty." Reprint No. 2604 from the *Monthly Labor Review* (Feb. 1969), pp. 42–49.

Irelan, Lola M., ed. *Low Income Life Styles.* Washington, D.C.: Division of Research, Welfare Administration, U.S. Department of Health, Education, and Welfare, 1966.

Jeffers, Camille. "Hunger, Hustlin' and Homemaking." *Journal of Home Economics,* Vol. 61 (1969), pp. 756–757.

Kain, John F. *Race and Poverty: The Economics of Discrimination.* Englewood Cliffs, N.J.: Prentice-Hall, Inc., 1969.

Katz, Carol Hecht, ed. *The Law and the Low Income Consumer.* Project on Social Welfare Law, Supplement No. 2, New York University School of Law, 1968.

Lynch, Jeanette. *30 Days on the Food Stamp Plan.* Cooperative Extension Service, Colorado State University, 1966.

Marion, Bruce W., Lois A. Simonds, and Dan E. Moore. *Food Marketing in Low Income Areas.* Cooperative Extension Service, Ohio State University, n.d.

Meyers, Treinah. "The Extra Cost of Being Poor." *Journal of Home Economics,* Vol. 62 (1970), pp. 379–384.

The Negro Family: The Case for National Action. Washington, D.C.: Office of Policy Planning and Research, U.S. Department of Labor, 1965.

Newman, Dorothy K. "Changing Attitudes About the Poor," in "Perspectives on Poverty." Reprint No. 2604 from the *Monthly Labor Review* (Feb. 1969), pp. 32–36.

Older Americans. Washington, D.C.: U.S. Department of Housing and Urban Development, 1973.

Orshansky, Mollie. "How Poverty Is Measured," in "Perspectives on Poverty." Reprint No. 2604 from the *Monthly Labor Review* (Feb. 1969), pp. 37–41.

Proctor, Samuel D. "Stability of the Black Family and the Black Community." *Families of the Future.* Ames, Ia.: The Iowa State University Press, 1972, pp. 104–115.

Rainwater, Lee. "Crucible of Identity: The Negro Lower-Class Family." *Daedalus,* Vol. 95, No. 1 (Winter 1966), pp. 172–216.

Reagan, Barbara B. "Definition of Poverty." *Journal of Home Economics,* Vol. 59 (1967), pp. 290–294.

"A Study of Prices Charged in Food Stores Located in Low- and Higher-Income Areas of Six Large Cities, February 1966." Bureau of Labor Statistics, U.S. Department of Labor, 1966.

"A Study of Prices Charged in Stores Located in Low- and Higher-Income Areas of Six Large Cities for Non-Food Items." Bureau of Labor Statistics, U.S. Department of Labor, 1966.

The Social and Economic Status of the Black Population in the United States, 1973. Washington, D.C.: U.S. Department of Commerce, 1974.

Stewart, Alice. "Making Homemaking Modern for Low Income Consumers." *1969 Report: National Home Appliance Conference.* Chicago, Ill.: Association of Home Appliance Manufacturers, 1969, pp. 45–48.

Sturdivant, Frederick D., and Walter T. Wilhelm. "Poverty, Minorities, and Consumer Exploitation." *Social Science Quarterly,* Vol. 49 (Dec. 1968), pp. 643–650.

Wickenden, Elizabeth. "The Legal Right to a Minimum But Adequate Level of Living." *Journal of Home Economics,* Vol. 59 (1967), pp. 14–19.

Working with Low Income Families. Washington, D.C.: American Home Economics Association, 1965.

chapter 10

---

the employed
woman

Industrialization dramatically altered the work role of
women in the Western world. Many of the productive
tasks that were formerly done at home are now done outside the household. As their work at home decreased,
women began to move out into the community. At first,
they took on responsibilities for the care of the sick and
education of the young, responsibilities that were very
much in the Judaeo-Christian tradition. In a sense, they
continued activities outside the home that had once been
confined to the home.[1] Gradually the scope of their
activities increased. Today women are found in just about
every field that employs men.

[1] Margaret Mead, *Women in Mass Society* (Boston: Beacon Press,
1962), p. 6.

Why Women Work

Women work for a variety of reasons. Some have no choice. They need the money badly. Perhaps they are the sole support of themselves and others. Maybe their husband's income is inadequate.

Others want to raise the family's standard of living, to provide luxuries, a better home, a college education for a child, or other needs.

Some women work because they want to be with other people. They may find that housekeeping doesn't keep them busy enough or that they are too isolated at home. Many women who are full time homemakers feel isolated from adult company during the day, particularly when the children are small.

Today many a young wife comes to marriage unprepared for the repetitive, routine nature of housework and child care. Watching her husband rush off to the office, well groomed and freshly shaven, some women presume that the outside world is much more exciting and glamorous than the one in which they spend their days at home. By comparison, cooking meals, picking up after children, and making the beds may seem like a dull round of tedious chores that have to be done all over again the next day.

"Among wives of high-income persons, paid jobs were fairly common,

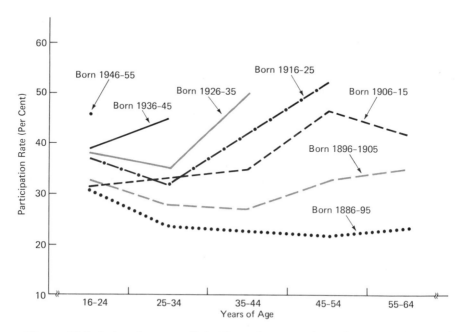

Figure 10.1. Labor force participation of women born between 1886 and 1955. (U.S. Department of Commerce)

but it appeared that financial necessity was seldom an important influence on those wives who did work."[2] Often women who are well educated—and many are in families with above-average incomes—feel a need to use their education outside the home as well as within it.

> Men have no alternative but to work and are considered asocial if they refuse to do so. This same ethical rule had not been widely applied to women. The latter have, to a large extent, retained the privilege, . . . of not taking part in the social effort. They have surprisingly long been held all the more respectable for not doing so.[3]

So long as society was organized in a way that women were fully occupied with their work in and around the home the role of women was not an issue for discussion. Only as women came to be needed less at home has concern developed about their place in society.

> At this juncture in our social history women are guided by two apparently conflicting aims. On the one hand, they want, like everybody else, to develop their personalities to the full and to take an active part in adult social and economic life within the limits of their individual interests and abilities. On the other hand most women want a home and family of their own. At a time when most social and economic life was carried on at home these aims did not conflict with each other. They appear to do so today.[4]

The major task left for today's homemaker is the care of children. To some extent the job has been eased by modern equipment, prepared foods, disposable products, and various types of services. But when children are very young there is still a great deal to do. One estimate is that it takes eight hours a day to care for a new baby even with good facilities and equipment. Babies need to be fed, changed, and played with. Their clothes and bedding require laundering. They need fresh air, which in many urban areas means that the mother must go out with them.

The homemaker with young children is a very busy woman. The immediate needs of her children take most of her time. As the children get older, however, the job of caring for them decreases. By the age of thirty-five most women have all their children in school. After a period of ten to fifteen busy years with little children there is a sharp drop in the hours per day that need be devoted to child care. And it decreases even more as the children mature. By the age of forty-five to forty-eight most women have all their children out of high school.

[2] Robin Barlow, Harvey E. Brazer, and James N. Morgan, *Economic Behavior of the Affluent* (Washington, D.C.: The Brookings Institute, 1966).

[3] Jean Stoetzel, "Une étude du budget-temps de la femme dans les agglomerations urbaines," *Population*, No. 1, Paris, 1948.

[4] Alva Myrdal and Viola Klein, *Women's Two Roles* (London: Routledge and Kegan Paul Ltd., 1956), p. xi.

With the present life expectancy most women will have many years when they are no longer badly needed at home. Generally, the bringing up of children occupies only a third of a woman's adult years. The span of years that remain ahead of a woman of forty-five today is about the same as the life expectancy of a man in his early twenties one hundred years ago.

Society recognizes that some women are in the same economic position as men: they need to support themselves or others. There is little controversy over whether unmarried women and widowed or divorced women should work. It has also become widely accepted for the young married woman to work before she has children or for the middle-aged woman to work after her children are grown. Today the big issue is whether a woman can hold a job and still be effective as a mother, particularly as the mother of young children.

Mothers in the Labor Force [5]

For many women, the birth of the first child means leaving the labor force for a time or perhaps even altogether. Others choose to remain on the job with time out for maternity leave. In 1972, more than 8 million women with children under 18 were in the labor force. More than a third of these women had children under 6 years old.

A mother's decision to be in the labor force involves many factors—cultural and family attitudes as well as economic considerations. Mothers continue to have the major responsibility in our society for care of children and thus are least likely to be in the labor force if home demands on time and energy are heavy—when children are young, for example, or if the family is large. About a third of the mothers of children under 6 are in the labor force, compared with half of those whose youngest child is school age. Among mothers with children under 6, the labor force participation rate is highest for those whose children are 3 to 5, for black women, and for women who are widowed, divorced, or separated. Also, women under 25 who have young children are more likely to be in the labor force than women 25 and over who have children in the same age group; in part, this reflects a trend to smaller family size.

The 1972 distribution of wives who expect to have more than two children illustrates the transition from the three-child to the two-child family. According to manpower experts, this trend is expected to have a continuing influence on the labor force participation of women and on the composition of the labor force.

State and Federal court decisions and equal employment guidelines have given women greater choice in their labor force decisions relating to child-

[5] Marilyn Doss Ruffin, "Mothers in the Labor Force," *Family Economics Review* (Fall 1973), pp. 13–15.

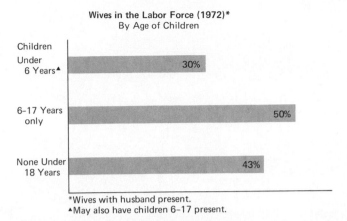

*Wives with husband present.
▲May also have children 6–17 present.

Figure 10.2. Of all the wives living with their husbands, those with children between the ages of 6 and 17 were most likely to be in the labor force, followed by wives with no children under 18. Wives with children under 6 years of age, and especially under 3 years, were less likely to be employed, although nearly one third of these women were in the labor force. (USDA)

bearing. The right of modern mothers of young children to participate in the labor force was upheld by the Supreme Court in 1971. In *Phillips vs. the Martin Marietta Corporation,* a case in which a woman was refused a job because she had preschool children, the court held that the law forbids "one hiring policy for women and another for men." Federal Equal Employment Opportunity Commission (EEOC) guidelines, intended for employers, labor unions, and courts, state that to dismiss or to refuse to hire a woman because of pregnancy violates Title VII of the amended 1964 Civil Rights Act. In addition, it is the woman, in consultation with her doctor—and not the employer—who may determine when in pregnancy she leaves her job and when she will return. The guidelines further state that employers must make

TABLE 10.1

Wife's Age	Per cent Having or Expecting to Have More Than 2 Births
18 through 19	29.7
20 through 21	27.4
22 through 24	31.3
25 through 29	39.7
30 through 34	55.0
35 through 39	63.4

Figure 10.3. Child care, particularly for young children, is a big problem for many working mothers. (U.S. Department of Health, Education, and Welfare)

maternity leave available. The Supreme Court, which ultimately interprets civil rights law, has stated that EEOC guidelines warrant "great deference."[6]

For many women the availability of suitable child care arrangements is a key factor in the decision to enter or leave the labor force. Some mothers are able to resolve the problem by working part time rather than full time. The mother of a school-age child, for example, may be able to eliminate the need for care arrangements by tailoring her work hours to the child's school day. For any age child, the hours of care services needed could at least be reduced. Employed mothers of school age and younger children work part time in about equal proportions (30 to 32 per cent, respectively). Working part time may not be the best solution financially, however, particularly for the mother who is the family's only earner. Working fewer hours means fewer hours of pay; moreover, employee benefits such as health insurance and pension credits often are not extended to part time workers. In addition, mothers who work part time are not eligible for the Federal Income Tax deduction for child care and household services. In 1972, about one third of employed wives with children under 18 compared with one sixth of mothers who were divorced, separated, or widowed worked part time.

Young mothers who use child care arrangements while they work most often take their children to someone else's home for care, according to a 1968

[6] *Griggs* vs. *the Duke Power Company*, 91 S. Ct. 849 (U.S. S. Ct. 1971) as reported by Carol Greenwald, "Maternity Leave Policy," *New England Economic Review*, Jan./Feb. 1973, p. 13.

TABLE 10.2

Type of Arrangement	Mothers Who Use Child Care	
	White	Black
	Per cent	Per cent
Own home by relative	18	26
Own home by nonrelative	7	7
Home of relative	28	34
Home of nonrelative	42	23
Group care center or school	5	10
Total	100	100

study sponsored by the U.S. Department of Labor.[7] Relatively small proportions used nursery school or day-care centers:

During the survey week, the median daily cost of child care was lower for black women than white women, . . . partly because black women were more likely to depend on relatives. A 1970 survey indicates that home care is preferred by parents but that more would use centers than currently if they were available and met requirements of quality, closeness to home, and cost.[8] The majority of the parents surveyed preferred care "next door" [for which they paid] . . . to "free and $\frac{1}{2}$ hour away" (58 and 33 per cent, respectively).

Women's Employment

"Women are playing an increasingly important role as members of the nation's paid labor force."[9] Many families have moved up from low to middle income status because of the wife's earnings. The mean income of families in which both husband and wife worked was higher than in families where the wife did not work.

Forty-four per cent of all women over age sixteen were employed or looking for work in 1972. This group of women comprised 38 per cent of the total labor force, as compared to only 29 per cent in 1950.

[7] Herbert S. Parnes, et al., *Years for Decision,* Vol. I. Issued as U.S. Department of Labor, Manpower Administration, Manpower Research Monograph No. 24, 1971. Chapter 6.

[8] *Meep (Massachusetts Early Education Project) Survey,* November 1970. Reported in *Child Care,* Hearings before the Committee on Finance, U.S. Senate, 92d Congress, 1st session, on S. 2003, Child Care Provisions of H.R. 1, and Title VI of Printed Amendment 318 to H.R. 1. 1971.

[9] Nancy Rudd, "Employment and Earnings of Women," *Family Economics Review* (Fall 1973), p. 3.

One of the important reasons for the greater employment of women has been the improvement in their educational attainment.

Women with higher levels of education, especially those with college degrees, are more likely to be in the labor force than women with less education; they have employable skills and are likely to earn higher wages and to perform more interesting work.

Changes in the marital status of women have also led to greater labor force participation. In both 1962 and 1972, the greatest proportion of women in age groups between 20 and 65 were married and living with their husbands. However, a greater proportion of women under 30 were single in 1972 than in 1962, and a greater proportion of women in all age groups 20 and over were divorced or separated. Many of these women were responsible for all or part of their own support and perhaps for the support of others.

.   .   .

Nearly three fifths of working women were married and living with their husbands in 1972; somewhat over one fifth were single. The remaining one fifth were widowed, divorced, or married but not living with their husbands.

Women are more likely to be white-collar workers than service, blue-

Figure 10.4. More women are employed in clerical jobs than any other kind of job. (American Telephone and Telegraph Company)

collar, or farm workers. In 1972—the greatest proportion were in clerical positions (35 per cent), followed by service (18 per cent), professional and technical (15 per cent), operatives (13 per cent), and sales (7 per cent). Smaller proportions were managers and administrators, craftswomen, transport equipment operatives, nonfarm laborers, and private household workers. . . . As women become qualified to hold higher paying jobs that demand greater skills, fewer are willing to engage in low paying, often unskilled, household service jobs.

.   .   .

Among the measurable factors affecting the size of income are occupation and level of skill required, total hours worked, and education. Women employed in full-time salaried professional and technical jobs had the highest incomes, followed by those employed as full-time salaried managers and administrators.

.   .   .

The mean incomes of full-time male workers were substantially higher than those of full-time female workers in every occupational group. A 1971 Department of Labor report indicated that much of the observed income differential between men and women is due to the specific kinds of jobs held by women as well as to the industries in which they tend to be employed. Within the broad category of professional workers, for example, nurses, elementary school teachers, and lab technicians, tend to be women, while doctors, college professors, and scientists tend to be men. Average incomes of the last professions are much higher than those of the first mentioned professions. Women are more likely than men to be employed in lower paying, labor-intensive industries such as apparel and leather products, while men are found in higher paying, capital-intensive industries such as petroleum products and transportation equipment.[10]

How long one stays on a job varies with the age of the worker. However, at every age over twenty-four, job tenure was less for women than men.

Families Headed by Women

Approximately 10 per cent of the working women in 1972 were heads of families. For more than two thirds of these families the woman was the only member of the family who was employed.

Historically the employment and income situation of such families has generally been bleak. Most of the women are ill-equipped to earn an adequate living. Many suffer from one handicap or more to successful competition in the labor market—lack of sufficient education or training,

[10] Ibid., pp. 4–7.

TABLE 10.3
Women at Work in Nonagricultural Industries, March 1972 [1]

Item	Total at Work	Working Schedule			Average Hours
		Full Time	Voluntary Part Time	Other Part Time[2]	Full-time Workers
	Thousands	*Percent*	*Percent*	*Percent*	*Hours*
Age					
16 and 17 yrs.	984	9.1	88.9	1.9	38.4
18 and 19 yrs.	1,591	53.6	40.9	5.7	39.2
20 to 24 yrs.	4,483	78.6	17.6	3.9	39.9
25 to 44 yrs.	11,226	73.3	22.8	3.9	40.3
45 to 64 yrs.	9,790	76.4	19.9	3.8	41.1
65 yrs. and over	968	49.3	46.9	3.8	43.8
Total 16 yrs. and over	29,042	71.1	25.0	3.9	40.6
Marital status					
Married, husband present	17,125	71.0	25.2	3.8	40.3
Widowed, divorced, separated	5,463	78.3	16.8	4.9	41.2
Single	6,454	65.2	31.5	3.4	40.6

Occupation					
White-collar workers	18,076	75.0	22.8	2.2	40.6
Professional and technical	4,461	77.2	21.0	1.7	41.8
Managers and administrators, except farm	1,351	85.9	11.6	2.4	45.3
Sales workers	1,974	51.6	43.9	4.5	41.3
Clerical workers	10,290	77.1	21.0	1.9	39.2
Blue-collar workers	4,428	81.5	11.2	7.3	39.5
Craftsmen and kindred workers	376	81.2	16.8	2.1	40.2
Operatives, except transportation	3,699	84.6	7.6	7.8	39.4
Transportation equipment operatives	127	22.8	69.3	7.9	38.7
Nonfarm laborers	226	64.1	29.2	6.6	40.4
Service workers	6,614	53.0	40.6	6.3	41.7
Private household	1,457	31.1	59.6	9.3	44.0
Other service workers	5,157	59.3	35.3	5.4	41.4

1 Nonfarm only.
2 Includes slack work, material shortages or repairs to plant and equipment, new job started during week, job terminated during week, could find only part-time work.

SOURCE: U.S. Dept. Labor, Bur. Labor Statis., *Employment and Earnings*, Vol. 18, No. 10, April 1972, pp. 40–41, table A-25, and pp. 42–53, table A-26.

irregular and unstable work histories, sex or racial discrimination in hiring, ill health, and the difficulty of arranging for satisfactory child care. . . .

Public assistance, a primary source of income for many of the families headed by women, has been expanding in coverage and in benefit levels, but payments are still generally very low—in most States below the poverty line.

The welfare system has been caught in a crossfire of public criticism. The target for most of the hostility is the AFDC program—Aid to Families with Dependent Children—designed to provide income assistance to the families of children whose fathers have died or deserted or are absent for a variety of other reasons. On the one hand, welfare programs are criticized because their payment levels are considered too low to provide economic security to families in need. On the other hand, the programs are criticized on the grounds that work, as well as need, should be a requirement for eligibility. The welfare system has also been faulted because of the widely disparate State benefit levels, because it may discourage some women from seeking employment, and because it may induce some families to break up.

The attacks have become sharper in recent years because of steady growth in the welfare population. By March 1970, about three fifths of the 3.4 million families with children headed by women were already on welfare and the rolls were still rising. These developments were placing a growing burden on the already hard-pressed taxpayer. One result of the resistance to the rising welfare bill has been a heightened interest in the possibility of employment for welfare mothers. One important aspect of welfare reform involves the development of training and job placement programs for able-bodied adult welfare recipients.[11]

Problems in Home Management

The woman who works outside the home adds responsibilities but does not usually relinquish the job of home management. Somehow she must arrange for someone to take care of it, or do the homemaking job herself in addition to her outside one.

[There are] several areas in which women commonly experience difficulty in combining employment with home responsibilities.

Isolation of families. The predominance of "nuclear families"—that is, families composed only of parents and dependent children—generally precludes the sharing of household duties and child care with grandparents or other adult relatives.

. . .

Child care. Lack of adequate care for the children of working mothers [which was discussed earlier] is not only a serious obstacle to the employment of women, it is a matter of social concern as to the welfare of the children.

[11] Robert L. Stein, "The Economic Status of Families Headed by Women," *Monthly Labor Review* (December 1970), p. 3.

Figure 10.5. Some women are the only wage earners in the family. (Sperry and Hutchinson Company)

Work schedules and practices. Present schedules and practices do not easily accommodate to family responsibilities. Opportunities for part-time work, for example, still fall short of the needs of working women. In the case of professional workers, part-time work may be associated with a reduction in status.

Sickness in the family and other family emergencies that may require a parent's presence are not routinely acceptable reasons for absence from work with—or without—pay. For some women, the problem is not only the absolute number of hours worked, but the inability to adjust work schedules to the demands of home. For example, lunch breaks may not be long enough to permit mothers to go home at lunchtime even though their school children are sent home at noon.

Transportation. Lack of convenient transportation sometimes impedes the meshing of home and work responsibilities, especially for part-time workers. Public transportation often is inadequate and erratic in off-peak hours, while in many urban areas parking space is scarce by midmorning.

The effect of role-attitudes. Husbands and wives often hold different views of women's role in marriage and in society, and these views are sometimes obstacles to employment. Studies of the labor force experience of women showed a strong correlation between husbands' attitudes and their wives' anticipation of labor force activity. For example, of white married women under 25 years of age whose husbands had positive attitudes toward their working, two thirds indicated they would accept a job offer. Of those whose husbands had strong objections, only one fifth said they would work. The pattern for blacks was similar, but the sample was too small to generalize. Among white married women aged 30–44, women who reported that their husbands strongly favored their working were three times as likely to have permissive views about working as those whose husbands opposed their working. The relationship was even stronger among black women.

One fourth of all married women age 30–44 were described as having

permissive attitudes toward the employment of mothers with schoolage chil
dren, while two fifths had ambivalent attitudes and slightly more than one
third were opposed. Black women were half again as likely as white women
to have permissive attitudes, and white women were 50 per cent more likely
than blacks to be opposed. The attitudes of husbands toward their wives
working is the factor most strongly associated with the women's attitudes toward the employment of mothers.

A small study[12] of couples where all the wives and most of the husbands
were employed in professional occupations found that the women generally
felt it possible to combine a profession and marriage as long as the husband
was not threatened by his wife's capabilities and achievements, as long as he
viewed it as adding to his stature and not as diminishing it, and as long as
the wife was not ambivalent toward her role. Nonetheless, these wives were
found to have limited their career ambitions in order to promote the smooth
running of their homes.[13]

There is also the pressure of meeting a time schedule. Working away
from home means that the mother must leave at a particular time. If
Susie isn't feeling well, her mother must decide by a certain hour what
she will do—whether she will go to work or stay home with her child.
Even when everyone is feeling well it is often very hard to get a whole
family organized and ready to go their various ways at an hour early
enough for the mother to leave for work. The mornings are apt to be
tense and hectic when a mother works, unless the household is carefully
organized and the morning routine planned in a way to avoid it.

Solutions

The following suggestions to better accommodate the needs of working
women with family responsibilities have been compiled from attitudinal
surveys and other literature.

Day care. One of the most frequently mentioned needs is more day care
facilities providing adequate services at feasible prices. The Administration-
initiated welfare reform legislation now before Congress authorizes $700
million to provide child care opportunities for 875,000 children.

Some groups, maintaining that child care is a legitimate business expense, have long advocated extension of tax allowances for such expenses to
workers at all income levels.

[12] Margaret M. Poloma, "Role Conflict and the Married Professional Woman," paper
presented at the annual meeting of the Ohio Valley Sociological Society, 1970. See also
Margaret M. Poloma and T. Neal Garland, "The Myth of the Egalitarian Family,"
paper presented at the annual meeting of the American Sociological Association, Washington, D.C., 1970.
[13] Janice Neipert Hedges and Jeanne K. Barnett, "Working Women and the Division
of Household Tasks," *Monthly Labor Review* (April 1972), pp. 10–11.

Upgrading househeld employment. Still another means that has been suggested to promote the smooth running of households in a nuclear family situation where the wife is employed outside the home is upgrading household employment to attract more workers into that occupation. Experimental and demonstration projects in the late 1960's funded by the U.S. Department of Labor indicated that trained household employees can provide needed services that command decent wages and good working conditions.

More efficient home management. Planning and organizing housework, utilizing labor-saving devices and convenience products, determining priorities, and taking a relaxed attitude toward chores of lesser importance have also been suggested as ways to reduce the demands of housework.

Adaptable work rules. The development of more part-time jobs has been suggested, as well as time off without loss of pay for such child-related activities as teacher conferences, doctor visits, or similar obligations and liberal maternity leave.

Recognition of life-cycle pattern. The problems of working women can be eased if employers (as well as educational and training institutions) come to accept and make provisions for interrupted education and employment patterns.

Fuller sharing of family reponsibilities. A more egalitarian family style, one in which the careers of husband and wife are equally important an the burdens of household tasks and child care are equally shared, has been pointed out as a way to enable more women to cope with responsibilities at home and on the job.[14]

The Dollar Value of a Second Income

As many families know, a wife's earnings can be very important. However, the net income available from a second worker's income in a family is greatly reduced by many expenses. Two incomes will put the family in a higher income bracket, resulting in a higher tax rate. Table 10.4 suggests some of the major expenses that may occur when a homemaker becomes the second worker in the family.

Fathers As Homemakers

A small but growing number of men are the heads of households in which there is no woman but there are children. The mother may have

[14] Ibid., pp. 11 12.

TABLE 10.4
A Paid Job: What's It Worth?

Income per Week $_____

═══

Expenses Resulting from the Job

═══

TAXES $

    Income, social security,
unemployment, etc.   _____

PERSONAL EXPENSES

    Clothes   _____

    Transportation   _____

    Lunches   _____

    Personal care   _____

OFFICE EXPENSES

    Parties   _____

    Gifts   _____

    Contributions   _____

    Coffee breaks   _____

FAMILY EXPENSES

    Child care (?)   _____

    Laundry service (?)   _____

    Meals out (?)   _____

    Higher shopping costs (?)   _____

OTHER   _____

    Total of All Expenses ....$_____

Net Income per Week ....$_____
(what can be spent)

Net Yearly Income ....$_____
(weekly income times weeks worked)

SOURCE: Marian M. MacNab. "Can Wives Afford To Work?" Home Economics Extension
Leaflet 11, Cooperative Extension Service, Cornell University, 1962.

died, or the parents are separated and the father has custody of the children. In this situation the home-management problems of the father are often similar to those of the employed mother with young children.

Summary

Women have worked from time immemorial to care for their families. As their work at home decreased women began to move out into the community. More than 40 per cent are employed outside the home today.

Women work for a variety of reasons. Some have no choice. They need the money badly. Others want to raise the family's standard of living. Or they may feel isolated at home. Many feel a need to use their education in a way that contributes to society.

The woman who works outside the home adds responsibilities but does not usually relinquish the job of home management. Somehow she must arrange for someone to take care of her home and children or do the job herself in addition to her outside one. Child care is one of the biggest problems. There is also the presence of meeting a time schedule and getting everything done.

CHAPTER FOLLOW-UP

1. In considering the employment of wives, are some goals more worthy than others? What about these?
   a. To provide a better living, cut down debts.
   b. To provide extra money (savings) for home, education, vacation.
   c. To provide extra money for luxuries.
   d. To get away from drudgery or boredom with housework.
   e. To train for a time when the children are grown, or possible widowhood.
   f. To develop or use special talents, abilities, or training.
   g. To help one's husband finish school.
2. What is an acceptable reason for working away from home?
3. What is an acceptable reason for *not* working away from home?
4. Assume that you are a mother who is considering working.
   a. If you decided to take a job next week, what is the first thing that you would eliminate or change in your homemaking routine? Why?
   b. If you decided to take a job next week, what is the last thing that you would eliminate or change in some way. Why? [15]
5. How might the growing trend for married women to hold paid jobs affect the location and size of new homes?

[15] Based on the discussion guide, "Can Wives Afford to Work?" Department of Household Economics and Management, Cornell University, mimeo., n.d.

6. Assume that you are a woman and planning to work outside the home whether you marry or not. How might you plan and furnish your household to make homemaking easier?
7. Have a committee investigate the child-care facilities in your community and report to the class.
8. Spend a day at a child-care center, from the time the parents start bringing the youngsters until they go home.

SELECTED REFERENCES

Bernard, Jessie, and Catharine Chilman. "Changing Lifestyles for Women." *Journal of Home Economics,* Vol, 62, (1970), pp. 575–583.

Bird, Caroline. *Born Female: The High Cost of Keeping Women Down.* New York: David McKay Co., 1968.

Daly, Margaret. "A Flexible Work Plan for Married Women." *Better Homes and Gardens* (January 1974), pp. 6–7.

Epstein, Cynthia F. *Women's Place: Options and Limits in Professional Careers.* Berkeley, California: University of California Press, 1970.

Friedan, Betty. *The Feminine Mystique.* New York: Dell Publishing Co., 1963.

Galbraith, John Kenneth. "The Economics of the American Housewife." *Atlantic Monthly* (August 1973), pp. 78–83.

Ginzburg. Eli. Chapter 18, "Work in the Lives of Women." *The Development of Human Resources.* New York: McGraw-Hill Book Company, 1966.

Gould, Elsie M. *American Woman Today.* Englewood Cliffs, N.J.: Prentice-Hall, Inc., 1972.

Hayghe, Howard. "Labor Force Activity of Married Women." *Monthly Labor Review* (April 1973), pp. 31–36.

Helmick, Sandra. *Employment and Earnings of Secondary Workers.* Doctoral thesis, University of Missouri, 1972.

Hoffman, Lois Wladis, and F. Ivan Nye. *Working Mothers.* San Francisco: Jossey-Bass, Inc., 1974.

Kievit, Mary. "Women in Gainful and Useful Employment." *Journal of Home Economics,* Vol. 60 (1968), pp. 697–702.

Linden, Fabian. "Women in the Labor Force." *Conference Board Record* (April 1970), pp. 37–39.

Mead, Margaret. *Women in Mass Society.* Boston: Beacon Press, 1962.

Melton, Neta Sue. "Comparison of the Homemaking Role Conceptions of Working and Non-working Wife-Mothers in Two Social Classes." Master's thesis, Michigan State University, 1966.

Miller, Francena L. "Womanpower: Rediscovering a Prime Resource." *Journal of Home Economics,* Vol. 60 (1968), pp. 693–696.

Myrdal, Alva, and Viola Klein, *Women's Two Roles.* London: Routledge and Kegan Paul Ltd., 1956.

Nelson, H. Y., and P. R. Goldman. "Attitudes of High School Students and Young Adults Toward the Gainful Employment of Married Women." *Family Coordinator,* Vol. 18 (July 1969), pp. 251–255.

Oppenheimer, Valeria K. *The Female Labor Force in the United States: Demo-*

graphic and Economic Factors Governing Its Growth and Changing Composition. Berkeley, California: University of California, Institute of International Studies, 1970. (Population Monograph Series No. 5.)

Rudd, Nancy. "Employment and Earnings of Women." *Family Economics Review* (Fall 1973), pp. 3–8.

Walker, Kathryn E. "How Much Help for Working Mothers? The Children's Role." *Human Ecology Forum* (Autumn 1970).

Young, Anne M. "Children of Working Mothers." *Monthly Labor Review* (April 1973), pp. 37–40.

chapter 11

---

the homemaker
with a
handicap

The problems facing the homemaker with physical limitations are complicated by the fact that family units have
gotten smaller in the past hundred years. The homemaker
with a disability often must choose between learning to
manage independently or living in a nursing home or
custodial institution. This is particularly true of the older
person.

Since the majority of homemakers are women, a large
proportion of the homemakers with handicaps are women.
However, numbers of men with disabilities are directly
involved in the care of a home. Many men share some
homemaking activities. Others are the sole homemaker.
They may be single, widowed, or divorced. Some have
older relatives or young children living with them.

The principal causes of physical disabilities are faulty
vision, arthritis, paralysis, and circulatory diseases. Among
the younger homemakers disabilities are often the result
of congenital defects, birth injuries, diseases such as polio,

or an accident such as an automobile injury. Older people tend to be limited by the degenerative effects of aging, such as glaucoma, cataracts, poor circulation, and arthritis, as well as by the aftermath of a heart attack, an operation, or an accident, such as a broken bone which heals very slowly or not at all.

In recent years a great deal has been done to prevent and cure diseases. We have also developed ways of helping many people with a disability to function independently. However, we still have many people with disabilities that limit their activities. Our accident rate is high. Injuries in the home are the leading cause of accidents. Automobile accidents rank second, and occupational injuries are common. Birth injuries and congenital defects also result in disabilities for some people.

As we increase the average life span more people are affected by the physical problems of old age. Not the least of these is the problem of decreasing energy. We all have less physical stamina as we move from the twenties to the retirement years. This doesn't mean that everyone loses vigor at the same rate. Many of us know physically and mentally active senior citizens. People vary tremendously in health and vigor, and individual differences occur at every age level. But with each passing decade we all tend to be less vigorous than we were in earlier years.

Persons Whose Activity Is Limited by Chronic Conditions

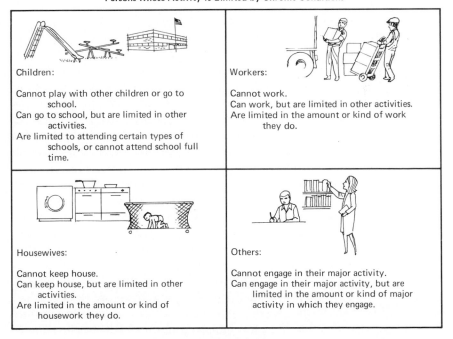

Children:

Cannot play with other children or go to school.
Can go to school, but are limited in other activities.
Are limited to attending certain types of schools, or cannot attend school full time.

Workers:

Cannot work.
Can work, but are limited in other activities.
Are limited in the amount or kind of work they do.

Housewives:

Cannot keep house.
Can keep house, but are limited in other activities.
Are limited in the amount or kind of housework they do.

Others:

Cannot engage in their major activity.
Can engage in their major activity, but are limited in the amount or kind of major activity in which they engage.

Figure 11.1.

Glaucoma, which was a relatively rare eye disease in the period when the average life expectancy was forty years, is a very common one today. It is the leading eye disease of people over the age of sixty.

Attitudes About a Disability

Some people are easily discouraged. They give up at the smallest obstacle. Others will overcome minor difficulties but give up at a major problem. Some people, however, cannot be discouraged by anything. Beethoven composed magnificent music long after he was stone-deaf. Helen Keller conquered the problem of being deaf, mute, and blind. Of course, these were people of great drive with unusual abilities. Nevertheless, it is amazing what most of us can accomplish if we really want to do so. How about the tired businessman who goes out and plays eighteen holes of golf, or the housewife who can breeze through her work if she is going out for the evening?

Most of us have reserves of energy and determination that we use only when we are highly motivated. Many people can learn to manage the job of caring for a home and family in spite of physical limitations if they are sufficiently motivated, and if they can be helped to learn how to handle these activities.

All too often the assumption is made that a person who has some disability is automatically doomed to a life of very limited scope. This isn't necessarily so. Franklin D. Roosevelt became Governor of New York and President of the United States after he was stricken with polio. During this period he was unable to walk well; he wore braces and used a cane, or sat in a wheelchair. A former president of the National Paraplegic Association lost the use of the lower half of his body as a result of an injury in the Korean War. In spite of being confined to a wheelchair he traveled extensively by airplane and car, held a responsible full-time position, married, and adopted children.

It is possible that a person with a physical handicap will be unable to lead a full life. But this is also true of many people without physical disabilities. A great many people are afraid to try new things or do something that is outside their usual pattern. People with disabilities must adjust to certain problems but this usually leaves a wide area within which they still can function effectively.

The attitude toward a disability on the part of the individual with the disability and his or her immediate family is often more limiting than the disability itself. In the case of the homemaker with a disability, studies have shown that there is often less of a relationship between the seriousness of the impediment and how one adjusts to it than might be expected.[1] The important thing to recognize is that a person with a physical disability is also a person with many abilities.

Most of us do not begin to use all our potential abilities. The individual who is limited in one way can often develop in some other areas. An injury to one hand might prevent one from playing the violin or piano but not from playing the trumpet or French horn. A leg impairment might make it difficult to play competitive football but would not prevent one from becoming a fine scientist. A tennis player who formerly was nationally ranked had a serious case of diabetes from childhood. Many people with this condition avoid heavy exercise because of concern about an imbalance in blood sugar. He checked his blood sugar carefully after each match and adjusted his medication accordingly. What one can do really depends to a large extent on the attitude one has.

One's self-concept plays a very important role in one's relationships with other people. If the person with a disability is able to accept his situation with a good attitude most of the people he meets will do so, too. Many people do not know how to treat a person with a disability. They may want to be helpful and end up by trying to be overly helpful. Or they may be afraid to approach the person with a disability.

The way in which a person meets the world will often determine how others will treat him. This is true of people without obvious disabilities, too. The person who exudes an air of cheer and confidence is better accepted by others than the timid, retreating sort of person.

Often the attitude of one's family will help determine how an individual learns to meet other people and problems. Families undergo many types of stress in the process of living together. The problems of a member with a disability are only one variety of these stresses. Some families fall apart when they encounter financial reverses. Others are shaken by job changes, or the marriage of a youngster to a person of whom they do not approve.

The homemaker with a disability needs to feel that her role is still important to the family. Deutsch and Goldston[2] point out that the best predictor of whether a patient with a severe disability will make the effort to manage at home is whether he or she can function in some useful way. The mother with a home and family can find many useful things to do even with a severe disability. She can participate in family decisions and spend time with her children, regardless of how little else she can manage.

A person who feels needed tends to make a much better adjustment

[1] Victor A. Christopherson, "Role Modifications of the Handicapped Homemaker," *Rehabilitation Literature*, Vol. 21, No. 5 (April 1960), pp. 110–117.

[2] Cynthia P. Deutsch and J. A. Goldston, "Family Factors in Home Adjustment of the Severely Disabled," *Marriage and Family Living*, Vol. 22 (Nov. 1960), pp. 312–316.

than the one who feels that he has no function. Thus the prognosis for a homemaker is often better than that for a man or woman who must make his way in the job market. His old job may not be there. Or it may be one in which he can no longer function effectively.

Management in the Home

Few homemakers have received any extensive education for the job of caring for their home and family. Among homemakers with disabilities only a small portion have been given help in how to develop work methods that will make it easier for them to care for their home and family.

Here are some ways to help homemakers with disabilities improve their management.

Develop New Standards

Realistic standards for home management need to be formulated. Often a choice must be made as to what will be left undone. The decision may have to be made that only those things that are vital to keep the family operating will be done.

Articles that take a great deal of upkeep may need to be put away: ruffled curtains that require ironing, bric-a-brac that needs careful dusting, or silverware that needs regular polishing. Fortunately, there are many things on the market that require very little care. Wherever possible one can try to replace household articles with others that require less work.

Eliminate Unnecessary Work

The homemaker with physical limitations has the same problems of home management as any other homemaker, plus whatever ones are caused by her handicap. If there are young children in the family there is apt to be a great deal of household work and time needed for child care.

Simplification of homemaking activities is even more important than for the homemaker without a disability, because every job is likely to take longer. Work needs to be streamlined wherever possible. Work-saving methods should be applied to almost every household activity.

Get rid of everything that is not really needed so that there will be fewer things to be cared for. Most of us tend to accumulate possessions with each passing year. The more crowded the house becomes, the harder it is to take care of.

Tools Can Help

The right tools can make a job go more quickly and easily. Small kitchen equipment that is designed for the general market can be selected to meet special needs. For instance, a portable hand mixer might be useful for a person who only has use of one hand. A carving rack that holds meat firmly in place would also be useful in the same situation.

In addition, there are many special aids that have been developed to help people with particular types of problems to do various things. A very long pair of tongs is a great help in reaching items on high or low shelves in the kitchen or a closet. These were developed for people who had limited use of their arms or were confined to a wheelchair. They are available commercially. With a little imagination some simple, inexpensive aids can be made at home.

Some things can be adapted to other uses. A laundry cart on wheels or a tea wagon can be used to carry things such as sheets, children's toys, or cleaning equipment from room to room.

Modifications in the House or Apartment

Some simple changes in the house may make it easier for a person with a disability to move around. For the person in a wheelchair, or the individual who has difficulty climbing stairs, a ramp can be placed over a short flight of steps, such as those leading to the entrance of many homes. A sturdy bar on the wall next to the bathtub can make it easier to get in and out of the tub. Handrails on both sides of a staircase often will aid the person who needs additional support in going up and down the stairs.

Remodeling may be needed to widen doorways and passageways for someone in a wheelchair.

If it is possible to arrange, moving to another house or an apartment may make it much easier for the homemaker with a disability. Many new houses, particularly those that are on one floor or planned for retirement communities, incorporate features that facilitate movement and save work.

Relocate Equipment

Household equipment can be put where it is easier to use. A first-floor laundry can eliminate going down to the basement to do the wash. A dryer might be set up off the floor so that there is no need to bend to get clothing in and out. Often there are many pieces of equipment that can be repositioned for easier use.

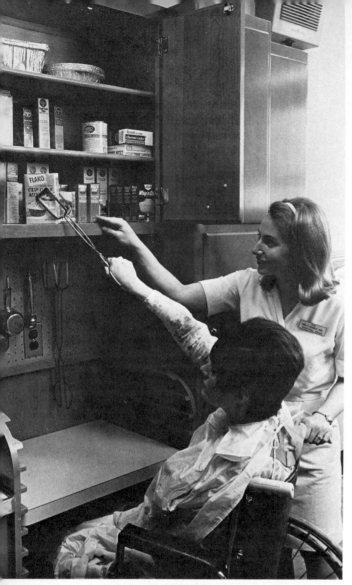

Figure 11.2. Using tongs to extend her reach. (*Training the Young Hemiplegic Homemaker*, Homemaking and Homeplanning Service, Occupational Therapy Department, Institute of Rehabilitation Medicine, New York University Medical Center)

Group Working Materials

Group as many work materials into work centers as possible. This may be useful for any homemaker, but it is particularly important when moving about is difficult and slow, or when one's energy is very limited.

Conserve Time and Energy

The management of time and energy is important to all homemakers, but it is especially so for the homemaker with physical limitations. Because he or she may take longer to carry out some activities, have less energy, or need a large block of time for therapy, careful use of both time and energy is crucial if one hopes to get the essential things accomplished. Caring for a home and family takes a lot of work.

Share Responsibilities

Most families are unable to secure outside help with the household work, even when the homemaker is disabled. Some limited public funds are available to assist an individual or a family by paying a homemaker who comes in daily or at intervals. But in most families those things that the homemaker cannot do which are important to the family welfare will need to be done by some other family member.

Other members of the family will probably accept the need to take on more responsibility for the household work if the development of plans to keep the home functioning are made by the family as a group. Most people, including children, are more willing to do their share if they feel that theirs is an important job and really needed.

However, the homemaker's emotional and physiological needs are so important that it may be more essential to her development for her to do tasks that could be performed more efficiently by another member of the family, particularly if this task gives her a sense of functioning. Depending upon the limitations of the situation, a homemaker with a disability probably needs to do as much of a normal work load as she possibly can manage in order to feel like a contributing member of society.

The Care of Children

A physical disability does not necessarily prevent a young woman from having children. Many do have a family after they are disabled. Also, some young women develop disabilities during the period when they have small children at home. It is particularly important to the family welfare that the homemaker with a disability be able to take care of her children if she can.

As soon as possible after the development of a disability it is psychologically important for the mother to take over at least some child care activities. A mother will often be highly motivated to function independently if she can care for her child. The confidence gained in taking care of a child's basic physical needs can carry over into other areas. It will also help the mother and child build a feeling of mutual trust and need, which is vital to every mother and young child.

Children are amazingly adaptable. Mothers with disabilities that limit their movement have proven that it is possible to care for young children. Even before they understand what the problem is, little children will clasp another person more securely if they feel that person's grip is not very strong. As they grow older a spirit of cooperation and independence can be fostered. This attitude on the part of the child is very important because the parent with a handicap may not be able to physically lift the child or remove him from difficult or dangerous situations.

It is always interesting to watch how a child whose mother does everything for him at home can manage quite well at nursery school where the attitude is "Now you can do it." Of course, there are many things that little children cannot manage. Still, they can be helped by the selection of clothing that they can get off and on easily. Large buttons are easier to handle than little ones. Zippers down the front of overalls are easier to do up than buttons on the shoulders. Lacing and tying shoes is often difficult for the preschool child. Buckle shoes and step-in styles like loafers are much easier to handle. Boots that are quite generous in size are simpler to slip on and off than snug fitting ones. Hats that pull on are more manageable than ones than tie under the chin. Clipping mittens onto coats and jackets makes it easier to find them.

Storing clothing within reach will help the child learn to take care of his own clothing. Inexpensive low closet bars that hang from high ones are available from mail order houses.

Time and patience are very important. Many little children can do a lot for themselves if they are not hurried. Learning to take care of oneself is a slow process.

Most of all, little children need encouragement and a sense of pride in their ability to do things for themselves. A little child may be just as pleased about learning to tie his own shoes as the teen-ager is about learning to drive a car.

Child-care equipment should be selected so that the mother can care for the child without assistance as far as possible. There is a wide variety of equipment on the market that can be used or adapted for special situations. For example, cribs and playpens can be bought with legs that raise and lower. Many feeding tables are also adjustable. Some cribs and feeding tables have wheels to move them about easily.

Children grow quickly. Therefore, in the interest of economy, most people try to limit their purchases to those things that are most important. Some equipment can be used for more than one purpose. Many carriages have bodies that lift out to serve as car beds. Some feeding tables can be converted to play tables when the child has outgrown a feeding table.

May, Waggoner, and Boettke suggest the following checklist in selecting child-care equipment for a homemaker with a handicap.

Is it manageable within the mother's limitations?

Is it adjustable in height? Can it be moved easily? Does it have easily manipulated controls?

Is it suitable for more than one use and over a long period of time?

Is it sturdy and durable? Is it adaptable to the rapid growth of the child? Is it easy to care for?

Does it help in promoting early independence in the child?

Is it safe for both the mother and the child? [3]

Try to do each activity in the least tiring manner. Do as much as possible sitting down if energy is limited. A baby can be diapered or bathed from a sitting position. Many mothers sit on a bed and diaper the baby on a waterproof pad. Bathing the baby can be handled in several ways. One can use a bar-height chair and a bathinette, one can use a basin placed on a table, and one can sit on a chair and bathe the baby in the bathroom or the kitchen sink.

Self-help Clothing

Homemakers with handicaps should be encouraged to keep up their appearance, if at all possible. Many women tend to be lazy about their appearance during the years when they are busy at home. Perhaps they feel that no one sees them, or that it isn't important. The years when children are small are busy ones for the mother, whether she is handicapped or not. But the psychological lift that comes from a good appearance may be particularly important for the homemaker with a handicap. Attractive clothing not only tends to raise the wearer's morale, but it also helps other people view the handicapped person as more presentable.

A person with physical limitations may need clothing that he or she can manage easily. Dresses that zip down the back are a nuisance for anyone, but they may be impossible for a woman who can't raise her arms fully. A leg brace may mean that a woman needs a skirt that is a little fuller than the current fashion. With some types of handicaps the homemaker may be able to use clothing that is on the market. Wrap-around skirts are easy to manage. So are blouses that button down the front and coat dresses that open all the way down.

Underclothes often pose a problem. Van Davis Odell produces garments for women with physical handicaps under the trade name of "FashionAble." These have Velcro-type closings instead of hooks and eyes. Girdles have extra zippers, which make it easier to get in and out of the garment. Slips have front zippers.

An effort has been made to produce commercially attractive garments that can be worn by women with handicaps. This effort grew out of a pilot project by the Institute for Physical Medicine and Rehabilitation of New York University. At present the Clothing Research and Development

[3] Elizabeth Eckhardt May, Neva R. Waggoner, and Eleanor M. Boettke, *Homemaking for the Handicapped* (New York: Dodd, Mead and Co., 1966), p. 29.

Foundation, which includes contemporary designers, approves garments that make dressing easier for women with a handicap. These clothes are sold as part of the regular lines of clothing available in stores around the country.[4]

Training the Young Hemiplegic Homemaker [5]

For the housewife who has suffered a stroke, retraining in homemaking techniques is an essential step in rehabilitation and also one of the most threatening because here she comes face to face with the practical realities of her situation. She must recognize that she may be returning to her homemaker's role without regaining the functional use of one side of her body. For many women, especially those who have been competent, this seems impossible to accept.

In the homemaking program at the Institute of Rehabilitation these handicapped women face their fears and begin to accept their limitations by actually cooking and working in a kitchen that is planned for their special needs. The Institute's training kitchen is divided into two units—one kitchen adapted to make it as convenient as possible for a woman in a wheelchair, and the other a standard height unit similar to the ordinary kitchen.

In the wheelchair kitchen the homemaker works at a continuous counter 31″ high (and open underneath for chair and leg room) that connects the refrigerator, sink and range so that she can slide all her utensils and food back and forth without ever lifting and carrying. Narrow shelves and pegboard at the back of this counter are carefully planned to store the frequently used supplies and utensils within her easy reach. Here she begins to learn one-handed cooking techniques, and regains some confidence in herself as a homemaker.

Soon the homemaker is ready to try working in the standard kitchen where she is faced with problems similar to those she will have at home. By this time she is usually doing some walking with the aid of a leg brace and a cane but because of poor balance and fatigue it will be difficult for her to stand for any length of time, and consequently she is taught to work sitting in a high chair from which she can reach both the standard height sink and range.

At about this time the therapist starts to guide their conversations toward the patient's kitchen at home. From the patient's description the therapist makes a rough floor plan to determine whether the patient will be able to follow her new working patterns in her own kitchen, as it is. If there are going to be problems a home visit is made, whenever possible, to check out

---

[4] Clothing and Research Development Foundation, Inc., 1 Rockefeller Plaza, Suite 1912, New York, N.Y. 10020.

[5] From *Training the Young Hemiplegic Homemaker: A Picture Study in Rehabilitation*, Homemaking and Homeplanning Service, Occupational Therapy Department, Institute of Rehabilitation Medicine, New York University Medical Center, n.d.

the kitchen's dimensions and details and to evaluate the feasibility of making changes. These changes are often such minor adjustments as removing the sink enclosure to make leg room and relocating appliances for the patient's one-sided approach, or they may require some new equipment and structural alterations. In every case the planning goal is to give the homemaker the working arrangement she will need to cook for her family.

At the Institute the homemaker training program is carried on by an occupational therapist and a home economist [who is also the kitchen planning consultant]—a logical combination to handle the many different kinds of practical problems that must be solved if the disabled homemaker is really going to go back to work in her own kitchen. The initial training approach and the overall responsibility are the occupational therapist's. She draws the home economist and planning consultant into the training sessions when the patient has gained some skills and her new kitchen requirements are known. The planning consultant . . . checks out the advantages and costs of different plans for changing the patient's home kitchen, and when the plans are final she makes the simple scale drawing and specifications that will be needed to carry out the changes.

. . . The home economist evaluates the family's living patterns and the changes that would be necessary for the handicapped homemaker to resume her familiar role. The home economist also follows the patient's progress in her training sessions and becomes thoroughly familiar with her particular way of doing things—cooking, cleaning, ironing, making beds, so that when the patient is discharged the home economist on home visits can help her use the skills she developed at the Institute in her own home kitchen.

Mrs. E., the homemaker shown in the following pictures, was aged 30 at the time of her stroke and the mother of three children under 8 years of age. She started her homemaking training just one month after the stroke and was treated three times a week for about eight months.

Mrs. E. started off with sewing. Because it was early in her rehabilitation program Mrs. E. was so confused and fearful that it was impossible for her to think about the problems she might have cooking for her family. However, she could face the difficulties of sewing—they were not so crucial to her family and Mrs. E. had special skills in dress designing. So she started off making a dress for her small daughter. As she learned to use heavy scissors and other objects to stabilize the material for one-handed pinning and cutting, and then found she could still handle a sewing machine . . . she began slowly to gain confidence so that she could start to think about her kitchen at home and ask questions about how she would ever manage by herself. At this point she was ready for homemaking training.

Soon she was ready to start cooking from her wheelchair. Working from a wheelchair is considerably slower and more tiring than ordinary cooking so patients are carefully trained to organize their work, first gathering all the materials they will need before they start to cook. This eliminates back-tracking and extra trips for things that were forgotten.

While the long range goal in training a handicapped homemaker is the meal preparation for her family, the best introduction to the one-handed techniques is usually in making something as simple as a plain cupcake mix. This takes just a short time and very little energy so it makes a realistic project for patients just starting in rehabilitation. It also gives the therapist an indication of the patient's ability to read and follow the printed directions, a good clue to possible perceptual problems or receptive aphasia. Baking the cake divides into four or five definite steps that are easy to follow. . . . The finished cakes, which are practically foolproof, prove very satisfying to a woman who has long been hospitalized and inactive.

Modern packages are the first obstacle to be overcome. The therapist guides Mrs. E. in opening the cake mix box with her one hand while holding it firmly between her knees. With this same technique she will be able to open different types of boxes as well as screw top jars. Then she learns to manage the electric can opener that is held and operated with one hand.

The next step is mixing the batter. First, while the bowl is empty . . . [so that] any bits of shell can be easily removed, she cracks the egg sharply on the side of the bowl with one hand, puts her thumb in the crack and pushes the shell apart. The mixing bowl, fitted in its own hole stays stable and the electric mixer can be partially supported on the work top.

Next Mrs. E. ladles out the batter rather than trying to pour it one-handed. With individual paper liners there is no need to grease the cake pan. From the way that she fills the cups the therapist can make another check on possible perceptual problems. As she puts the pans into a hot oven, Mrs. E. feels safer with elbow length mitts to protect her arm.

Mrs. E. begins to use the standard kitchen when she can walk safely. When Mrs. E. began to make real progress in her physical therapy and ambulation programs it was soon followed by a definite "breakthrough" in her kitchen activities. Walking with a short leg brace and a cane, she feels more confident so she begins to plan ahead and relate what she is doing in the Institute's kitchen to the problems she will have at home. Here, she continues her training in work organization and collects all the food and utensils she will need, using a wheeled table to carry them—and to give herself extra support in walking.

In the standard kitchen at the Institute Mrs. E. parks her wheeled cart in front of the range. For greater safety and to conserve her energy, she works sitting down in a comfortable chair-stool with sturdy arms and back and a swivel seat 24″ high. Her feet rest on a small movable stool 5″ high and the space under the sink is open for knee room. In this position she can easily reach both the 36″ high sink and the standard range as well as the wheeled table beside her. The 31″ high table top provides the low work surface that she needs for cutting, chopping and slicing. The therapist shows Mrs. E. a one-handed cutting board with heavy rubber suction on the back to hold it in place. On the top side the board has a pair of pointed stainless steel nails to hold the food. In one corner there is an L-shaped molding to hold bread and sandwiches for spreading.

Washing, cleaning and ironing are basic chores in homemaking and present a variety of problems to the disabled. Mrs. E. "corners" her pan in the sink and uses a wet spongecloth underneath to keep it from sliding. She practices with a long handled dust pan and broom that she can use without

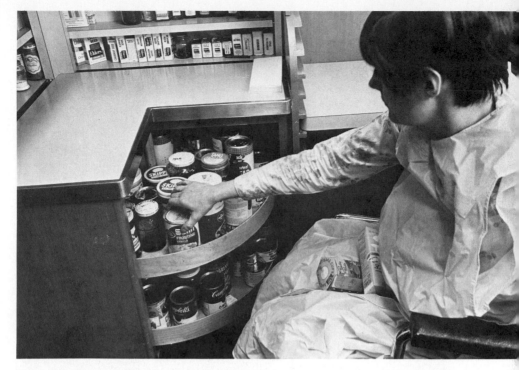

Figure 11.3. Collecting supplies she will need. (*Training the Young Hemiplegic Homemaker*)

bending. Also, she finds that ironing in a comfortable sitting position helps her balance and save energy.

The next problem is rearranging Mrs. E.'s kitchen at home. After six months' training Mrs. E. is working safely and independently in the Institute's standard kitchen. At about this time she begins to spend her weekends at home and from her reports it is plain that her own kitchen will have to be changed to enable her to use her new skills to cook for her family at home.

Mrs. E. is able to describe her kitchen and explain that it is the arrangement rather than the equipment that makes it impossible to cook by herself. Her range, refrigerator and dishwasher are all usable but she has to carry things back and forth across the room. The work space is overcrowded and badly placed and she can't reach the upper or the lower storage cabinets.

A home visit clarifies her explanation and provides the outline and definite dimensions needed to rearrange this kitchen to match Mrs. E.'s new working pattern.

If there is no money available for kitchen changes and the homemaker can qualify for assistance under the public program of vocational rehabilitation, the necessary adaptations can be financed with the participation of the local office of the State Rehabilitation Agency. This help is available because homemaking is classified as a "remunerative occupation" under the State-Federal partnership program of vocational rehabilitation. Consequently,

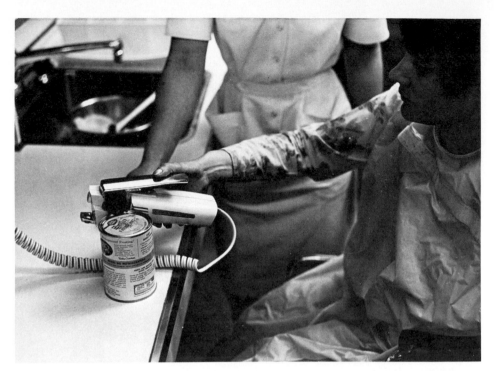

Figure 11.4. She learns to manage the electric can opener with one hand. (*Training the Young Hemiplegic Homemaker*)

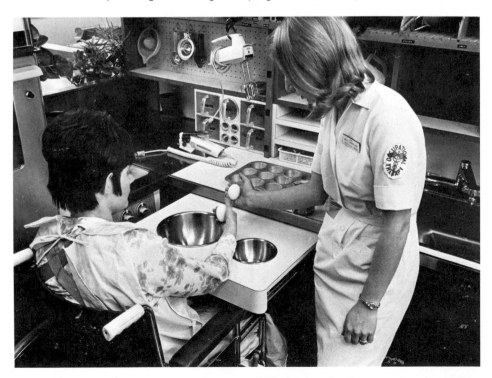

Figure 11.5. Special pull-out stabilizes bowls for one-hand mixing. (*Training the Young Hemiplegic Homemaker*)

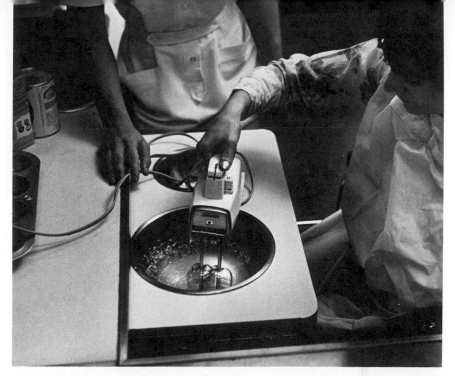

Figure 11.6. The mixing bowl fitted in its own hole stays stable and the electric mixer can be partially supported on the worktop. (*Training the Young Hemiplegic Homemaker*)

Figure 11.7. Mrs. E. ladles out the batter rather than trying to pour it one-handed. (*Training the Young Hemiplegic Homemaker*)

Figure 11.8. Mrs. E. feels safer with elbow-length mitts to protect her arm. (*Training the Young Hemiplegic Homemaker*)

in addition to counseling, diagnostic and physical restorative services, handicapped homemakers are eligible for the training, tools, equipment, and "other goods and services necessary to render a handicapped individual fit to engage in a remunerative occupation." For homemakers this can mean the necessary kitchen changes, including both equipment and labor costs.

In Mrs. E.'s case the State agency authorized the purchase and installation of the new storage cabinets and an L-shaped counter with a sink-top. This new equipment was carefully combined with Mrs. E.'s appliances to create a new kitchen that she could use.

In her new kitchen Mrs. E. can go on with her homemaking. With the new cabinets that she can reach and a continuous counter so that she can slide food and utensils back and forth, Mrs. E. finds that she can manage very well by herself. Now that her balance is better and she doesn't tire so quickly she prefers to work standing up, but she must plan ahead to give herself regular rest periods.

With the help of the home economist, Mrs. E. has carefully stored the utensils and food for her greatest convenience. Because she can't bend over to reach into the lower storage cabinets these units are equipped with roll-out storage drawers and racks and back-of-the-door shelves that swing out into easy reach. The upper corner cabinet has "lazy Susan" shelves attached to its revolving door and behind the sliding doors at the back of the counter is an 8″ deep storage space for the foods and utensils in everyday use.

Figure 11.9. With a wheeled cart Mrs. E. begins to collect everything she needs. (*Training the Young Hemiplegic Homemaker*)

Mrs. E. finds new ways to mother her children. Small children being what they are—all different, lively and growing so fast that they change from day to day—there can be no easy rules, no one-handed techniques for the handicapped mother to follow in caring for them. Her mothering must be of her own pattern, homemade and matched to her particular children, but if it is to be successful she will quickly learn to make the most of whatever help her children can give at different stages as they go along together.

All of Mrs. E.'s children, the two girls aged 8 and 5 as well as the 3 year old boy, seem to be very aware of their mother's limitations but perfectly comfortable when they are with her. They are quick to see her needs, unbuttoning her coat, running errands, picking up the things that she can't reach, but they also accept her caring for them just as naturally as any other children. With this kind of give and take, Mrs. E. and the children have their own very definite parts to play in such combined performances as dressing, bathing, hair combing, etc. The children know that they are the ones who do the moving while their mother stays still. They know exactly where to sit or stand, when to move and how to hold themselves so that Mrs. E. can do her part easily and quickly. Because Mrs. E. can't bend over to them, the youngsters automatically climb up on a chair to get themselves level with her for hair brushing, clothes fastening—and a good-bye kiss as they leave for school.

In her relations with her children Mrs. E. tries to be honest about the

Figure 11.10. Planning ahead, Mrs. E. Selects the right sized utensils. (*Training the Young Hemiplegic Homemaker*)

Figure 11.11. The "one-handed" cutting board. (*Training the Young Hemiplegic Homemaker*)

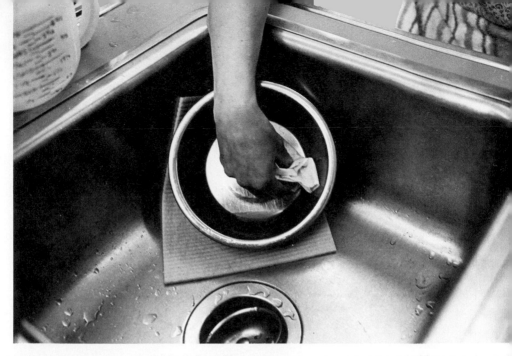

Figure 11.12. Mrs. E. "corners" her pan in the sink and uses a wet sponge-cloth underneath to keep it from sliding. (*Training the Young Hemiplegic Homemaker*)

limitations of her handicap. While she was a patient in the Institute she encouraged the children's visiting her, and she answered their questions about her own as well as the other patients' disabilities with simple factual explanations. At home she points out to them her gains in skill, balance or energy but she also freely admits the many things she cannot do by herself, and she has never given them that old familiar assurance that she would "be all better soon." Although the children seem to have accepted her disability easily, Mrs. E. finds that they now want extra mothering, often coming to her for things that they can do themselves. She recognizes this as a natural need for reassurance and tries to give them all they ask, and a little more.

Other Rehabilitation Programs

A number of government programs and private agencies help pay for the rehabilitation carried on by medical teams. As was mentioned earlier, the Vocational Rehabilitation Administration finances rehabilitation and education for disabled persons, including homemakers. Workman's Compensation Insurance aids insured workers, some of whom are also homemakers. Automobile insurers are also a source of aid for people who are injured in automobile accidents.

Figure 11.13. Mrs. E. and the therapist sit down at the drawing board with the home economist to consider the new L-shaped plan with a continuous counter that has been worked out to fit her kitchen space and to use the appliances that she already possesses. (*Training the Young Hemiplegic Homemaker*)

There is a growing recognition that rehabilitation is not only good for the injured person but good economics and good for society. Here is the story of the rehabilitation program of a young teacher who is also a homemaker.

Even before she arrived at the hospital, the young home economics teacher had begun to suspect the real extent of her injuries. Conscious, Diane Grzymko was aware she had no feeling in the lower half of her body. And because she and her husband (a high school physical education instructor) had often worked with handicapped children, Diane knew the significance of spinal cord injury.

Only minutes before she had been driving along New Jersey's Garden State Parkway when a sudden tire blowout rammed her car into a bridge abutment. Diane, at 22, was permanently paralyzed below the waist.

Because of the nature of her injury, Diane's emergency admission to the

Figure 11.14. *Above:* Mrs. E. can go on with her homemaking in her new kitchen. *Below:* Back of the counter storage is eight inches deep. (*Training the Young Hemiplegic Homemaker*)

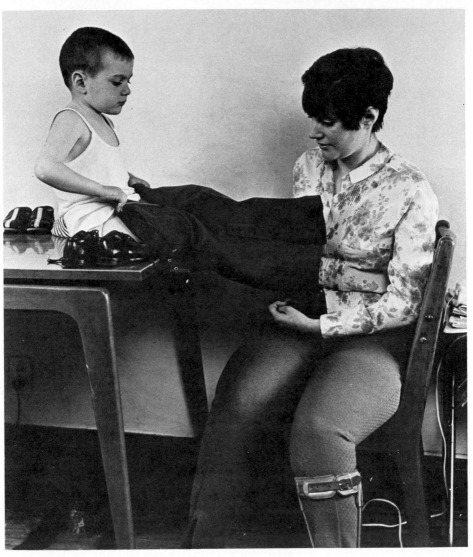

Figure 11.15. Together David and his mother solve the problem of the long pants. (*Training the Young Hemiplegic Homemaker*)

Somers Point (New Jersey) Shore Memorial Hospital was only the first step toward maximum recovery. It was May 13, 1973. Still ahead of her were more than three months of intensive medical and rehabilitative care—much of it in a facility half-way across the nation. It would be a long summer, but in the end the young teacher would be prepared to continue a full and productive life at home and in the classroom.

Because Diane sustained her injuries in a car crash, her automobile insurer (a member company of the American Mutual Insurance Alliance) did much more than just sign the checks for the $22,000 in costs associated with her accident.

Figure 11.16. Diane shows a young girl how to fold dress material according to the pattern instructions. The 22-year-old home economics teacher returned to the classroom despite permanent paralysis resulting from a car crash. ("Coordinated Care: Strength of the Casualty Insurer,") *Journal of American Insurance* (Winter 1973–74)

The person most closely involved with Diane and John Grzymko was Patricia Smith, R.N., a rehabilitation nurse on the insurance company's New Jersey professional staff. Mrs. Smith was assigned to Diane's case after early investigation by insurance representatives revealed that an injury to the spinal cord had occurred.

A consulting physiatrist—a specialist in physical medicine and rehabilitation, recommended that Diane go to Craig Rehabilitation Hospital in Denver, a facility directed toward returning the spinal cord injured to as normal a life as possible.

The rehabilitation nurse describes Diane's case as extraordinary: "Really, she was marvelous—all of them (the family) were. It was like working with professionals. They didn't take time to feel sorry for themselves. They were sympathetic to Diane, but theirs was a constructive sympathy to assist her in the big job to be done.

"Diane herself had the perfect mental attitude. She didn't waste any time. Even before she went to Craig, while she was still at Shore Memorial, she was working with weights to use her muscles. Once, when her physical therapist was out of town for several days, John [her husband] took over the therapy so that Diane would not lose her exercises."

Diane was transferred to Craig in Denver as soon as her condition was stabilized so that her rehabilitation treatments could begin immediately. The trip was made June 7 by air ambulance; Diane was accompanied on the flight by her husband and a Craig rehabilitation nurse. John Grzymko went to Colorado so he could work with his wife at the hospital and learn what kind of care and support she would need when she returned home.

Diane Grzymko did not allow her disability to limit her as a teacher. Today she is as deeply involved with her students as ever, often participating in after school activities as well as her regular class duties.[6]

What Can Be Done for the Handicapped? [6]

By the Individual

1. Become interested in the handicapped persons in your community—with an awareness of needs for assistance.
2. Find out the kinds of programs, both private and public, that are available for helping the handicapped.
3. Determine what needed services are not available in your community and work with others to provide them.
4. Encourage the handicapped to seek and accept rehabilitation services that will increase their abilities to function as fully as possible in the home and community.
5. Boost community acceptance of the handicapped through publicity of the capabilities of the handicapped—as through the various news media.
6. Involve the handicapped persons in community activities as they have special interests and abilities.

By Groups

1. Conduct a survey within your community to find the disabled who need help in rehabilitation within the home environment.
2. Locate the rehabilitation services available within your community. Contact your state director of Rehabilitation Services for a list of what is available—and what is further needed.
3. Encourage the disabled to contact appropriate facilities—taking advantage of those offering the needed assistance.
4. Include the handicapped in your own group—arranging for transportation, if needed. Work to remove the architectural barriers in the church, public buildings, theater, library, school—that keep the handicapped from participation.
5. Increase interest in health–related professions—through funds for scholarships, trips to rehabilitation centers, etc.
6. Cooperate with local rehabilitation and health agencies to provide appropriate facilities and personnel for retraining in the home environment.[7]

[6] Condensed from "Coordinated Care: Strength of the Casualty Insurer," *Journal of American Insurance*, Vol. 49 (Winter 1973–74), pp. 1–4.

[7] From the brochure, "Help on Wheels," which describes a film produced by the School of Home Economics, University of Nebraska, in cooperation with the Women's Committee, President's Committee on Employment of the Handicapped.

The Homemaker Rehabilitation Consultant

Homemaker Rehabilitation Consultants assist the disabled homemaker to create more emotionally satisfying, energy-saving, independent daily activity patterns that lead to happier and more productive lives.

Homemaker Rehabilitation Consultants are Home Economists with special training to

1. Help physically handicapped individuals find ways to do necessary home-making tasks such as preparing foods, dishwashing;
2. Aid in selection, arrangements, use, care, and storage of equipment;
3. Plan with the disabled person for the best heights for working surfaces, especially in the kitchen where so much time is spent;
4. Show ways in which bathroom fixtures can be used with safety and comfort;
5. Plan adaptation of home through adding ramps, adjusting work centers, and adding devices;
6. Demonstrate ways in which clothing can be functional and easy to manage;
7. Help schedule time for work, rest, and vacation with the family;
8. Stimulate interest in the experimental approach and encourage effort to find new ways;
9. Encourage self-confidence, pride, and satisfaction in achievements.[8]

Summary

More than four and a half million women who are homemakers have disabilities that limit their activities in some important way. Some of the principal disabilities are faulty vision, arthritis, paralysis, and circulatory disease. As we continue to increase the average life span, it is likely that more homemakers will suffer from some of the disabilities of older age.

People with disabilities must adjust to certain problems, but this usually leaves a tremendous area within which they can function effectively. A person with a disability is also a person with many abilities.

The attitude toward a disability on the part of the individual with the handicap is often a determinant of how limited his activity will be. The prognosis for a homemaker with a handicap is better if she feels that her function, however limited, is still important to the family.

Effective management for the homemaker with a disability is particularly important because work in the home may take her longer and her energy may be more limited. Decisions about what really needs to be done

[8] Excerpt from "Homemaker Rehabilitation," The President's Committee on Employment of the Handicapped, Washington, D.C., 1968.

and what should be omitted are basic. Realistic standards must be formulated.

The household can be streamlined by eliminating unnecessary articles and replacing others with easy-to-care-for items. The right tools can make a job go more quickly and easily. Simple modifications of the house may make it easier for her to move around. Other members of the family may need to take on more responsibility for household work.

Many women with disabilities are the parents of young children. Like women the world over they find child care satisfying and rewarding. The homemaker with a handicap is apt to be highly motivated to function independently if she can care for her child. Mothers with disabilities that limit their movement have proved that it is possible for them to care for young children in spite of their limitations.

An attitude of cooperation on the part of the child helps immensely. Also, many things can be done to enable a child to do as much as possible independently, such as providing clothing that is easy to put on and take off and low storage shelves for clothes and toys.

The psychological lift that comes from a good appearance may be particularly important for the homemaker with a handicap. Attractive clothing also helps other people view the person with a handicap as a presentable person.

CHAPTER FOLLOW-UP

1. Make believe that you are planning to furnish your first home. Assume that you want to be able to take care of it with the least amount of effort. What type of furnishings would you buy in order to have the least possible upkeep.

2. Visit a local nursery school when the children are getting dressed to go outdoors. Watch them get into their clothing. What are the things with which they have difficulty? How could clothing for this age group be planned to make it easier for toddlers to put on their own outer clothing?

3. Try working in the kitchen from a sitting position. What will need to be moved to make it possible for you to do so? How could you rearrange equipment to be more efficient?

4. Imagine that you are a young mother who has had polio which left you with limited use of your left arm. How much can you manage with one hand? What things would help you manage better?

5. Visit an older person and watch how he or she gets around. Does he have difficulty lifting and reaching? Does he tire easily? What would be important in planning a household to make it easier for him to manage?

6. Injuries resulting from accidents at home are one of the leading causes of disability. What can you do to avoid accidents at home?

7. Many public school systems have special classes for children with

various types of disabilities. Some of these youngsters take homemaking classes. What things might you need to do to help youngsters from a sight conservation class (children with poor vision) manage better in a homemaking class?

SELECTED REFERENCES

Conwell, Donald P. "Future Directions." *Journal of Home Economics*, Vol. 61 (1969), pp. 425–427.

Coulter, K. J. "Characteristics of Consumer Behavior of Physically Disabled and of Non-Disabled Homemakers." *Journal of Consumer Affairs*, Vol. 6, (Winter 1972), pp. 170–183.

DiMichael, Salvatore G. "The Voluntary Health Agencies' Stake in Rehabilitation." *Journal of Home Economics*, Vol. 61 (1969), pp. 421–423.

Fish, Marjorie. "The RSA Training Program." *Journal of Home Economics*, Vol. 61 (1969), pp. 423–424.

Fisher, Gerald H. "Challenge of Full Service by '75." *Journal of Home Economics*, Vol. 61, (1969), p. 417.

Friend, Shirley E., Judith Zaccagnin, and Marilyn Bartak Sullivan. "Meeting the Clothing Needs of Handicapped Children." *Journal of Home Economics,* Vol. 65 (1973), pp. 25–27.

Grant, Linda J. "The Community Adaptation of Physically Disabled Homemakers." Master's thesis, University of Nebraska, 1971.

Green, Gerald W. "The Potential for Home Economics in the Rehabilitation Services." *Journal of Home Economics*, Vol. 61 (1969), pp. 418–420.

Hall, Florence Turnbull, and Marguerite Paulsen Schroeder. "Effects of Family and Housing Characteristics on Time Spent on Household Tasks." *Journal of Home Economics*, Vol. 62 (1970), pp. 23–29.

Homemaker Rehabilitation: A Selected Bibliography. Washington, D.C.: Women's Committee of the President's Committee on Employment of the Handicapped, 1972.

Homemaking Unlimited Bulletins. Lincoln, Nebraska: School of Home Economics, University of Nebraska, n.d.
  EC–66–2200 "Easy–to–Use Kitchens"
  EC–66–2201 "No–Stoop, No–Stretch Kitchen Storage"
  EC–66–2202 "Easy–to–Use Sink Center"
  EC–66–2203 "Easy–to–Use Cooking and Serving Center"
  EC–66–2204 "Easy–to–Use Mixing Center"
  EC–66–2205 "Streamlining Household Tasks"
  EC–66–2206 "The Bathroom Made Safe and Usable"
  EC–66–2207 "Cleaning Supplies—Keep Them Handy"
  EC–66–2208 "Easy Fashions for You"
  EC–66–2210 "Food and Your Family"

Jones, Alpha H., and Lois O. Schwab. "Rehabilitation for Homemakers with Cardiovascular Involvements: Changes in Attitudes and Ability." *Home Economics Research Journal*, Vol. 1 (December 1972?), pp. 114–118.

Judson, Julia, ed. *Home Economics Research Abstracts 1963–1968: Rehabilitation*. Washington, D.C.: American Home Economics Association, 1969.

Kaarlela, Ruth. "Home Teachers of the Blind." *Journal of Home Economics*, Vol. 61 (1969), p. 416.

Lacey, Lee. "The Home Economist—Team Addition." *Journal of Home Economics*, Vol. 61 (1969), p. 415.

Lowman, Edward, and Judith Lannefeld Klinger. *Aids to Independent Living*. New York: McGraw-Hill, Inc., 1969.

Manning, Sarah L. *Time Use in Household Tasks by Indiana Families*. Experiment Station Research Bulletin No. 837, Purdue University, 1968.

May, Elizabeth Eckhardt, Neva R. Waggoner, and Eleanor M. Boettke. *Homemaking for the Handicapped*. New York: Dodd, Mead and Co., 1966.

——, ——, and Eleanor B. Hotte. *Independent Living for the Handicapped and Elderly*. Boston: Houghton Mifflin, 1974.

Mc Cullough, Helen E., and Mary B. Farnham. *Kitchens for Women in Wheelchairs*. University of Illinois Bulletin, Circular 841, University of Illinois, 1961.

Mealtime Manual for the Aged and Handicapped. Prepared by the Institute of Rehabilitation Medicine, New York University Medical Center. New York: Simon and Schuster, Inc., 1970.

Merchant, M. H. "Homemaking Time Use of Homemakers Confined to Wheel Chairs." Master's thesis, University of Nebraska, 1969.

"Resources in Rehabilitation." *Journal of Home Economics*, Vol. 61 (1969), p. 428.

Snyder, Nancy V. "The Utilization of the Management and Decision-Making Processes in Homemaker Rehabilitation." Master's thesis, Ohio State University, 1968.

Trotter, Virginia Y. "Dimensions of Home Economists in Rehabilitation." *Journal of Home Economics*, Vol. 61 (1969), pp. 405–407.

Wang, Virginia Li, and A. June Bricker. "Extending Home Economics to Health Care Services." *Journal of Home Economics*, Vol. 63 (1971), pp. 350–353.

index